Romanian and Chinese Cinemas

Romanian and Chinese Cinemas

Socialist Affect and Cultural Politics from Maoism to the New Waves

Lucian Țion

EDINBURGH
University Press

Edinburgh University Press is one of the leading university presses in the UK. We publish academic books and journals in our selected subject areas across the humanities and social sciences, combining cutting-edge scholarship with high editorial and production values to produce academic works of lasting importance. For more information visit our website: edinburghuniversitypress.com

Edinburgh University Press Ltd
13 Infirmary Street
Edinburgh EH1 1LT

First published in hardback by Edinburgh University Press 2026

Typeset in Janson and Neue Helvetica
by Cheshire Typesetting Ltd, Cuddington, Cheshire, and
printed and bound by CPI Group (UK) Ltd,
Croydon, CR0 4YY

A CIP record for this book is available from the British Library

ISBN 978 1 3995 1278 7 (hardback)
ISBN 978 1 3995 1279 4 (paperback)
ISBN 978 1 3995 1280 0 (webready PDF)
ISBN 978 1 3995 1281 7 (epub)

Contents

PART TWO

Figures

Introduction

When telling a friend from the former Yugoslavia that my research involved Romanian and Chinese films of the socialist era and that I would be scouring the archives for evidence about the relationship between them, he thought it amusing to recount an anecdote which, by his own account, had happened to his father a few years earlier and was slightly relevant to my topic. On a brief visit to China in the early 2000s, when his father once took a taxi from Beijing airport to the city, he found himself in the car with a Chinese driver who looked roughly the same age as him. While neither he nor his driver spoke much English, after a few attempts, the father managed to communicate to the driver that he was coming from Belgrade, the capital of former Yugoslavia. This immediately caused the driver's face to light up, and he broke into a song. The tune that he was singing in exhilaration was from a Yugoslav war movie that he had seen in China as a young man. The father, surprised that he could hear the theme song of a long-forgotten film in a taxicab on the other side of the world, gladly joined in and sang the lyrics in Serbian while the driver sang in Chinese.

The film was *Walter Defends Sarajevo* (*Valter brani Sarajevo*, Krvavac, 1972), one of the many antifascist war dramas exported from Eastern Europe to China during the long haul of the twentieth century.[1] This film, along with the Romanian ones shown in China, as well as the Chinese ones screened in Romania, helped create a now forgotten affective community of once socialist subjects who, even though they did not know each other physically, rejoiced watching the same films in unison.

The transcultural community thus created represents the central theme of this book, which tries to understand how Romanian and Chinese films produced from 1949 to 1989 managed to connect, at least virtually, two cultures that were otherwise linguistically and historically very dissimilar. Therefore, in addition to presenting an analysis in film studies, this book also takes an anthropological and historical approach to the two regions. Connecting

[1] It was customary in Maoist China to issue illustrated booklets of popular films, which narrated an abridged version of the plot's diegesis, including artist-painted renditions of movie scenes. *Walter* was honored with such a booklet as well, proving the popularity of the film among Chinese audiences at the time. This also explains the driver's knowledge of the film.

socio-political events from Romania's and China's pasts to the many films that were produced and exchanged as a token of friendship and solidarity, it describes in (almost) chronological order the paths that the two members of the Eastern Bloc followed as they gradually drew politically closer to each other and away from the Soviet Union.

The Romanian films of the socialist era that make up the corpus of the first part of the book will be analyzed in their historical contexts, via the socialist realist style as well as what I have termed the *social* realism which bookends them. I will begin my comparative discussion of mainland Chinese cinema with the first film produced by the Communist government after Mao's rise to power in 1949, and I will conclude the first part with an analysis of the fourth generation, who in their work discussed the tumultuous period of the Cultural Revolution. In the second part, I will contrast and compare the fifth and the so-called sixth generation of filmmakers in China with the Romanian anticommunist 1990s films and their New Wave counterparts in the 2000s, respectively. This is because filmmakers of these otherwise distinct cinematic trends created an aesthetic, ideology and filmmaking style surprisingly similar to one another.

Although I sometimes selected films that may be known to scholars of Romanian and Chinese cinemas for their aesthetic and historic value, not all the movies discussed here are validated by the so-called national canons of their respective countries. My purpose oftentimes is that of reviving a film from unwarranted oblivion. Despite their datedness and, in some cases, their alleged political indoctrination, my aim is to make all films discussed here more accessible to a wider audience. Another important purpose is to explore the subtleties of Communist politics which have been hastily categorized as totalitarian and thrown onto the garbage heap of history, alongside the many masterworks that the Romanian and Chinese socialist cinema produced.

A recent challenge in teaching material related to the history and culture of Eastern Europe in general, and Romania in particular, has been the stark resistance with which local as well as international students treat media objects from the socialist period. It is somewhat understandable why this is so. Educated in a capitalist system which has taught them that all socialist-era cinema was a form of indoctrination and propaganda, students researching Communism are predestined to become biased in their educational pursuits. Another effect of this pedagogical narrative is that students all over the world are becoming increasingly apolitical, content to consume a Western reading of Eastern European and Chinese histories that uncritically agglutinates Communist authoritarianism with artistic expression and even the overall lifestyle of the people who have lived in these countries for more than half a century. This understandably makes history (that of cinema included) appear less and less interesting or important. Claiming that the past does not represent them, students move on to develop a highly narcissistic attitude *vis-à-vis* history, which – fed by their individualstic, neoliberal upbringing – is dominated by the overpowering capitalist present. From such a viewpoint, the films of early Béla Tarr, Andrzej Wajda, Lucian Pintilie, Miloš Forman,

Dušan Makavejev and Rangel Valchanov, among others, become boring relics of a bygone era. Lacking the context to appreciate the complexity of these both tragic and funny cinematic works of the socialist period precipitates an unjust forgetting of the past and these films' hurried incorporation into the binary constituted of propaganda filmmaking, on the one hand, and "dissident" cinema, on the other.

Because the word "propaganda" itself has recently become a catch phrase that encourages uncritical thinking, akin to Slavoj Žižek's warning that "totalitarianism" is now a stopgap for thinking about the past altogether (Žižek 2001), part of my book will deconstruct the meaning of the term "propaganda" and analyze the degree to which allegedly propagandist works can be relegitimated from both a historic and an aesthetic point of view. These works act not only as markers of historical events, but also as products leading to collaboration among countries of the Second World,[2] following precepts active during the socialist era, such as those of the "friendship of nations." While it is not the purpose of this book to change public consciousness in relation to the alleged wrongdoing of Communist regimes around the world, I will attempt to find subtextual divergences laying under the veneer of blunt authoritarianism. In that sense, I read some films produced under socialism not as vehicles to fight state oppression, as Romanian postsocialist critics have done, but as representatives of lifestyles and cultures situated on a common geographical continuum in approximately similar times. Drawing on Third Cinema theories enunciated in the 1960s (Solanas and Getino 1969), this should challenge the commonly held binary view that cinema was entirely propagandistic and devoid of artistic merit or, to the other extreme, occasionally dissident.

As we shall see in this book, responsible for the Western propagation of an oftentimes ideologically skewed version of history are sometimes the Romanians and the Chinese intellectuals themselves. Appropriating readings of the socialist past propagated during and after the Cold War, including those advanced by CIA propaganda meant to destabilize various socialist regimes in Eastern Europe (Paddington 2000), this attitude was made possible by the stringent wave of anticommunist ideology that proliferated in postsocialist countries after the downfall of Communism, as well as by intellectuals belonging to the Romanian and Chinese diasporas. Over time, this gave rise to an uncritical and ultimately amnesic understanding of history. The uneven, Westernized and one-sided treatment of the past eventually started to replace local identity with one derived from a purportedly global

[2] The term has been coined in reference to the theory of Alfred Sauvy, a French sociologist who in 1952 called attention to the existence of an underdeveloped 'Third World' which he has linked to the third estate of revolutionary France. This came to be associated roughly with the areas in which socialism became the dominant political philosophy in Eastern Europe and parts of Asia. Furthermore, Mao Zedong elaborated his own theory about the 'three worlds' in the early 1970s – a theory that became influential in Third World countries.

capitalist character shared by all of humanity, which – held to be non-ideological and natural – is currently promoted as panacea for the ills induced by socialism and its aftereffects. Unfortunately, this can only mean one thing: that the postsocialist future is bound to be as tragic as the Eastern Europeans and the Chinese portend their recent past to have been.

Central to a vitiated understanding of the past was the anticommunist creed holding that the only valuable cinema under socialism was the cinema produced in contestation to Communist power. This prejudiced view of Eastern Europe's cultural past ensures that half a century of cinema history – in Romania's case, more than half of its entire history – has become uncritically buried in the waste pile that anticommunism scurried to heap up as soon as Communism collapsed in 1989. Even if one were to endorse Hannah Arendt's comparison of socialism and fascism, the cinema of the Nazi era did not meet the same fate as the Communist one. This is verifiable because Leni Riefenstahl's films have long been accepted as part of the canon illustrating the effective use of propaganda filmmaking. And while Sergei Eisenstein's and Dziga Vertov's indubitable contributions to montage theory also feature in the syllabi of most introductory film courses, Soviet and Soviet-inspired cinema is treated with suspicion and oftentimes disgust in many Eastern European countries, where socialist films are considered propagators of an ideology that brought together poverty and authoritarianism.

While Third Cinema won more appeal in the West because of the centrality of its anticolonialist message, instead of playing up its own anticolonialist card (which was inadvertently Communist), postsocialist Eastern Europeans chose to take their anticommunism to extremes, going far beyond curtsying approval from the West to become one of the most feverish supporters and enablers of neoliberal capitalism. Moreover, anticommunism helped erase half a century of objective local history which, as a whole, has been buried alongside Stalin's purges, even though such purges never actually took place outside of the Soviet Union on any such scale. This has pushed Eastern Europe into a position of complete and utter ignorance of its recent past, an ignorance which helps feed the younger generation with inaccuracies, clichés, vulgarizations and half-truths.

The tendency of the elite capitalist establishment to teach the next generation a film history of Eastern Europe that is cobbled together as a series of monolithic encounters between the freedom-starved Communist subjects and the culturally rich West is aligned with Western film education, which is largely based on David Bordwell's cognitivist theories. Moreover, such binary interpretations of their cinemas are perpetuated by the Eastern Europeans themselves, particularly by Romanian theorists, who overstate the "dark times" of socialism or their aftermath. They do so in order to curtsy approval and validation from a distant and largely indifferent Western cultural establishment.

This forces us to consider whether the "Western canon," in as much as this applies to film studies, is in need of reconceptualization. With students hailing from places that are increasingly non-Western and with a multipolar world that does not consider the problems of the USA to be its own, issues such as racism (as it has been understood in the US) increasingly fade in importance, in favor of an ethnic-based discrimination which threatens the entire social and political fabric of the European project. While the type of racism discussed in North America remains a pressing concern for that part of the world, this discourse cannot be exported to a continent in which most of the non-natives in academia today are Eastern European, Chinese, Turkish, Eurasian and, of course, of Arabic descent.

The East is no longer red; indeed, it is more capitalist than Western capitalism itself, despite the presence of state-sponsored programs and facilities such as health care and a (largely still) free education system. If I emphasise this geographical division between the East and the West, this is because nowhere did capitalism gain more ground more quickly and swept people off their feet more abruptly than in Eastern Europe for some thirty-odd years after the collapse of Communism. In this context, it is important to establish that the part of the large landmass I refer to as Eurasia (for reasons which I explain in this book as having to do with common national histories and aesthetic movements) has a history of its own, and this history has been skewed by the dominant capitalist discourse. This has given rise to a self-destructive tendency that makes of Eastern European cultural history a subaltern field studies, in contrast to the hegemonic one of the West.

Including Asian cinematic values in the reconceptualization of an ontology of Eastern European aesthetics would favor a transnational paradigm meant to discontinue the depreciative and discriminatory view of Asia and Asianness in Romania. This is especially important in today's neoliberal climate, since Eastern Europe's distancing from Asia was perceived as central to the self-identification of the region as a capitalist promontory of the West (Deletant 1999), despite the region's forced rupture from socialist states such as China, which once were its close cultural, political (Szalontai 2014) and cinematic partners.

Considering that Second-to-Second and Second-to-Third World cinema connections were as powerful in shaping cultural identity during the socialist era (Verdery and Chari 2009) as Europeanism arguably is today, I focus on Romanian and Chinese cinemas because they are my area of expertise and because a book emphasizing all the connections between the cinemas of the former Eastern Bloc would be too large and cumbersome to undertake as a single research project. That said, I agree that future efforts involving multinational and transnational scholars would greatly advance the field of Eastern European and Chinese cinemas.

Aside from a lack of local research available to the English-speaking public, my motivation also comes from the commonplace demonization of anything Communist and everything China – from the authoritative form of government to human rights abuses. While I do not condone either and consider these forms of political leadership inadequate and disturbing, I believe that there are enough gray areas in Western discourses and East-West polemics that would force a researcher to unearth some nuances that the legacy of socialism has left open to interpretation. In this vein, the work of both Romanian and Chinese New Wave directors is illuminating because it treats the popularly demonized past with a professed neutrality that is different from that of their predecessors and provides an understanding of the past that many film critics and theorists lack.

As stated above, in addition to film analysis proper, this book offers a socio-political and anthropological view of two spaces that are not usually associated with each other. Against perpetuating clichés and reprising worn-out themes treating Communism as evil, in the first chapter I will explain the notion of socialist affect and how this permeates the veneer of two postsocialist cultures that, although ruled by different political systems and on vastly different economic footing, share a cultural history that makes them surprisingly similar to each other. In order to demonstrate this theoretical angle, I will use films from both Romania and China, starting with the early productions made during the brief socialist realist episode from the 1950s to the social realism of the 1980s.

The second chapter will explain the emergence of anticommunism, claiming that 1990s cinema was more heavily influenced by politics than by aesthetic concerns. Going back to the roots of socialist filmmaking, I will discuss the performativity that certain Korean War films enacted in China during the 1960s in order to support and instill a sense of dignity for the new country that China was at that time, and I will parallel this with the performativity of the first socialist Chinese and Romanian films, *The Bridge* and *Reverberates the Valley*, respectively.

I will then proceed to analyze the cinema of both cultures in a chronological manner, highlighting similarities between political events, such as Ceaușescu's denouncement of the Soviet invasion of Czechoslovakia in 1968 and Mao's distancing from Khrushchev during the Sino-Soviet split. I will similarly compare the Cultural Revolution in China with the alleged cultural and economic austerity that Romania experienced after Ceaușescu's visit to Beijing in 1971, following this bifurcated analysis until the societal changes brought about by the anticommunist revolution of 1989 and China's gradual liberalization under Deng Xiaoping. Seeing how these events influenced filmmaking practices, the last two chapters will compare the sixth-generation Chinese director Jia Zhangke to what I consider to be his New Wave counterparts in Romania, Cristi Puiu and Cristian Mungiu. Here, I will also discuss the debate on abortion, which Mungiu's *4 Months, 3 Weeks, and 2 Days* managed to bring to the public forum, while contrasting it to *Unforgettable Life*, a little-known Tian Zhaungzhuang film on the same topic, which precedes it by over a decade in China. I argue that, although Tian technically belongs to China's fifth generation, some of his works, such as *Unforgettable Life*, prefigure the work of Jia Zhangke.

In conclusion, I will dig the trope of Eurasia out of the dustbin of geopolitics. Following Dipesh Chakrabarty in his suggestion of "Provincializing Europe" (Chakrabarty 2008) – rather than the neonationalist theories of the likes of Aleksandr Dugin, which distort early Russian anthropological research, such as that of Lev Gumilev (Bassin 2015) – I conceptualize Eurasianism as a cultural trope birthed from the influence of historical traditions and Communist ideology. I will show that Eurasia is a region still connected by the former socialist-era goals of internationalism, via an old Soviet slogan vying for fraternity between nations, even though that fraternity has been watered down (if not destroyed entirely) by the penetration of Occidentalism into both cultures. This, however, puts the cinema of Romania and China on a par subaltern footing, which endorses a reading of the Eurasian continuum as predicated on a certain alterity that makes all Eurasian cultures, those in Eastern Europe included, more similar to each other than to the West.

Aside from discussing the strict comparison between Romanian and Chinese cinemas, in the book's finale I will expand my point of view on affective similitude to incorporate the way in which both Eurasian cultures relate to the West. Drawing on Ray Chow and Xiaomei Chen, as well as Maria Todorova and Alxsander Kiossev's self-Orientalism, I will show that the identity of subaltern nations with a semi-colonial past is contingent on the description that Western Orientalism has advanced and then incorporated into the national imaginary of subaltern cultures. Films made during the 2000s in both Romania and China reflect this Orientalism by, in turn, Occidentalizing their view of the West and demonizing one another. Indeed, instead of seeing each other as partners in the reconstruction projects meant to drive their transition from socialism, the former Eastern Bloc countries after the downfall of socialism entered in competition with one another to gain access to and win the favor of the West.

The tacit hope of the book is that, instead of only looking admiringly towards Western cultures, Romania and China would find each other again and recognize that they have more in common with each other than either of them has with the Western world (with which they expect to catch up). If socialism forced film directors in both countries more or less to rely on their originality to create films that, most of the time, did not follow Hollywood's formulaic plots, catching up in postsocialism requires a laborious process of copying and following the trends of Hollywood formulas to ensure commercialization for cinemas that barely have the experience and finances to compete. While China's status as the second-largest world economy is moving in this direction already, albeit by creating mostly simulacra of Hollywood films, Romania continues to promote its "arthouse" for lack of other aesthetic and stylistic resources.

The Westernization of culture promoted in both countries has only been exposed in postsocialism by the Romanian New Wave and by China's so-called Sixth-Generation film directors. While socialism gave both countries plenty of opportunities to discover each other in a similar ideological world, the realism of the New Wave and that of the Sixth Generation presents a renewed offer for dialogue for both partners. I only hope that this would be taken up by the critics and theorists of aesthetically similar cinematic movements, and that it would span a communication bridge between two cultures that are both dissimilar and yet have so much in common.

Part One

1 Film and Socialist Affect

In the first scene of *4 Months, 3 Weeks and 2 Days* (*4 luni, 3 săptămâni și 2 zile*, 2007), Cristian Mungiu's famous abortion drama set in the late years of the Ceaușescu era, the Romanian director takes his audience into a student dorm room, which allows viewers to participate intimately in the everyday lives of two female undergrads for whom living in the dorm is akin to living in a large family. This "family" is shown sharing the basic necessities (such as hair driers, medicine, videotapes, soap and cigarettes) and appears to be running more like a happy commune. When recalling Mungiu's film, it is not only the dim hallways and white-tiled public restrooms typical of socialist buildings that come to mind, but also the interpersonal warmth present in the midst of an otherwise austere environment made even poorer by the hardships of the 1980s. Responsible for this lighter mood is the affective solidarity that describes the student collective as an organism animated by friendliness and mutual support.

In a film made only one year earlier on the other side of the world, Chinese director Lou Ye painted a similar atmosphere in his much-acclaimed, hotly debated and ultimately banned *Summer Palace* (*Yi He Yuan*, 2006). Describing a student collective at a fictitious educational institution styled after Beijing University, Lou contrasts the happy lives of students in the shabby-looking dorms and dilapidated halls to those that the same people would experience later in the film, in the more liberal years of the Deng Xiaoping era and in Berlin. The Romanian and Chinese directors both portray the affective environment of their characters in the first part of their films as warm, caring and friendly, despite the challenges associated with that era, which gives the two films an uncanny similarity.

Despite this, Mungiu's film is usually read in a different key. This is understandable given that *4, 3, 2* (as it is known for short) depicts the tragic aftermath of Ceaușescu's 1966 decree outlawing abortion in Romania. After discovering that Găbița, one of the roommates, is pregnant against her will, she and her friend Otilia must band together to arrange an illegal abortion, which they entrust to the shady wannabe "doctor," Mr. Bebe, who runs the risk of being found guilty of murder if discovered. The abortion proper is prefaced by the misadventures of the protagonists when they try to book a hotel room to perform the illicit act in a collapsing economic system in which neither hotel personnel nor relatives or passersby appear trustworthy or helpful. Furthermore, family and friends, who normally would offer much-needed support, antagonize the protagonists, as the senior generation is bent on criticizing the disappearance of traditionalism and patriarchy. To make things worse, Otilia's very boyfriend opposes abortion in principle, which complicates the girls' drama and makes the web of entangled relationships more dangerous.

In this world of traditionalism and superficiality, the two friends' loyalty to each other seems to be the only beacon of hope. In addition to taking numerous chances when assisting her friend Găbița with the abortion, Otilia submits to sexual assault in the name of their friendship, after Mr. Bebe all but coerces her. The audience is shocked by Otilia's commitment to her friend, which highlights the tenacity and resilience of their attachment to one another – something which ultimately appears as a positive quality in a socialist culture that endorses togetherness in opposition to Western individualism. The habit of sharing, which Otilia and Găbița have learned as members of the social collective, and their learned responses to adversity (including that of the strong party state) are the elements that sustain that friendship. If there is a metaphor at work here, it is that the tightly-knit, mutually supportive student community reflects the closeness of the masses living in the socialist state.

Because he ignores this fact, American film scholar Chris Robé's take on the film, celebrating the reaffirmation of freedom embedded in its anticommunist message, fails to convince us. Robé has claimed that the "Romanian New Wave relates a communist structure of feeling of immense oppression, surveillance, and homogenization not only through its characters' actions and words, but also through its cinematic style of using long takes, oblique and distant framing, and sparse mise-en-scene" (Robé 2017, 3). While it is undoubtedly true that the film's chiaroscuro lighting, the jerky camera and the highly charged performances help render the last years of Ceaușescu's dictatorship eerily real, employing the notions of "oppression, surveillance, and homogenization" in an anti-authoritarian sense, Robé has read the film solely as personification of Foucault's concept of *biopower* – namely, as the state's ability to survey, dictate and produce the lives of its citizens (Foucault 1978). But that is to misrepresent the contingency, arbitrariness, unpredictability and (why not?) the warmth of Romanian Communism, with its ironies and tragedies, which Mungiu clearly tries to capture in his film. Moreover, while Foucault's analysis refers to the rather subtler ways in which capitalist power shapes and determines lives through institutions such as the school, the prison and the mental hospital, Mungiu's film is focused on the way in which common people created solidarity in the face of patriarchal structures of power.

Lou Ye makes a similar point in *Summer Palace*. He opens his film with a touching portrayal of student life at the time of the Tiananmen "democracy movement"[1] in Beijing, focusing on a sexual triangle between the rebellious

[1] Although this is the name by which it is known in the West, the movement started as an anti-corruption protest against the abuses by certain party officials. As in

Yu Hong, her boyfriend Zhou Wei and her best friend Li Ti. Despite the betrayals and jealousies which they experience, it appears that the three develop a very strong friendship, marking their lives for the remaining film. Although they were born in the throes of a challenging political climate, what casts a surprising shadow on their relationships is the three characters' subsequent encounter with change a few years after Yu moves to Wuhan in post-1989 China and after Zhou Wei and Li Ti emigrate to Berlin. The film follows their troubled destinies: Li Ti ends up committing suicide in Germany, and Yu Hong attempts to fill the emotional void created by Zhou and Li's departure with a meaningless sexual relationship, secretly waiting for Zhou's return. When Zhou finally does move back to a China that has been drastically altered by Deng Xiaoping's Southern tour leading to more liberalization and opening up to Western capitalism, the lovers cannot reconnect emotionally. Because their brief repeat encounter does not offer either of them the satisfaction which they seek, they end up following separate paths in the film's finale. In his option to end the film on a sour note, Ye clearly contrasts the emotional distance of his characters in the political climate of the early 2000s to the interrelatedness that they experienced as students in Beijing, all the while pointing out the pluses and minuses of pre- and post-1989 China.

While the film has rightly been hailed as antiauthoritarian by several critics (Shen 2006, Li 2021), the same critics have failed to notice that the friendship which bonds the film's characters in the beginning describes the nature of a unique generation born in the midst of a particular political environment. While Qinna Shen has admitted that the film gives "authentic representations of campus and dorm life and of the romantic and sexual relationships of average students" (Shen 2006, 52), she has gone on to focus on the film's political message and placed disproportionate importance on the film's ban, which is indicative, as both Shen and Li have argued, of the CCP's unwillingness to remember inconvenient truths and create a sense of amnesia around the events of 1989 (Shen 2006, 74; Li 2021, 276). While this is certainly true – and very similar to the critical reading of Romanian films of the socialist period, as I will discuss shortly – neither of the two critics has valued the affective environment created before the time of change, which is a core attribute of the so-called "Tiananmen generation." This is despite Lou's clear intentions of depicting that generation as a cohesive collective predicated on togetherness and friendship.

What my reading of the two films suggests is not that Communism was not oppressive, surveillance-happy and homogenizing in its ideology, but that both Mungiu and Lou focus on the way in which citizens of the state, oppressive as it might have been, created a safe, intimate space in response to an allegedly authoritarian leadership. The phrase "communist structure of

---

Yugoslavia's anti-red bourgeoisie student protests of 1968, the students demonstrating in Beijing in 1989 were not there to overthrow the government, but to ask for dialogue.

feeling" (Williams 1977), which Robé has borrowed from Raymond Williams to refer to life under Communism in his critique of the Romanian film, should therefore be read less in reference to the politically-dictated homogenization of Romanian society before the anticommunist revolution of 1989, and more in relation to the universe engendered by commonplace responses to economic challenges and material scarcity. To stereotypically assign this structure of socialist feeling solely to the category of "oppressiveness" is to caricaturize real-existing socialism, something which amounts to selling Eastern suffering to a Western audience (Grossman 2009). As it appears in both films, everyday life in socialism seems to be distinctly different from that in a capitalistic, individualistic society, in that it generated an affectivity now lost to the age of capitalism that became prevalent in both countries.

In this book, I treat lived realities and power – that is, life under socialism and the political authority of the state – as two distinct categories. Because, interestingly, both films show strong female friendships resulting in response to the state's authoritative structures, I hypothesise the existence of a socialist affect extant in both Romania's and China's Communist-ruled societies. In the hopes of recontextualizing the comparative histories of the two countries, I introduce the phrase "socialist affect" in order to comprehend better the socialist era outside the confines of anticommunist (re)interpretation. For this reason, the phrase "socialist affect" is predicated on the affective turn in the humanities, in the context in which socialist cultures endorsed not Communist ideology *per se*, but a form of socialism that created a unique response at the level of intrapersonal relationships.

Socialist Affect: The Theory

Applying affect theory to literary criticism, various scholars who have drawn on Baruch Spinoza and Gilles Deleuze have theorized affect as a state that provides "an understanding of how texts and images work beyond – or before, or below – signification" (van Alphen 2019, 163). Sara Ahmed, Eugenie Brinkema and Sianne Ngai have articulated that texts are not there solely to be interpreted but to be felt emotionally – that is, experienced – in the sense of entering into certain relations with the reader (Ahmed 2017, Brinkema 2014, Ngai 2005). Powered by specific triggers from the texts, readers feel an urge to act, via the emotions which texts elicit. This leads to a state of potentiality in the readers which can be described as "affect."

In my reading of "affect," I see state power ruling the lives of its subjects as similar to the power that texts have on their readers. Exercising power in this paradigm becomes a way of entering a dialogue between the state and its citizens. Citizens treated to state power in this way are therefore given the potentiality of reacting, and their reaction births a special type of interrelational dynamics charged with a specific type of affectivity. As in the similar inter-character relationships formed in the films analyzed above, this affectivity, so I claim, is recognizable in both China's and Romania's social environment.

Philosopher Jan Slaby has applied the understanding of affect to the field of politics. Believing that affect transgresses individual responses to triggers, such as those elicited by a text, Slaby has written about "relational dynamics between individuals within social domains" (Slaby 2019, 59), which he describes as "sophisticated dynamic arrangements that act as local conducers and channeling devices for affective interactions" (75). Although he has not described it in detail, Slaby has expanded this relational affect to include forms of response to other "applicable domains," such as "organizations, even subcultures, perhaps even entire nations or historical epochs" (77). Coupling this with Daniel White's understanding of feelings as "the primary field for strategising, measuring, and more generally experiencing politics" (White 2017, 177), I describe socialist affect as a political form of emotion generated by the interrelation between forms of political power and the citizens of the socialist state. This interrelation is the crux of what we proverbially refer to as the "national psyche," which in a socialist society describes the feelings and behaviors of citizens experiencing life in a socialist state.

To exemplify, Otilia and Yu Hong's reactions to their surroundings in both Mungiu's and Lou's films are predicated on societal values that are distinctive to China and Romania's late socialist era environments. Both films describe a social climate in which the lack of material resources and government investments (recall the dilapidated dorms in both films) create a reaction to state structures which is one of both opposition and accommodation. When this reaction is shared by a large group of people living in the same space, it becomes the basis of an emotional closeness that empowers the characters and confers upon them the unique ability to contest their surroundings jointly, which ultimately leads to the Tiananmen "democracy movement" in Lou's film and to the implied fall of the regime in Mungiu's. In fact, applying the theory of shared arousal found in crowds, which has been described by Elias Canetti, the Hungarian philosopher Endre Kiss has directly related the agency of the crowds to the Romanian uprising of 1989. Kiss has seen the masses in this context as instigators of change, moved by the affective current empowering them to commit the act of rebellion that led to the 1989 revolution (Kiss 2004).

Unlike in a capitalist society, such emotions would not exist outside the collective. Otilia and Găbița in Mungiu's film are after all powerless to oppose the patriarchy of the establishment. This is shown in the overbearing attitude with which Otilia is treated by her boyfriend's family during the dinner scene. Furthermore, the girls are equally powerless to oppose Mr. Bebe's domineering attitude, which points to a subtle connection between patriarchy and state power. Lou's film equally portrays political power as patriarchal, in the way in which authorities ultimately decide to unswervingly put down the Tiananmen protests. This, however, empowers the characters in both films to forge the affective bonds which will eventually shape their destinies. To put it another way, Yu and Otilia sublimate their opposition to the state and refocus it on building a sturdy friendship. It is impossible for both Mungiu's and Lou's characters to become anything but heavily emotionally involved, whether in a shockingly close friendship or a dangerous love triangle, and to lead any lives other than those dictated by the political contexts which birthed their affective relationships.

Extrapolating this relational affectivity to regional and transnational frameworks, one finds that people from cultures and nation-states in which the concept of private property was almost foreign, people who learned to address the state's economic and social requirements in a similar way, are more likely to relate to each other from congruent positions, yet differently from someone who has been raised in a capitalist economic climate. The above-mentioned similarity bridges the linguistic and cultural gap between such vastly different countries as Romania and China and imagines a way in which both Otilia and Yu could ultimately inhabit the same cultural and affective space. This makes visible the power of socialist affect to bridge differences, and it makes the comparative reading of films from both cultures possible.

In order to understand properly the inner workings of socialist affect in Romania and China, one has to understand the cultural environments of both countries, which in turn requires a short summary of the two countries' historical development of socialist practices.

The Political and Historical Background

When they entered the Communist era in the aftermath of World War II, both China and Romania left behind centuries of poverty during which, particularly in the rural areas, landowners and aristocrats accumulated great wealth while oppressing a large mass of landless peasants, who were oftentimes coerced to work on their masters' fiefs until death. More importantly, in the late 1940s both countries put an end to a century of colonialism. In China, colonialism was exerted by all the major capitalist stakeholders (Maddison 2006, Karl 2010), via the so-called "concessions areas" such as Shanghai, Beijing and Guangzhou, which were freely exploited from the mid-nineteenth century onwards, leading to what the Chinese would later call the "century of humiliation" (Karl 2010, 2). In a similar position, Romania was the victim of an even longer economic exploitation carried out by the surrounding Ottoman, Tsarist and Habsburg Empires (which over time owned various parts of the country) and in the interwar period indirectly by the neocolonial regimes of the United Kingdom, France and Germany, which turned the country into nothing less than their economic dependencies (Ban 2014, Turnock 1970, Liehm and Liehm 1977). These developments advanced the horrific fascism of the interwar period and World War II, when Romania, led by Hitler's friend Marshal Ion Antonescu, allied itself with Nazi Germany and entered the so-called "enlargement war" on Hitler's side, managing to temporarily expand its territory after winning several battles against the Soviet Union. Despite heavy casualties and the ongoing genocide perpetrated by the country's military against the Jews, the "enlargement war" was accepted as righteous by the majority of the Romanian population (Harward 2021).

Even though most historians do not agree that the Communists came to power in Romania with the consensual agreement of the masses,[2] leftist forces managed to cobble together a motley coalition of both liberal and Communist supporters called the Democratic Bloc (*Blocul democrat*), which brought them a majority of votes in the first republican-held elections of 1946. Because of Romania's war against the USSR on the side of Nazi Germany, however, the country was forced to pay reparations to the Soviet Union. Consequently, Soviet companies practically exploited the Romanian soil for more than a decade while the Red Army watched on, until the leadership of Gheorghe Gheorghiu Dej, Romania's first secretary general of the Communist Party,[3] managed to oust the Russian troops from the country in 1958.

Given their relatively similar socio-political prewar history, it is not surprising that China and Romania followed similar paths to postwar reconstruction and shared comparable timelines as People's Democracies. Romania turned Communist in 1947, when the government strengthened its hold on power by forcing the former king to abdicate, while in 1949, following a speech in which he declared that "the Chinese people have stood up" in front of a large popular gathering in Tiananmen Square, Mao declared that the country would follow a revolutionary road to Communism.

In 1949, China emerged from various wars in ruins. It had fought the "War of Resistance against Japanese Aggression" and also endured the longest Civil War in history, between Mao's Communists and the nationalist Kuomingtang forces, a civil war which had lasted nearly twenty years and claimed millions of lives. To make things worse, in 1950 China became involved in yet another conflict – the "War to Resist US Aggression and Aid Korea" – because the United Nations, headed by the US, was trying to drive Communism out of the Korean peninsula. Following three years of warfare that nearly wiped the town of Pyongyang from the map and led to the extermination of a large number of civilians, Korea would finally become divided along the thirty-eighth parallel, and it remains so to this day.

While Mao tried to rebuild what was left of the Chinese economy in the early 1950s, the assistance of the Soviet Union which he had previously enjoyed started to diminish after 1956, when Khrushchev condemned Stalin's atrocities in his well-known "Secret Speech." Because Mao adhered to a more traditional view of Marxism (and was personally deterred by his hostility to Khrushchev), cooperation between the two countries decreased. This brought about what historians called the "Sino-Soviet split" in the early 1960s. As result, Mao was left to reconstruct the nation by himself. Determined to quickly reduce the differential in economic development

---

2 This is contested by a majority of historians today. The degree to which this view is influenced by political preferences in postsocialism and does not constitute an unbiased historical fact remains to be debated. For more on this matter, see Tismăneanu, Solonari, Totok and so on.

3 In this book, I capitalize the 'Party' when describing the Communist Party but do not do so when referring to the concept of any party in general.

between China and the West, with the help of those people who genuinely admired him, he launched the "Great Leap Forward" in 1958. The initiative aimed to "turn villages into factories and peasants into steel producers" (Dirlik 2017, 391), by enlisting the populace in methods of production never seen before in a modern country. Although the movement, which lasted approximately four years, spurred productivity, it drew harsh criticism from the West, adding more reasons for the Western media to denounce Mao's alleged personality cult.

China and Romania established diplomatic relations in 1949, with Romania being the third country in the world to recognize the Chinese Communist Party and the People's Republic (Xu 2006, 6). Historian Qiang Zhai has believed that "[a]t a time when the United States and many other Western countries refused to recognize Mao's government," this gave China "international legitimacy and empowerment" (Zhai 2013, 35). Interestingly, what brought the two countries together was shared distrust of the Soviet Union, and it was under this affective spell that part of the Sino-Romanian friendship was built. This shared distrust and, later, the special relationship that Romania enjoyed with the US caused the historian Wang Taiping to call Romania the country with which China had "the least ups and downs, and the longest friendly cooperation," besides North Korea (Wang, quoted in Liu 2006, 14).

Dej's enthusiasm for Mao's defiant approach to the Soviets ultimately precipitated Romania's ideological alignment with the Chinese Communists. Furthermore, as China often found itself in conflict with both Cold War superpowers, the Soviet Union and the US, Bucharest was happy to mediate between them. Nicolae Ceaușescu – a young, aspirational leader who had served in the military before becoming the minister of agriculture – took over as secretary general after Dej's death and was proud to promote such a policy of mediation. Outspoken in his criticism of Soviet meddling in Romania's economy, Ceaușescu continued Dej's plans to industrialise the desperately poor country. The first results became apparent in the 1960s, when economic growth finally allowed the government to abandon food-rationing policies that had been in place since the previous decade and to increase market liberalization. As one of the fastest-growing countries in Eastern Europe, Romania espoused a policy of what some authors have called "reform communism" (Eyal et al. 1998), which represented the polar opposite of the Stalinist 1950s, when the Party-held media abounded in declarations of political and cultural commitment to the Soviet line. By the end of the decade, Romanian radio waves were abuzz with the Italian pop hits of Gianni Morandi and Rita Pavone; women's hairstyles rivaled those of their Western counterparts; and movie theaters were showing John Wayne and Clint Eastwood Westerns, as well as Elvis Presley musicals, thus reversing a 1950s' trend in which 75 precent of foreign films screened in Romania were imported from the Eastern Bloc.

2 The Story of Romanian and Chinese Socialist Cinemas

The Beginnings

China and Romania began exporting films to each other as early as in 1952, as a means of fostering their cultural and economic ties and as a sign of friendship. At that time, there was little mutual knowledge of the two countries' cultures, and even less so of their cinemas. The exchanges would continue for the entire duration of the socialist period, in which the Romanian government acquired approximately 140 Chinese film titles used for archival and documentation purposes, about ninety of which were screened in theaters. By contrast, approximately seventy Romanian films were shown in China between 1949 and 1989, although the number of acquired titles by the Chinese government may have been higher.[1]

While during and after Khrushchev's Thaw[2] between the late 1950s and the early 1970s Romania opened its screens to imports from Western European countries, China usually, albeit not exclusively, favored Soviet, North Korean, North Vietnamese and Eastern European movies. Researcher Jing Li has argued that, "of all the films at the time, Romanian films were the most courageous in their display of a relationship between a man and a woman" (Li 2010, 35), which meant that, for young people in love, watching Romanian (and sometimes Albanian) films was similar to tasting the "forbidden fruit" (36). Chinese audiences interpreted Romanian films as emancipatory as well as progressive, because aside from boldly expressing love and romance onscreen, some Romanian films also tackled political topics considered delicate in China, such as land nationalization and the punishment of the kulaks. This goes to show not only the influence that Romanian films had on an entire generation of Chinese viewers, but also demonstrates that these movies opened a channel for affective communication between China and Eastern Europe. This channel then tightened connections between cultures

[1] Screenings after 1989 are not considered here, because the availability of videocassettes, the advent of television and the liberalized market significantly increased the number of films and venues available for viewing in both Romania and China.

[2] An initial period of liberalization in the Soviet Union following Stalin's death in 1953, which later spread to other Eastern European countries.

that were otherwise dissimilar and, to a certain degree, incomprehensible to one another.

While roughly half of Romanian imports were screened in China before 1976, the year of Mao's death, the remaining were shown between 1978 and 1993 and represented almost 6 percent of all foreign film imports during this period. Although apparently small, this figure is important in a country as large as China. After Japan, France, the United Kingdom, North Korea and the USSR, in that order, Romania came in sixth among the countries which sent their films to China (Li 2010, 41). This reflects the great popularity that Romanian films enjoyed among audiences as well as Chinese officials, even after China had opened up its market to Western imports and capitalist-produced films in the post-Mao era. Furthermore, it reflects the power that socialist affect had in creating transnational affinities.

Socialist Realism

The socialist filmmaking history of both Romania and China emerged in the throes of socialist realism, or, as the Chinese used to call it, Revolutionary Realism and Revolutionary Romanticism. The difference between Stalin's mid-1930s' "socialist realism," which I will describe presently, and Revolutionary Romanticism is significant for the development of the style in China, because the concept suffered a process of alteration and transference from Soviet Russia to Mao's China. In the late 1950s, Mao stressed that, in the fashioning of an erstwhile "qunzhong wenyi" (culture of the masses), a combination of "Revolutionary Realism" and "Revolutionary Romanticism" was necessary in order to capture both "revolutionary passion, revolutionary ideals and practicality" (Mao, quoted in Wang 2014, 94). Film historian Zhuoyi Wang has offered a clear understanding of this combination, which he has abbreviated as 2RR, explaining that the style was meant to create a distinct Chinese feel for the times, so as to differentiate it from post-Thaw Soviet socialist realism. While these differences should indeed be made clear, it is also my goal in this book to stress the similarities rather than the marked differences between the Chinese and Romanian cultural spaces – similarities that, so I argue, ultimately created common themes and aesthetic practices predicated on socialist affect and a similar outlook on national history.

It is generally accepted that socialist realism originated in Stalin's founding decree of 1934, announced during the meeting of the Soviet Writers' Union. Following this announcement, socialist realism is thought to have smothered the pioneering and distinctly "superior" avant-garde of the 1920s, only to spread its gangrenous influence in the coming decades over the entire art of the Eastern Bloc. Prominent film historians of Soviet, Chinese and Eastern European cinemas (such as Jay Leyda and Antonin and Mira Liehm) have indicted socialist realism for producing nothing but mass-numbing, dogmatic works that exasperated, bored and turned away from the screens a vast number of viewers (Leyda 1972, Liehm and Liehm 1977). The reason behind this – so it is implied – was that art was strictly subordinated to politics; or, in Walter Benjamin's words referencing the rise of fascism in the culture of 1930s Germany, the outcome was the classic *aestheticization of politics* (Benjamin 2008). Frightened by the Soviet experiment with Communism, Western powers rebuffed the politics of the Eastern Bloc and in retribution chose to denounce Communist culture as unpopular. Aided by the US Congress, which during the Cold War funded the CIA to carry out a continuous assault on Communist culture (Paddington, 2000), the Western condemnation of art and literature originating in the Eastern Bloc led to an outright demonization of socialist realism.

In *Dreamworld and Catastrophe*, US cultural theorist Susan Buck-Morss has contended that what turned Western attention in the 1960s to the avant-garde of the Russian 1920s was a politically grounded reinterpretation of early Soviet art. This reinterpretation sanctioned the work of Kazimir Malevich (whose "Black Square," so Buck-Morss has insisted, represents the birth of postmodernism in the West) as a revered object in an increasingly polarized East-West political divide. Buck-Morss has further claimed that the Western apotheosis of Malevich was a political act that only later would become associated with art proper. In other words, it was cultural politics first, and culture later (Buck-Morss 2000).

I contend that a similar process sealed the fate of socialist realism: as Stalinist politics became increasingly questionable in the eyes of the West from the late 1930s until the dictator's death, it was the art of El Lissitzky, Alexander Rodchenko, Dziga Vertov and Vsevolod Mayerhold – all artists somehow associated with formalism and experimentation – that the West continued to see as "unadulterated," while socialist realism became associated with a corruption of the original goals of the revolution and, ultimately, with propaganda. Boris Groys has explained in *The Total Art of Stalinism* that socialist realism, however, represented a continuation rather than a break with the avant-garde, arguing that "Stalinist poetics is the immediate heir to constructivist poetics" (Groys 1992, 36). Indeed, if compared to the utopian, forward-thrusting designs of the constructivists, the stylized image of the low-angle, triumphant socialist worker of early socialist realist films appears as an actualization rather than a defeat of the avant-garde.

By glorifying the mundane yet magnificent aspect of war or daily manual labor – as well as Communist revolution in the case of the Chinese revolutionary operas – socialist realism is not only populist (proletkultist) or dictatorial (fashioned by diktat from the top), but also, as Katerina Clark has contended, surprisingly and disarmingly simple (Clark 1981). Whether featuring cooperative-farm-related love stories, as in the case of the so-called kolkhoz musicals in the Soviet Union, or glorifying the People's Liberation Army in China, socialist realism, not unlike the ideology of Communism itself, has nothing "to hide"; it comes with no strings attached. While simplicity never amounted *ipso facto* to "bad art" previously, it is precisely this simplicity, however – the very core of what the bourgeoisie referred to as their unrefined aesthetics and disarming honesty – that became grounds for attack from the modernist and postmodern camps: How can an art designed by a vicious dictator like Stalin have been inoffensive? How can it be simply taken at "face value"? How come socialist realism did not actually lead to the Gulag?

What we witness, in fact, is a splitting of theoretical discourses to serve political ends: while in the East what is being recuperated from classicism, as in Andrei Zhdanov's description of the mission of socialist realism, is the heritage of "all nations" to "inspire the working people" (Zhdanov, quoted in Groys 1992, 40), in the West there is a recuperation of both European naturalism and Russian formalism to oppose the later ideology of Communism – that is, to paraphrase Walter Benjamin, neither an aestheticization of politics nor a politicization of art, but a simple process of instrumentalization for political means.

Aside from Boris Groys, other authors have recently attempted to re-evaluate socialist realism. Anikó Imre and Constantin Parvulescu in their work on Eastern European cinema (Imre 2016, Parvulescu 2015) have both shown not only that cultural policies in each country of the region differed from those of Soviet Russia (particularly during the Thaw), but also, as Paul Coates has demonstrated in reference to Poland, that socialist realism and the kinds of films which it engendered were a complex phenomenon that does not fit its current clichéd interpretation as indoctrination. In fact, in *TV Socialism*, Imre has discussed the case of several TV series that sprung from the early genre and were later made during socialism, such as militia-driven action dramas, which were genuinely loved for their entertainment value (Imre 2016). As will be discussed shortly, this also made audiences enjoy early Romanian socialist realist films, since they swallowed the ideological content for the sake of their pure entertainment value.

Although impacted by the style of the Soviet Union, it is up for debate to what degree the socialist realist films in China and Romania were directly influenced by it. In an intriguing analysis of what she has called a "Chinese socialist road movie," film scholar Ling Zhang has implied that the 1959 ethnic film *Five Golden Flowers* (*Wu duo Jinhua*, Wang Jiayi) – which, so she has written, "encompass[es] ethnic inclusivity, agricultural collectivity and consolidat[es] community" (Zhang 2018, 151) – is also indebted to the road movie and musical tradition; it "incorporat[es] folk and traditional culture as a source of inspiration" and "fuses traditional rural and local cultural forms with ideological commitment" (158). Similarly, although themes such as the anti-kulak campaign promulgated in the Soviet Union found some traction with early Romanian socialist dicta, 1950s films undeniably chose to highlight the particularities of local tradition and lifestyle rather than to reproduce those from Soviet Russia. Moreover, the style of the first socialist films in Romania and China, despite having elements in common with the Soviet socialist realism of the 1930s, determinedly resemble each other, more so than they do with the better-known films of their bigger neighbor and political mentor.

A Comparative Analysis of the First Socialist Films in Romania and China

In analyzing the outcomes of socialist realism outside of the Soviet Union, it will be helpful to identify similarities and differences between the first two films produced in 1949 by the Romanian and Chinese Communist film industries, respectively. Rather than judging only the poor technical standards of Paul Călinescu's *Reverberates the Valley* (*Răsună valea*) and Wang Bin's *The Bridge* (*Qiao*), as other authors have done (Nasta 2013, 13), in looking at the two films side by side, I try to ascertain whether the socialist realism that they promoted did not perchance play an entertaining as well as educational role, while engendering a transnational affectivity recognizable in both cultures. The two films clearly intended to spread the ideologies of their governments, but they also played the significant role of creating and molding a new type of affectivity and, ultimately, a new audience who would subsequently come to love the tone, character types and situational humor that films such as these popularized for the remainder of the socialist era.

Reverberates the Valley was created in response to a then-current economic necessity. Cut off from its main sources of energy at the time, the new Romanian nation needed a steady supply of fuel from the coal mined in the remote mountainous Jiu region to guarantee its survival. Soon after taking power, the Communists started the reconstruction of a railroad left unfinished by the bourgeois government and needed volunteers to see it through to completion. For this reason, the Bucharest Politburo hired the bourgeois-era film director Paul Călinescu to document the construction process. Since replicating the construction site in the studio was out of the question – for once, this would have been financially unfeasible, and secondly, the country did not have a film studio yet – Călinescu traveled with his crew to the Jiu Valley to use some of the actual brigadiers already working on the site as actors. Shooting on location and using real-life characters as actors turned the film into a neorealist experiment, a first for Romania.

The opening sequence of *Reverberates the Valley* features triumphant classical music as the credits roll over stunning images of the breathtaking Jiu region in the Carpathian Mountains. In a clear effort to popularize volunteerism, a title card announces that the film is dedicated to the "thousands of young people who answered the call of the Romanian Workers' Party […], thereby contributing to the completion of the Bumbești-Livezeni railway." This railway's construction would reconnect the region with the rest of the country and improve living standards in the area.

Next, two spirited young men are seen writing down the names of young volunteers while hunched over a massive logbook in a recruitment office. When they are asked about the number of people who have answered the call, one of them closely inspects the logbook, which dissolves via an iris-shot into a montage of factory workers, peasants and students introduced as the "hundreds of thousands of young people from all parts of the country heading over to the construction site with full enthusiasm." The montage later shows youthful groups of people walking with the Communist and Romanian flags in their hands, illustrating the great distance that the brigades had to travel on foot from the urban to the mountainous areas. We can see faces of determined yet unassuming young men and women in casual clothing crowding the screen from all directions, as eye lines intersect with each other. Eisenstein's dialectical montage theory, according to which a number of opposing camera perspectives and intersecting orientations provide an atmosphere of energy, is combined with Dziga Vertov's pioneering montage style to exude optimism and to incorporate as much documentary material into the metanarrative as possible.

Not as specific in its propagandist message as the Romanian film, the Chinese film *The Bridge* generally aimed to raise the morale of the exhausted working class at the end of the long Sino-Japanese war. Although released in 1949, the film takes place in the spring of 1947, before the coming to power of the Communist regime. During the last years of the war, a bridge previously destroyed in battle needs fast rebuilding so that the army can carry the wounded across the waters of the Sungari River in Manchuria. In a busy montage of wintry landscapes, we see soldiers fighting fierce battles in the snow while we hear energetic marching music. The atmosphere is vivacious, and the shots are reminiscent of early Soviet montage scenes as in Eisenstein's *October*. The shots, of course, also remind one of Călinescu's film, especially when, as in the beginning of *Reverberates the Valley*, intertitles call to mobilization "for the war effort and for the sake of victory."

If Călinescu's film starts in a volunteer recruitment office, in almost eerie likeness, Wang's drama opens in a crowded room in which a soldier busily answers phones while his comrades bombard him with questions about the status of the bridge. Mirroring the scenario of *Reverberates the Valley*, the conflict emerges early in the film, as a skeptical engineer of apparent bourgeois persuasion clashes with the Communist steel plant manager over the way in which the bridge repairs should be carried out. While the Communist manager insists that the work needs to be finished in fifteen days because of the imminent thaw of the river, which would lead to dangerously high water-levels, the engineer asks for four months instead. Without necessary supplies such as electricity and steel, so the bourgeois engineer reasons, the project is scientifically unsound. This forces the workers – inexperienced but well versed in eight years of anti-Japanese warfare – to attempt the impossible and by means of a collective effort repair an electric furnace in order to produce steel, the most precious resource.

Unlike the workers who are usually portrayed in long shots, the bourgeois engineer in *The Bridge* is framed in medium close-ups, which in the audience's minds cast doubts about his honest intentions. The engineer in Wang's film, moreover, wears a Western suit and smokes a pipe, much like the former bourgeois in *Reverberates the Valley*, who also wear felt hats. Furthermore, like the Romanian antagonist himself, Wang's engineer sports a mustache, which, in the context of the Sino-Japanese War, makes him appear suspicious and more like the Japanese enemies.

A similar pair of engineers – the bourgeois and the Party-mandated one – confront each other in *Reverberates the Valley* over differing timeframes concerning the construction of the railroad. While the bourgeois engineer thinks that the job needs seven years to complete, the Communist retorts that they could finish the task in seven months. Unlike in *The Bridge*, this rather abstract conflict is, however, supplemented with a more dramatic one, which contrasts a comical bourgeois dandy type with the more serious collective of experienced workers. A banker's son from Bucharest wearing a tuxedo and a top hat, Nikki volunteers on the construction site mainly to attract women and have a good time. Using Eisensteinian contrasts to describe the corruption of the rich, Călinescu juxtaposes Nikki's lavishly decorated house, replete with servants carrying liquor glasses on fancy trays, with scenes in which lean brigadiers crack well-natured jokes while toiling in the blazing sun.

Nikki's attitude almost puts him in the same league as Crețu, a reactionary laborer on the worksite, who is unhappy with the new regime and usually portrayed as lurking in the shadows, making unwanted passes at the female brigadier Sanda. When Crețu is demoted by his supervisor for touching Sanda inappropriately, this establishes a clash between the progressiveness of Communism and reactionary toxic masculinity, and it also introduces the topic of women's liberation, a crucial subplot of the movie, and an episode prophetically foreshadowing subsequent discussions in academia and political discourses. Crețu's dismissal from the site leads him to commit an act of sabotage. To the sounds of a brooding classical tune appropriate for a thriller, Crețu blows up a mountain wall the collapse of which causes the death of a young volunteer. This acts as a deterrent for other workers, who decide that the effort is not worth their lives and head home – that is, until the dead volunteer's brother signs up to replace him, which serves as a motivation for the rest to return.

Both films focus on the resilience of the workers in the face of adversity. Their optimism is permanently contrasted to the former bourgeoisie's generally stand-offish attitude. Furthermore, even though unkempt and untidy, Communist workers almost always wear a smile. As in Călinescu's film, shots indicating friendly relations among them in *The Bridge* point to an affective solidarity and enthusiasm, which communicate that it is not the individual, but the collective that is more important in this conflict. In *The Bridge*, the selflessness and altruism of this collective are sublimated in the figure of Liang Risheng, the prototype of the calm, accommodating and unaffected worker who is prone to self-sacrifice. Skipping lunch breaks and refusing the medicine that his wife gives him, Liang is obsessed with making the furnace produce steel, despite a lack of resources. After replacing the old dolomite used to reinforce the furnace walls with refractory bricks, Liang finally succeeds in heating up the furnace to the required temperature to produce steel.

If the volunteers are shown as brothers-in-arms in both films, in *The Bridge* female characters are few and primarily utilized in supporting roles – such as that of Liang's wife. In contrast to the wife's rather submissive attitude, Sanda in the Romanian film is independent and self-driven, even though she is doubly solicited, by her job as laborer on a difficult construction worksite and by her male coworkers who exert upon her unwanted sexual pressure. This pressure comes to a culminating point when Crețu, in a demonstration of bestiality, decides to rape Sanda for revenge. Although he is caught by a volunteer before carrying out his actions, Crețu continues to hold a grudge. In order to receive satisfaction, he plots to detonate the last railway tunnel which his coworkers are about to finish that night. Just as he is about to blow up the gallery, he is apprehended by a progressive co-worker and killed, following a long physical fight that provides tension and suspense. After a well-staged vaudeville number in which Nikki is humorously ridiculed in a moment of comic relief, the dénouement shows a locomotive donning Communist insignia, pulling a train full of volunteers along the valley. The engine-mounted camera pans to show the spectacular sights of the mountain gorge to the sounds of triumphant music, while a peasant in traditional clothes, who in the beginning of the film was introduced as opponent to Crețu's reactionary ideas, watches from afar in admiration.

The Chinese film features a finale highly similar to the Romanian one. The ice on the river melts with the arrival of spring, which requires an increased number of workers to complete the bridge repair work in time. Although a small-sized replica is used to show the progressive rebuilding in extreme long shot, the various low-angle close-ups of construction workers perched on dangerous scaffolding on top of the bridge, struggling to complete the work as the icy waters flow underneath are effective. When the bourgeois engineer arrives by train to inspect the work nearing completion, his attitude changes. This is a double-edged victory for the Communists who not only finish work on time, but also win a victory over the bourgeoisie. In the inauguration ceremony, a train engine with workers perched on each side and carrying red flags crosses the bridge to the cheers of a crowd chanting Mao's name. Even though by then he has well earned a break, Liang once more refuses to rest, claiming that the reconstruction work which the people have only started needs to be carried through to the end.

In the film's finale (Figures 2.1 and 2.2), one of Liang's coworkers asks the manager to join the Party. This is Old Hou, an endearing, bearded worker wearing a sheepskin overcoat, who is the equivalent of the old man in traditional garb saluting the train engine in admiration at the end of *Reverberates the Valley*, as the train rolls past him. While Old Hou earlier gave several speeches in which he compared the poverty of the Chinese proletariat to that of orphaned children, the Romanian farmer was mostly silent – his function still is as important. Considering both countries' experiences with colonialism and the millions of dead in World War II, these two older characters bespeak optimism for change while also playing a performative role which prefigures their young governments' ambitions to enter the big politics game in the years to follow. While in China's case this was predicated on the referenced lack of resources and feudalist mentality, which Mao had identified as the

Figures 2.1 and 2.2 The similar train engines rolling on the new tracks in the finales of *The Bridge* and *Reverberates the Valley*.

main reason for China lagging behind the West, foreshadowing the sacrifices of the Great Leap Forward some ten years later, in Romania's case it described the badly needed industrialization that the country would undergo starting in the 1950s.

Style and Criticism

Not only is Călinescu's editing in *Reverberates the Valley* sometimes amateurish, but his shots are generally static and close-ups almost absent (Popescu 2011, 65), evidencing theatricality and a lack of continuity editing that clearly betrays the film's educational function. Moreover, conversations look staged, and the subtext is oftentimes too obvious to be believable. This clearly shows the Romanian film industry's lack of experience until that moment, as well as the attempt, on behalf of the crew, to overcome the limitations of rudimentary professional equipment. In his own defense, Călinescu later stated that he fully acknowledged his "mistakes inherent to beginnings," but believed that the film should be seen primarily as a historical document (Călinescu 1982, 105). The press of the time praised the film, noting from a political perspective that *Reverberates the Valley* marks a break with the "scorn and indifference" that the bourgeois regimes had shown for the Romanian film industry. The 1950s film critic Emil Suter has also written that the former regime's servility to the West ensured that filmmaking lacked the necessary means to develop into a proper industry in Romania, and that the country remained primarily an outlet for dumping mediocre Western products (Suter 1950).

These conditions made viewers curious to watch the first Romanian-made production after the collapse of capitalism, and Suter's quip that the proletariat "looks forward enthusiastically to the production of fiction films" as expression of an art that is "national in form and socialist in content" (Suter 1950) is not only verbiage. This was the mood that captured the nationalistic trend of the time, according to which Romania wanted to make a name for itself as a viable competitor for Western film products. Political concerns aside, the film directly affected some of the movie-goers of the 1950s. In a 2013 article[3] reminiscing about life in socialism, a certain Mr. Ilie has written that "in the mid-fifties the supreme 'fad' was to be seen on a volunteer construction site wearing a brigadier's uniform." A 1950s volunteer himself, Ilie has proudly confessed over half a century later that he was one of the "millions of youths – almost a child at the time – who filled the country's demand for volunteer labor, and one who fondly remembers, among other titles conferred to [him] later, the designation of 'brigadier'" (Teodorescu 2013).

Volunteer construction sites were enormously popular in the Soviet Union and Eastern Europe after World War II. Aside from filling their countries' need for manual labor, these sites also fulfilled the need for socializing that many teenagers acutely felt following the privations of the war. That young people were driven to sign up on volunteer construction sites, as Ilie has written, by "the spirit of adventure" (Teodorescu 2013) and not by coercion is confirmed by the British commander of a volunteer brigade during the construction of another railway, the Sarajevo-Šamac line in Yugoslavia, in 1947. Working amidst the volunteers, the commander noticed that his workers' dedication was not necessarily to an ideology, but to the genuine desire to rebuild their war-torn country (Karamanić and Momčilović 2017, 225). *Reverberates the Valley* therefore catered to the young generation of baby boomers who made up the thickest ranks of movie-going audiences in the 1950s and who could genuinely relate to the film because their experiences coincided with those of their onscreen heroes. This proved the government right when appreciating that some audience members were highly interested in seeing a version of their own selves on the screen. Since the youngsters of the 1950s largely became the proletarians of middle-period socialism, the government also appreciated correctly that a film about the social experiences of volunteers would slowly lead to the emergence of a proletarian cinema to which most of the masses and future audiences could relate.

In 1971, film critic Radu Cosașu wrote in Romania's most important film monthly, *Cinema*, that *Reverberates the Valley* had "a clean and healthy schematism" in that the "puerile force of the construction site scenes prefigured the achievements of the investigative documentary" via shots of "uncontrived beauty" which mixed "documentary style with invention, ciné-vérité with fiction, and realism with surrealist photomontage." He has further appreciated Călinescu's sincerity of showing workers wearing patched shirts, sweating and not looking their best, even though his direction of actors was minimal and the acting theatrical (Cosașu).

Although postsocialist critics indicted the film for its ideological normativity – Popescu has called it "virulent propaganda" (Popescu 2011, 76),

[3] This article was written in response to an invitation by *Evenimentul Zilei*, one of the rabid anticommunist dailies founded in the 1990s, which asked readers to recount their socialist-era experiences in a column sarcastically titled "Memories from the Golden Age," drawing on the name that Ceaușescu popularized in reference to the late socialist period.

while Jitea finds it ironic that a bourgeois filmmaker was chosen to direct the first Communist film (Jitea 2021, 30) – younger Romanian critics such as Iulia Necșulescu have correctly identified a "predominantly contemptuous attitude toward 1950s Romanian cinema," which is "prevalent among the general public, and sometimes even among movie-goers" (Necșulescu 2022). Seeing through the postsocialist propaganda condemning the socialist propaganda, as it were, Necșulescu has recommended a less impassionate reading of socialist-era cinema, opining that a monovalent interpretation of these works in a disparaging key is due to the "unrealistic expectations that modern audiences have of these films, considering the place and historical context in which they were made." Instead of deconstructing these films by using the overly sophisticated methods of contemporary cognitivist analysis, Necșulescu has suggested overlooking their so-called "technical or structural shortcomings" and using alternate tools to "investigate the portrayal of gender roles predicated on the ideology of the period." In this reading, Necșulescu has seen the film as progressive for its ability to call out toxic masculinity and stand up for the independence of women in a context in which few other national cinemas, including those of the West, were prepared to do something similar (Necșulescu 2022).

As prefigured by Suter's political reading, a more thorough investigation of the film's political content would reveal that *Reverberates the Valley* is a deeply national response to Romania's subjugation in the postcolonial postwar context.[4] This represents an important performative gesture that would insure the country's independence, from the Soviet encroachment of the 1950s on the Romanian economy as well as from the country's former neocolonial regimes.

It is interesting that, although it decried the colonization of the country by Western powers and the Soviet Union, socialist realism fails to be appreciated today, despite promoting the country's economic independence, whose disappearance politicians bemoan in postsocialism. While, as Liehm and Liehm have put it, Romania passed from the semi-colonial hands of Great Britain, France and the US in the 1930s into those of the Soviet Union after the war (Liehm and Liehm 1977, 139) and considering moreover what David Turnock has called the interwar "autarchic industrial policy by the liberals"

[4] Ironically, the dogmatism of the Romanian film reminds one of the 1937 US Department of Interior production of *Boulder Dam*. Documenting the building of the Hoover Dam on the Colorado River in the mid-1930s, the film served as a propaganda piece meant to soften the environmental impact of the dam and the news of the 112 workers killed on the immense construction site. As one scholar has put it, the film's voice-of-god narration and its rigid omniscient style helped "shape (and exploit) public perception of and attitudes towards the dam project," attempting to "influence the public 'image' of the dam, that is, to fix it in the American social imaginary" (Arrigo 2010, iii). A similar sententiousness is felt in *Reverberates the Valley*, which, even in the absence of a voice-of-god narration, manipulates the viewers' sympathies, aligning them rather quickly with the government's position on the postwar reconstruction effort.

and the "stranglehold of German trade," which forced Romania to buy overpriced German manufactures (Turnock 1970, 542), it is not surprising that the postwar Communist regime was determined to take economic matters into its own hands and reverse the slow growth of the 1930s. Above all, the film intended to performatize and glorify the Romanian effort against the Axes forces and provide some dignity to a country that had moved from being a fascist dictatorship to being a Soviet satellite in only a few years.

If one accounts for the railway's historical significance, the film presents a surprising lesson. As the mountainous Jiu Valley in the center of the country hosted mines which had been the property of the Austro-Hungarian government until 1918,[5] the multiethnic brigades made up of Romanian, German and Hungarian units validated not only the country's rich multiculturalism, but also demonstrated that Communism did more than only pay lip service to internationalism. Downplaying the extraordinary effort put forth by the multiethnic brigades of nearly 29,000 volunteers, the articles and documentaries produced under postsocialism have stated that, although the brigadiers built the railroad by moving 2.5 million tons of rock, sometimes with their bare hands (BZI 2016), they did so because they were "indoctrinated" and thus overzealous (Povestea et al. 2014). With thirty-nine tunnels completed in seven months, however, the Bumbești-Livezeni railroad appears to be a comparative triumph in human engineering and sheer willpower, especially in a country whose infrastructure construction work largely stalled during the thirty years after the fall of Communism,[6] due to fiscal mismanagement, corruption and embezzlement. Despite its vilification today, the railroad line is still in use, even if mishandling of the country's rail system, the closure of the mines due to structural adjustment plans signed with the IMF and a lack of funding under postsocialism renders it less active than it was during the socialist era.

The film style in *The Bridge* harks back to the leftist productions made in pre-Communist Shanghai, such as Shen Xiling's *Crossroads* (*Shi zi jie tou*, 1937) and Zheng Junli's 1949 *Crows and Sparrows* (*Wuya yu maque*). Similar to these early socialist movies which, among other things, fiercely championed workers' rights, equality between classes and public housing availability for all, there are few stylistic innovations in *The Bridge*, and the cinematography

[5] The former Austro-Hungarian provinces of Transylvania and Bukovina, as well as Bessarabia, which had belonged to Russia since 1812, were joined after World War I to the other Romanian provinces to create what Romanian nationalists called "The Greater Romania."

[6] Bent on replacing rail with road transport, the postsocialist Romanian state contracted the American company Bechtel to build Romania's first highway in 2004. Due to endemic mismanagement, the state and Bechtel took almost ten years to build 35 kilometers of an unfinished motorway (about the same length as the Bumbești-Livezeni railroad line) and put the project on hold shortly after the beginning of 2013. Chinese construction companies, however, which have proven their efficiency in such projects in other parts of the world are, with few exceptions, banned from accessing tenders that involve transport infrastructure works, be they road or rail (Radu 2021).

follows the precepts of classic figure behavior and lighting, favoring storytelling over aesthetics. Aside from a few innovative shots taken from inside the steel furnace and aside from a scene in which the picture turns blurry and shaky to denote Liang's exhaustion, most of the scenes are shot indoors, using a camera that rarely moves. When it does move, it is to frame its subjects in classical positions. Furthermore, the music is largely illustrative and repetitive, figuring primarily in montage sequences, while the dominant grays of the steel works and the planning offices create an otherwise tense atmosphere. Finally, the film inherits a certain theatricality from the pre-socialist era. This is understandable since before the Communist take-over Wang Bin had directed the film version of Cao Yu's bourgeois-era play *Sunrise* and, apart from a few films, had worked primarily in theater.

In the pre-industrial, traditionalist landscape in which *The Bridge* was produced, its educational and inspirational value is not to be taken lightly. As literary critic Yingjin Zhang has written, "considering the fact that many filmmakers as well as military and rural audiences had lived through years of battles and that the Korean War was raging on, it is not surprising to see the immense popularity of the war or military genre during this period" (Zhang 2004, 192). Even though its focus was on industrial rather than military action, the fact that most of the population at the time was involved in the restructuring effort made even the inner working of an industrial factory suitable dramatic material. *The Bridge*, in fact, introduced the so-called peasant-soldier-worker style (*Gongnongbing*) to Chinese audiences, a style which drew its inspiration from the lives of everyday people who in turn recognized themselves onscreen. As in *Reverberates the Valley*, the situational conflicts and the characters in *The Bridge* were entertaining to a large part of the audience because they addressed concerns and featured characters with which spectators were familiar from their own working environment. This made the clearly stated propagandist message easier to swallow and less pompous than it appears today.

Even though *Gongnongbing* would be utilized *ad nauseam* by filmmakers in the following decades, it created a community both on- and offscreen. The characters in Wang's film are diverse: from an enthusiastic and handsome young man who taxes the laziness of a coworker to a passive comic sidekick only interested in his wages, all the characters exude energy. Because film in socialist cultures became the subject of debate and instigated the masses to action, and because everybody, from the most uneducated members of society to the highest placed, could see and relate to films, this energy gave rise to a collective affect derived directly from the silver screen. This socialist affect in China would allow the future enactment of late-1950s economic policies urging the Chinese to sacrifice their wellbeing for the country's economy, sacrifices which, incidentally, did drive the country to economic success eventually, if only half a century later.

In that sense, the focus of *The Bridge* was surprisingly economic for a motion picture, and therefore Marxist, in that the conditions which the film assumes as formative are those of the postwar reality of scarcity. Not so much a film about Stakhanovism proper (Liang is rather hesitant and less outspoken than one would expect of a working-class hero), *The Bridge* serves a social function – one that subsequent "war movies" would perpetuate: it reinforces working class concerns with acquiring and developing resources, dealing with scarcity through ingenuity and employing the fairytale motif of developing lack into abundance. In that sense – as in the case of the Romanian film – it addressed the audience's desire to build a better life, and it offered the poor and downtrodden masses hope, which played a part that was no less important than a saccharine Hollywood happy ending. Unlike their American counterparts, however, the endings that the early socialist masses watched onscreen were still potentially implementable in real life in those early days, through the sheer power of exerted effort and willpower.

Referencing the iconic message of the rather educational Soviet film *Road to Life* (*Putyovka v zhizn*, Nikolai Ekk, 1931), which reflects the partial influence that Soviet cinema had on both Chinese and Romanian directors, the almost identical endings of *Reverberates the Valley* and *The Bridge* – a train rides into the new world built by the fruits of Communist labor – show that, in addition to fostering hope, the interest in national economic recovery was serious on both sides of the Communist Bloc. This interest – mediated via a cinema that featured common themes, similar characters and a comparable narrative – helped shape the identity of a transnational socialist audience educated in the spirit of optimism, despite horrendous working conditions and a generalized lack of resources.

Rather than representing a recruitment poster for manual labor, both Călinescu's and Wang Bin's films attempt to demonstrate that personal happiness hinges on the effort to rebuild the national economy, which, in turn, bestows pride upon the individual who undertakes the effort to engage in physical labor. These conditions generated a type of forward-looking enthusiasm, which over time became recognizable to Romanian and Chinese audiences alike. The films also show that private and group interests can coalesce and lead to collective happiness, whose existence is predicated on the dismantling of bourgeois relations and the emergence of socialist affect.

Reverberates the Valley also had an enduring legacy for the way in which film and TV directors subsequently criticized mismanagement and inefficiency in the workplace. Numerous TV sketches featuring prominent Romanian actors – among them Radu Beligan, the thespian who had played the reformed bourgeois Nikki – thenceforth employed satire to denounce common socialist-era practices such as nepotism, corruption and theft. Painting factory directors in a negative light by way of comedic treatment helped show the trustworthiness of the common folk and paved the way for a satirical style that would survive almost unscathed into the postsocialist period.

The film's vestige of Neorealism also impacted filmmaking practices in the coming years. Drawing on Călinescu's interest in and employment of real-life characters, Lucian Bratu, Andrei Blaier and Mircea Mureșan, among many others, further employed the motifs of proletarian cinema to develop stories focusing on the real-life experiences of factory workers. These stories featured characters who, in early socialism, were confronted with class inequality, discrimination and the shock of moving from the countryside to the city, as shown by the ingénue peasant who leaves his home in a traditional village to join a construction site in *Partea ta de vină* (*Your Part of the Blame*, Mircea Mureşan, 1963) and becomes the victim of mockery and theft perpetrated by the wannabe socialites already present on site. Mureşan's theme is featured in a long series of now demonized construction site epics falling under the category of "actuality films," to be discussed below.

Although the enthusiasm for a better future, which is amply foregrounded in *Reverberates the Valley*, lasted a good twenty years, film directors in the 1970s began to question the basis of socialist realism upon which this early enthusiasm was built. This is the moment when erstwhile socialist realism was transformed into *social* realism. As I will discuss below, social realist films critiqued the continuing lack of resources that socialist labor markets faced in the 1980s, as well as the lack of improvement in living conditions which the working class found unsettling two decades into the socialist period.

Unlike in literary theory, I use the term "social realism" to denote the power of Romanian and Chinese films to truthfully represent the social and working conditions of the proletariat in socialist societies. Although derived from literary theory to refer to nineteenth-century psychological realism and despite its resemblance to Italian Neorealism and the British New Wave in cinema, social realism describes conditions that are decidedly different from those of the worker in a capitalist society. Since the particular lifestyles of socialist subjects are most intricately connected with the way in which the state imparts power, the individual in social realist films, unlike that in Hollywood-made populist entertainment, is not only a vital pawn in the economic rebuilding machine, but also an important member of the collective.

In the words of Thompson, "[i]n England some may smile when they hear of shock worker and heroic feats of labor. And yet there can be a heroism in labor equal to that in war. Its fruition and recognition appear to arise only in a society whose values are strange to those who have learnt the code of capitalism" (Thompson, quoted in Karamanić and Momčilović 2017, 226). Criticism of *Reverberates the Valley* in postsocialism is justified only because it used this very "code of capitalism" – in which economic growth became subjugated to personal wealth accumulation – as a guiding principle for a largely superficial and ahistorical analysis. As propaganda-driven as the film's heroism may appear today, it is clear that the style of early socialist realist films indeed fit the definition of proletarian cinema because it gave a sizable portion of the masses – to whom the volunteer brigades of the early 1950s belonged – the chance to truly identify with their own enthusiasm.

Feminism in Early Romanian Socialist and Maoist Cinemas

Early on in various Eastern European nations, Communist regimes became interested in what they called "actuality films." Drawing on the "actualities" of the Lumière brothers' early shorts, the concept was meant to describe the real living and working conditions of ordinary people, including those of women. In that sense, actuality films are comparable to the Chinese peasant-soldier-worker style, or *Gongnongbing*, which *The Bridge* started to popularize in the early 1950s. Although *Reverberates the Valley* essentially initiated a long run of Romanian *Gongnongbing* or *actuality films*, Călinescu's female-centered approach did not yield a comparable female-driven narrative until the mid-1960s, in contrast to the subsequent development of feminism in Chinese cinema.

Despite the relative lack of female presence in *The Bridge*, Wang Bin gave the young actress Tian Hua the important opportunity to play a female warrior seeking liberation from patriarchy in his very next project, *The White Haired Girl* (*Bai mao nü*), in 1950. This role, which Tian Hua would reprise in Lin Nong's 1958 film *Daughter of the Party* (*Dang de nu er*), would enable the actress to join a long list of heroines such as Bai Yang in *New Year's Sacrifice* (*Zhu Fu*, Sang Hu, 1956), Zhu Xijuan in *The Red Detachment of Women* (*Hong se niang zi jun*, Xie Jin, 1961) and Xie Fang in *Two Stage Sisters* (*Wutai jiemei*, Xie Jin, 1964) – all female figures who would become recurrent symbols of women's empowerment on Chinese screens. This empowerment was of course made possible by the 1949 Communist revolution, which valued the role of women in the class struggle, in the national liberation from foreign imperialism and in the process of abandoning unequal feudal relations.

Describing different social realities from those of capitalist cultures, feminism in socialism was based on the collective rather than the individual emancipation of women. In this sense, women were not meant to emulate their male rivals and compete for social advancement in order to close the gap undergirded by unequal pay and opportunity but to perceive themselves as equal in gender terms. Communist ideology perceived women as equally important in fostering the change in social relations that Communism was supposed to adduce. For that reason, although I refer to feminism as an integral part of socialist-era filmmaking, women's liberation in socialism should be understood differently from bourgeois feminism in capitalist cultures.

Similarly, patriarchy in socialist societies referred not only to the dominant male role in society, but also to the oppression caused by feudalism (in which the landlord oftentimes had the right of life and death over his indentured servants), as well as to imperialism and capitalism. This in China and Romania was a multipolar form of subjugation which rendered social realities for women in the two cultures eerily similar to each other, yet vastly different from those of women in Western societies.

The White Haired Girl marks the beginning of a long series of feminist and female-centered works spanning the entire duration of the Maoist era, which would also influence the fifth generation of Chinese directors working in the 1990s. It tells the story of an elderly farmer who, unable to pay his landlord's debts, is forced to sell his daughter into slavery. While a hallmark of propaganda illustrating the Party's emancipatory role in women's liberation, the film intuited the strength that women could marshal in a patriarchal, traditionally structured society based on feudal economic relations of productions.

Another iconic feminist film of the socialist era is *The Red Detachment of Women*, which was shot as both a feature film in 1961 and a revolutionary ballet performance in 1970. Not unlike *The White Haired Girl*, it tells the story of a female slave who plots her escape from a warlord's cruel grip, only to find liberation in a fortuitous encounter with a Communist women's army whose leader she becomes over time. In the film's finale, her humiliations are avenged when, helped by her female soldiers, she kills her former oppressor. The use of the color red in the film, coupled with energetic music, an abundance of effective low-angle shots and the fairytale-like plot structure where good overpowers evil, helped make the film (as well as its even more daring and expressive ballet version) very popular with Chinese audiences.

While the classic Lu Xun adaptation, *New Year's Sacrifice*, is a film set after the 1911 revolution,[7] during a time of peasant exploitation, which gives its female lead yet another chance to contest surviving feudal mores and traditionalism,[8] the 1963 movie *Struggles in an Ancient City* (*Ye huo chun feng dou gu cheng*, Yan Jizhou) constitutes a significant marker of Chinese feminism. Leaning towards a noir aesthetic, this spy film[9] has the feel of a thriller shot in contrasting shades of black and white against the oftentimes nighttime scenery of a small provincial town. The stylistically innovative film emphasizes the role of a young woman in an underground operation aimed at defending the provincial capital from Japanese troops and their collaborators. Coupled with dramatic music and suspense, as well as period costumes harking back to 1943, the time in which the film is set, it makes Yan's effort not only worthwhile to watch, but also historically memorable.

By contrast, in Romania, although not addressing women's liberation head-on, a truly feminist film came out only in 1964, treating for the first time a subject which the rather traditionalist Romanian culture of the time considered risqué. *Love Ended at Dawn* (*Dragoste lungă de-o seară*, Horea Popescu) is visionary for its time and bold in its subject-matter, because it discusses the issue of unwanted pregnancy in a remote, traditionalist village community. Although 1964 criticism has indicted the film for being less accomplished than the script from which it was adapted (Săraru 1964), the theme demonstrates undoubted progressiveness: one of three sisters becomes pregnant from the village boor, who avoids responsibility for his act and is in the film's finale condemned by the entire community for his irresponsible behavior. Romanian postsocialist criticism of films made in the 1950s and 1960s ignored the production, because – unlike *Reverberates the Valley*, which has a propagandist message – it apparently did not serve the

[7] Also called the Xinhai revolution, this was the movement that led to the collapse of the Qing dynasty and the establishment of the republic of China, an era marked by frequent conflicts between warlords, which did not put an end to the feudalist exploitation of the landless pesants. This would only be accomplished, after a long struggle, by Mao's Communist revolution in 1949.

[8] Due to delays, the film would be seen by Romanian audiences only in the 1980s.

[9] Most literally, the Chinese term for this genre is "anti-spy" film, or *fantepian*.

cause of anticommunist opprobrium with which films in this period tend to be treated today.

Aside from Popescu's film, Romanian cinema would have to wait more than fifteen years for *Charming Girl* (*Un film cu o fată fermecătoare*, Lucian Bratu, 1966) before a female-driven plot would emerge, and that only until Elena Ceaușescu,[10] the wife of the secretary general, precipitated the film's removal from theaters due to its alleged excess focus on bourgeois morals. Played by the country's most popular female singer of the time, Margareta Pîslaru, the heroine's extravagant physical appearance and overindulgence in personal care, as well as her abuse of charm to obtain favors from men, made the film unpalatable to the socialist establishment. Despite its apparent feminist message, *Charming Girl* only superficially focused on the topic of women's liberation, instead concentrating, like most actuality films of the 1960s, on the uncertainty that a young female would encounter after graduation in a world dominated by men. Nevertheless, the emotional confusion of the protagonist and the film's depiction of "the pleasures of the sophisticated-urban youth of a new Romania" (Gorzo 2018) made for a progressive turn in filmmaking, which opened up actuality films to themes which they had not tackled before. Unlike the praise it received in its native country, however, the film was not well received by critics elsewhere. In a review conspicuously entitled "Story of a Modern Idiot," a Polish critic has described the female lead as a girl with "a chicken brain" who "thinks that she is extremely clever," even though she obviously is a simpleton, while the film's director was blamed for "the inept and unconvincing characterization of the human environment" (Wilczynski 1968).

What the examples of both Romanian and Chinese early-period socialism films show is that the Communist authorities paid close attention to the issue of women's liberation, which they saw as integral to the effort of national rebirth. Although few in number, sometimes formulaic and treating some of their female protagonists without the depth they deserved, these films popularized gender equality and challenged the dominance of patriarchy in a deeply traditionalist society, which still foregrounded male figures as sole enablers of social change. They showed a female perspective of the reconstruction effort, which early socialist films such as Dinu Negreanu's *Nepoții gornistului* (*The Bugler's Grandsons*, 1953) and *Răsare soarele* (*The Sun Rises*, 1954) lacked. Negreanu's films feature anti-kulak plotlines favoring collectivization and are styled on typical Soviet socialist realist scenarios, such as those seen in Oleksandr Dovzhenko's *Earth* (*Zemlya*, 1930) and Fridrikh Ermler's *Peasants* (*Krestyane*, 1935). Despite their innovative cinematography and oftentimes captivating drama, as in their Soviet counterparts, women in Negreanu's early works held peripheral functions in the struggle staged by the peasants against their landowners.

---

[10] Like her husband, Elena Ceaușescu rose from poor origins to become increasingly influential in political life from the mid-1960s onwards. She oftentimes interfered in cultural matters, and sometimes she even had a say in decisions that affected the fate of films and the careers of certain filmmakers.

Whatever their conceptual or aesthetic shortcomings, the films made by Horia Popescu, Lucian Bratu and, not least, Călinescu himself showed, however, that women could not only hold the screen with a story of their own, but that they also could instigate social change by way of raising awareness about the stark inequality that women faced under early socialism. The fact that a majority of scholars, in their postsocialist readings of these early films, have tended to focus on the authoritarianism of the Communist government, on the issue of nationalization of private property and on the lack of artistic freedom about which some film directors complained in later years does not minimize the power that these films had in shaping a more just world for women at the time.

In contrast to the rather noticable absence of female-driven narratives in the Western cinema of the 1950s and 1960s, these Communist-made screen works demonstrate the parallel effort of both Romanian and Chinese early socialist cinema to increase awareness of the role that women played in Communist societies. This paved the way for later films which openly discuss child abandonment and abortion, as in the dramas of Aurel Miheleș, Tian Zhuangzhuang and Cristian Mungiu, to be discussed in the second part.

Finally, the increasing awareness about female-centered topics featured in the early Romanian films discussed above made possible the works of women directors such as Elisabeta Bostan and Malvina Urșianu, who became important names in Romanian filmmaking as early as in the 1960s, as well as Ada Pistiner and Maria Callas Dinescu who helmed social realist dramas in the 1970s and 1980s. Aside from focusing on female characters and their personal dramas, as Urșianu's *Gioconda fără surîs* (*Smileless Mona Lisa*, 1968) did, the films made by these women auteurs diversified the offer of cinematic genres available in the 1960s and 1970s. Bostan's musicals, such as *Veronica* (1973) and *Ma-ma* (1976), infused national cinema with a local version of magic realism, which helped make the films' phantasmagoric universe highly popular with child audiences. These innovative qualities helped introduce women's cinema to a wide audience and rendered their authors important in the social environment.

Romanian Anticommunism

As seen in the conciliatory reaction to *Reverberates the Valley* promoted by Necșulescu, who appreciates the film's proto-feminist approach despite its propaganda, it is the anticommunism of the postsocialist-era critics that irremediably sealed the fate of early socialist productions. Considered formulaic and uncreative, anticommunism indicts *Reverberates the Valley* for what is unilaterally seen as indoctrination in postsocialism. In order to understand this tendency, it is necessary to briefly define how anticommunism came into being in the socio-political turmoil of the first capitalist decade.

Katherine Verdery, an anthropologist working as a researcher in Ceaușescu's Romania has believed that "the years between 1947 and 1989 were the locus of a battle between two powerful discourses: Marxism, and the discourse on the nation" (Verdery 1991, 11). She has correctly observed that manipulating the German-derived concept of "nation" allowed Ceaușescu to exert excessive control over the populace. While many authors have seen the slippage of the regime into nationalism in the 1980s as the sole result of Ceaușescu's maniacal tendencies and authoritative style, Verdery has argued that the "nation" gained traction with the general public long beforehand, because of the abundant use of the concept in public discourse before World War II. This was because nationalism, unlike Marxist discourse, was so ingrained in the national psyche that anyone who tapped it was sure to strike gold (Verdery 1991, 125). Verdery has concluded that it was not top-down totalitarianism that allowed nationalism to become over-dominant in the Ceaușescu era, but that it was the masses – here the "cultured masses" themselves – who allowed nationalism to change the signification of Marxism. In Verdery's own words, ...

> Intellectuals who engaged in arguments about national identity were not doing so because they were told to, or because they were allowed to (although that was of course a necessary ingredient): they were doing so because by these means they could give vent to passionately held resistance to Soviet and/or Marxist-Leninist rule (126).

The attachment of right-wing intellectuals to the concept of the "nation" pitted them against the advocates of Marxism-Leninism, driving a wedge between Communists and anticommunists from the interwar years onwards. Although they only opposed each other directly for the first time in the free elections of 1990, Communist supporters and anticommunist opponents had clashed along ideological lines since the interwar conflict between Communism and fascism. In the late 1930s and early 1940s, the country was successively governed by the fanatical Iron Guard and Antonescu's military dictatorship, both fierce right-wing governments that exacerbated the ethos of the nation in relation to atavistic designs of continuity with an illusory ancient past and exuberant mysticism and militarism.

Even though the emergence of anticommunism lies in this period, anticommunism would gradually become a dominant political force only after the 1989 revolution. In 1992, a group of intellectuals who rallied behind the prominent anticommunist author Gabriel Liiceanu – a disciple, in turn, of right-wing interwar philosophers Constantin Noica and Mircea Vulcănescu – took the socialist-era polemic into the open and identified a distinct class of Communist collaborators, who had allegedly derailed the national cultural project under socialism only to pose as democracy-abiding citizens thereafter. As literary critic Mihai Iovănel has written, Liiceanu's accusations were vague and unspecific, but appealed to the emotional (rather than rational) side of his readers. Instead of founding his denunciations against Communism on fact, Liiceanu based them on personal resentment related to his being marginalized by the socialist regime, according to Iovănel. Although rhetorical, filled with pathos and unspecific, Liiceanu's discourse found a large following among the post-revolutionary intelligentsia and went on to become the flagship of the anticommunist cause (Iovănel 2021, 46).

Sociologist Florin Poenaru has taken the criticism of anticommunism to another level, giving it a class-based reading. He has identified the supporters of the anticommunist cause with the winners of the economic transition to capitalism, and those with leftist sympathies with the losers. For Poenaru, these winners were the grumbling (but not vocal) critics of the Communist system who were frustrated with their lack of upward mobility under socialism. Poenaru has equated the anticommunist discourse with the autobiographies of anticommunist dissidents, who allegedly used this negativist platform to enrich themselves after 1989 but gave anticommunism neither programmatic values nor an ideology (Poenaru 2017).

In a parliamentary assembly of a kind never witnessed before in Eastern Europe, the nation's center-right political government officially put Communism on trial in 2006. Then president Traian Băsescu and a group of right-leaning intellectuals declared that Communism was an "illegitimate and criminal regime" (Comisia prezidențială 2006) in the presence of Lech Wałęsa and Adam Michnik, well-known anticommunists from Poland and the Czech Republic, who played significant roles in their countries' transition to capitalism after 1989. While Ovidiu Țichindeleanu has felt that the report which the committee produced was un-academic and smacked of political performativity (Țichindeleanu 2017, 164), and while Alex Cistelecan has found the event to be theatrical and well-staged (Cistelecan 2019, 161), Florin Abraham has noted that the trial "literally reached a pre-established conclusion" rather than offering a competent analysis (Abraham, quoted in Cistelecan 2019, 164). This places the verdict in the same league as the mock trials of the 1950s, employing moreover a vocabulary that was just as evocative of authoritarianism as the "wooden language" of the previous government (169).

The above authors have substantiated the performative nature of the trial, arguing that its language was sentimental and arbitrary rather than rigorous; that it used the term "genocide" incorrectly; that it produced no evidence of Communist crimes but used rhetorical devices to win over its audience; and most importantly that, instead of investigating the past, the trial served the political needs of the center-right government and further legitimized the status of the governance in the eyes of the population. Finally, it was a melodramatic and populist act. For this reason, Poenaru has observed that, although the report purported to engage with the past, it actually disregarded the past completely, because anticommunism does not want the past "investigated and remembered, but controlled, rewritten, and forgotten" (Poenaru 2017, 149). According to him, anticommunist ideology – which was developed as a crude denial of a nuanced historical phenomenon – only takes into account the consequences of Communism on the resentful intellectual class, ignoring the historical reasons that at the start of the twentieth century sparked the internationalist movement, which struggled against widespread poverty and inequality. Anticommunism is therefore a type of Nietzschean resentment, or, at best, a political instrument for the legitimization of liberalism. Put bluntly, anticommunism instrumentalizes communist history to serve capitalist ends.

Literary and film theorist Claudiu Turcuș has also believed that anticommunist radicalism is an expression of political inexperience and an overreaction to the already exaggerated line holding that Romania suffered "the most repressive variety of communism" (Turcuș 2017, 168). Ignoring the complexities of the socialist period, anticommunism thus prevents the postsocialist generation from accessing genuine historical data about its own historical past. Moreover, as Cistelecan has written, anticommunism attempts to treat the absence of political consciousness in postsocialism as the norm rather than the exception (Cistelecan 2019).

The anticommunist cause continues to be widespread in Eastern Europe, affecting the majority of the former socialist states. Critical theorist Nataša Kovačević has written that anticommunism has normalized the "alienating violence of the transitions to capitalism, [...] a phenomenon which would typically only help intensify stereotypes of barbarous and crime-ridden Eastern Europe which must be placed under control and civilised" (Kovačević 2008, 121). In *Imagining the Balkans*, anthropologist Maria Todorova has argued that Eastern Europe adopted the tropes used by foreign visitors to paint the region as backward in relation to Western Europe, thus favoring an implementation of Orientalism to describe themselves. The postsocialist transition to capitalism has repopularized Todorova's vision of the Balkans as the Wild East, favoring the emergence of violent capitalist elites, nationalism and the obsession with Europeanization and forging a new (rich, white) European imaginary built on the exclusion of non-Europeans from the Balkans' midst. Speaking of the former Yugoslavia, Kovačević has described the fragmented country's journey toward European integration as one of rejection of everything Oriental (Kovačević 2008, 163). In Romania, this journey was based on the rejection of everything connected to the Communist past.

The transition in China was similarly traumatic. After the events of 1989 in Tiananmen Square, film director Wu Tianming wondered "why, all of a sudden, Chinese people seem to have grown so cold" (Camhi 1999). The same complaint could be heard in Romania after the 1989 revolution. However, in contrast to Romanian anticommunism, which partially explained the coldness referenced above, the Chinese transition from Maoism to Deng Xiaoping's era of "Reform and Opening Up" was characterized by a relative acceptance of the past, and an acknowledgement of the limited but profound changes that Communism had wrought in social and economic life. In other words, while the Romanians threw the baby out with the bathwater, the Chinese attempted to at least preserve the embryo.

Historian Arif Dirlik has stated that it was immediately after Mao's death that the Communist Party in December 1978 decided "to leave revolutionary aspirations behind, and open up to capitalism" (Dirlik 2017, 388). The Turkish-American historian has further written that, "with the socialist project abandoned in all but name after 1978, the Communist Party's victory in 1949 appears most impressive in hindsight not as a harbinger of communism but for the organizational revolution it engineered" (391). Even though China's liberalist transition in the 1980s was predicated on capitalism more than on revolutionary Communism, and even though it mirrored the authoritarian capitalism of Singapore's Lee Kwan Yew more than Mao's Communism, the Communist past greatly contributed to the so-called capitalist reorientation (389).[11] Although Dirlik has criticized the corruption of the Chinese elites who would profit from the transition, he has correctly warned that "it is the height of arrogance to offer the advanced capitalist societies of Europe and North America as inspiration or models for emulation" (394). In other words, criticism against Chinese authoritarianism is misplaced when coming from cultures which themselves are corrupt.

In contrast to the Chinese acceptance of Communist values and their gradual morphing into "socialism with Chinese characteristics," Romania has treated its past in a monovalent key. This has allowed anticommunism to decisively influence postsocialist cinema and literature, leading to a drastic re-evaluation not only of economic goals, but also, via sheer negation of half a century of Communism, of the entire identity of the country.

Propaganda and Entertainment in the Films of the 1950s

Despite the villainous charges filed against them by anticommunism, which accused them of pro-Bolshevik propaganda, the films of the 1950s in China and Romania had mass audience appeal. Because they were scarce (the government could not afford to produce more than a handful of films a year for the entire decade) and because they spoke in the mother tongue of most audience members instead of in a foreign language, films such as *Reverberates the Valley*, *Life Triumphs* (*Viața învinge*, Negreanu, 1951) or *Alarm in the Mountains* (*Alarmă in munți*, Negreanu, 1956) – that is, films pitting the builders of the new society against the reactionary elements of the old regime – made up for straightforward "good guys" versus "bad guys" plotlines that were more entertaining than they were ideological.

Before delving into a brief comparison of Romanian and Chinese films produced during that decade, it is worth identifying the general motifs, narrative practices and themes, as well as aesthetic concerns, that characterized film production in both countries. Pointing out similarities and differences in films produced on a comparative basis will help us to understand the ways in which the two cultures reflected each other's ideological, political and societal concerns, generating that socialist affect which, so I argue, helped the countries both encounter and recognize each other as culturally comparable.

[11] It is for this reason that in this book I will refer to Dirlik's definition to describe the age after Mao's death in China as postsocialist, even though there exists some debate as to whether this should be described as "Socialism with Chinese Characteristics," as the official historiography holds.

This mutual reflection is based on an affective experience made even more similar due to the comparable economic context.

Life Triumphs, like *The Bridge*, focuses on a chemical engineer who is determined to discover the formula for a sturdier alloy that would give a Romanian factory an edge over its foreign competitors. Yet, he is thwarted in his efforts by the treacherous machinations of a mysterious employee. After some hesitation, the lead engineer (who, of course, is also a Communist) unmasks a saboteur who has infiltrated the factory at the behest of fascist forces loyal to the old regime. Although the saboteur temporarily thwarts the engineer's attempts to create the new alloy, the engineer is ultimately successful. In the film's finale, he turns the saboteur over to the people's militia.

As ideological as the plot may seem, the story adheres to the narratological style that David Bordwell has derived from cognitivism, more so than to a strictly socialist realist aesthetic. In what appears to be the longest and broadest-reaching theory of cinema launched and made famous in the 1980s, Bordwell has identified character development, plot and dialogue as the universal ingredients necessary for any form of cinematic representation to make sense for viewers of any cultural background. For audiences watching *Life Triumphs* in the 1950s, the film came across not so much as promoting an ideology, but as simply entertaining, in as much as a screenplay is well-written and solidly structured and, in that sense, fully adhering to Bordwellian cognitivism. Featuring somewhat understated acting that does not make the film seem "over the top" and on some occasions even using innovative cinematography, Negreanu utilizes all the ingredients of a formulaic "whodunnit" to turn his film into a veritable suspense thriller written with all the required Hollywood references in mind. As such, the legionnaire[12] character selling trade secrets to his fascist collaborators in order to detract from the findings of the Romanian engineer is nothing but a pure Hollywood-style villain acting against the interests of the progressive leadership of the factory, which happens to be Communist. If the clear ulterior motive of the film is to legitimize the Party line, this ideological dressing is easily sacrificed for the narrative structure, driving the plot with such agility as to make the "message" not only inconspicuous but irrelevant for the audience. Anticommunist engineer-turned-film-critic Cristian Tudor Popescu has believed that the triumph of life in the film equates to a loss of quality for cinema, seeing propaganda in "every inch of the celluloid" (Popescu 2011, 222). Moreover, he has regarded the lead engineer as an unfortunate archetype that would serve as a foundation for propagandistic figures in the subsequent history of Romanian cinema.

In spite of this caustic postsocialist criticism, in prefiguring the function which this film would play in developing political relations between the two countries, it is important that, after winning a diploma of merit at the 1952

[12] A legionnaire in this context is a member of the fascist wartime organization The Iron Guard, which continued to subvert Communist power after the regime change. In this case, the character does fall to a measure of ethnic profiling, as the actor playing the legionnaire (Fory Etterle) is an ethnic Hungarian.

Bombay International Film Festival, *Life Triumphs* went on to be the first Romanian film screened in China. Film historians Tan Hui and He Yuan have written that, "on this occasion, the China Ministry of Culture held a grand premiere in the Capital Cinema of Beijing in August 1953. The audience from the two countries comprised over 1000 people, including famous Chinese writers, dramatists, directors, and the ambassador along with the embassy staff of Romania in China" (Tan and He 2018, 106). This reception would bode well for the future of cinematic screen relations between the two countries and open an era of dialogue that few other nations enjoyed on such an intimate level as China and Romania.

Life Triumphs reifies a maddening fascination with spy thrillers that took audiences by storm on both sides of the Iron Curtain as early as in the 1950s. From Hollywood to Europe, political themes suddenly became entertaining, as long as the "good guys" in the capitalist camp prevailed over the "bad guys" of the socialist camp, while the reverse happened across the Iron Curtain. Film scholar Ling Zhang has observed that "(counter)espionage narratives developed in parallel across the Cold War ideological divide," and although Western thrillers and film noir "were imbued with anti-communist and even neocolonialist messaging," the Chinese *fantepian* genre, as it was commonly known, "drew on popular crime fictions and 1950s spy films originating from the USSR and other socialist countries, rather than on detective stories and espionage films coming from the capitalist camp" (Zhang 2021, 1310). *The Letter with Feathers (Ji mao* xin, Shi Hui, 1954) was the first Chinese "spy film" to be screened in Romania. The rather sedate tone of the film, however, which features the heroic behavior of a child in the face of danger, in contrast to his cowardly adult peers, did not quite hit the spot for Romanian audiences. Neither did *Mysterious Travelling Companion (Shen mi de lü ban)*, a rather stagnant and verbose film directed by Lin Nong and Zhu Wenshun in 1955. Audiences had to wait for Lu Jue's *Secret Post in Canton* (*Yang cheng an shao*, 1958) to change this.

Lu's film was translated into Romanian as *Agent secret la Canton* (Canton Secret Agent) and enjoyed great success with Romanian audiences. Not only did the movie have a catchy title, but it also featured dramatic battle scenes augmented by an exotic South Chinese landscape setting. For instance, in the opening scene a young man, emerging triumphant from a duel with unnamed opponents, makes his way through dense jungle in order to establish contact with his fellow, similarly unknown comrades. With these components in place, the movie stood a good chance of captivating viewers in Eastern Europe, since Romanian spectators would have easily overlooked the fact that the young, attractive man from the opening sequence was a Communist agent on a mission to find a mysterious female connection, who would later help him uncover nationalist spies in Guangzhou. Despite their differences in language and culture, Romanian audiences were able to relate to the film's characters with ease, and the plot proved to be compelling despite ideological overtones. Furthermore, as Ling Zhang has made clear, "most Chinese *fantepian* were set in Chinese territories and emphasized anti-spy (*fante*) activities as righteous gestures of self-defense of national sovereignty" (Zhang 2021, 1310); therefore, they were not "out to get" political enemies, like their Western counterparts. In that sense, they shared a defensive standpoint with such Romanian films as *Life Triumphs*, which made Chinese plots additionally relatable to Romanian audiences.

The same defensive attitude is central to *Alarm in the Mountains* (Dinu Negreanu, 1955), a spy thriller in which a fascist agent, returning from abroad after the war at the head of a right-wing legation meant to topple the Communist government, deceives a Romanian soldier serving as a border guard in the mountains in order to quickly infiltrate the state defense system. The guard, however, discovers the scam when he suspects that the woman with whom he was romantically involved is in cahoots with the spy. This causes him and his girlfriend to get into a heated argument, followed by a dangerous ambuscade via which the guard hopes to exact revenge on the woman he used to love, while also showing his devotion to the nation. After a dramatic battle between the guard and the spy during a scene featuring suspenseful moments set against a magnificent mountain backdrop, the Communist guard prevails and thwarts the fascist scheme. Of course, romance and action are used as a tool to forward the government's propagandist agenda calling for defending the country from fascist spies. It would be naive to think, however, that audiences in the 1950s were more susceptible to ideological manipulation than audiences of the present day. It would be safer to infer that the film's dramatics, rather than its politics, were what the audience found enjoyable.

To better understand the way in which ideology and drama were intertwined in some cinematic products, it is useful to briefly consider again Anikó Imre's description of a film franchise from Hungary's socialist period. She has focused on a particular series named *Blue Light* (*Kekfeny*, 1965) which "started out as a public affairs series that focused on real-life crime cases that had been solved, using dramatic reenactments as well as interviews with criminals, law enforcement, and other professionals. In 1969, it began to solicit the public's help with solving unresolved cases" (Imre 2016, 67). Surpassing its Western sources of inspiration in audaciousness, Imre has made the case that, "because of their fairly uncontrolled flow and unanimous popularity across borders, crime appeal programs require a transnational comparative historical examination, to which socialist formats made a significant, so far unacknowledged, contribution" (67).

It is in this light that early Romanian Communist spy thrillers should also be regarded. *Alarm in the Mountains*, for example, featured popular talent that the audiences had started to like and follow: the lead, Iurie Darie, a young handsome actor of mixed Russian and Romanian heritage, would go on to become something of a Romanian male sex symbol, playing the lead in most musical films that the studios would start to produce in the 1960s. These attributes in fact transformed the ideological imperatives of the Communist Party into nothing but – to use basic Hollywood parlance – a good show. As such, the wartime squabbles between communists and fascists literally became sources of film material following either the gangster or the war genre.

Although these themes and genres were to be found equally in Chinese films of the period, Romanian and Chinese films of the 1950s are generally associated with the state-planned monotony of socialist realism themes and further correlated to Soviet Russia. Joining other scholars who have regarded Stalinism in the Soviet Union as opposing artistic freedom due to the top-down planning of the cinema industry, film scholar Jamie Miller has affirmed that "one of the fundamental problems of thematic planning was that its attempt to convey […] differing political messages to the masses often neglected the need to do so in an entertaining manner" (Miller 2010, 98). Without engaging with the reception of early Soviet films by the general public – even though Miller has admitted the durability of *Chapaev* – it is debatable whether socialist realist films in Romania and China were as unpopular with 1950s audiences as postsocialist critics have claimed.

This research has reified the epitome of cultural politics and cannot be taken at face value because, as we have seen above, most of these films conveyed universal narratives of good versus evil with which audiences could identify, just like those advanced by the formulaic Hollywood films that inspired them. On closer inspection, it seems that these films offered a decent degree of entertainment despite their ideological wrapping, contrary to Miller's claim that "the politicization of films often tended to overwhelm the entertainment element" (98).

When discussing the films of Vladislav Pudovkin, Australian film scholar David Gillespie, has seen *Deserter* (*Dezertir*, 1933) as a film that glamorizes the "utopia of Communism," yet comes from a "pure" representative of the avant-garde. Gillespie has written: "This is of course, blatant propaganda of the most ferociously pro-Bolshevik type, but Pudovkin's film is *notable for its stylistic experimentation*" (Gillespie 2014, 109, my italics). Engaging once again with Buck-Morss' argument, "stylistic experimentation" in Pudovkin's case is categorized as a superior class of art, even though it is in fact an eminently political procedure coeval with Othering. Gillespie's indictment thereof amounts to the ultimate denial of socialist-made films to be political, while, at the same time, encouraging the West to be not only political, but also deceptively pass its apoliticism for entertainment. While Gillespie has previously claimed that "the true task of the Soviet comedy writer was not to be funny but to educate" (44), he ignores the fact that, by allowing only Western culture to be political, he in fact endorses the West's right to be perfectly educational as well.

Gillespie has accepted the ideological implications of an avant-garde film only as long as the artist's hand was "forced," and only if his art had "stylistic experimentation" written all over it. Ironically, this is the same argument that rescues from damnation the works of Nazi sympathizer and ideology-enabler Leni Riefenstahl, whose films continue to be taught and propagated in Western academia for their alleged technical progress and the enrichment of film language that they contributed, which ultimately aided the development of Western cinema. One indeed wonders whether this kind of cultural politics does not influence both art and scholarship, and whether the erstwhile depiction of the yellowface Chineseness of Yellow Peril fame (in the works of none other than Griffith, among others) does not still inform the constituency of what we have come to appreciate as the Western canon. It also begs us to trace the ontology of this canon in the developments of Western culture.

The failure of the West to allow socialist realism its ability to poly-signify does not connote artistic concerns but political ones. The Western knee-jerk reaction to socialist realism in Romania and revolutionary romanticism in China occurs because the West sees in socialist realism the fear of the quintessential Other. And still, this is not enough: the Other is frightening not because s/he is the carrier of a precise ideology – that would mean only a friendly war of words. What lies beneath the Western disqualifying perorations on the East is the precise *obverse* of ideology as the West knows it, the fear of absolute chaos and indetermination, the pure contingency of the Orient hiding under the condemned façade of the shiny socialist realist image. This means that what continues to inform the Western understanding of Eurasia, the enlarged continent where these films were made, is the most basic conception of Otherness as theorized by Said, with the Communist project adding to the confusion rather than subtracting from it.

Children's and Young Adults' Films

A popular genre in the 1950s, which has fallen into disrepute because of its allegedly indoctrinating message, was that of children's and young adults' films. State communism in the Soviet Union after World War II put great efforts into its educational programs. Since teaching fundamental human values such as camaraderie, mutual care and deference to the elderly was an integral part of every communist school, Soviet cinema often examined the lives of children and young adults with interest. Due to their unexpectedly thin propagandist plots, films candidly portraying the adventurous lives of young children and adolescents became extremely popular in the Soviet Union as well as in the countries of the Eastern Bloc, which sometimes – though not always, as we will see in the case of musicals – followed in the footsteps of their bigger and more developed neighbor.

The trend was set in the 1960s by Georgiy Daneliya's somewhat light portrayal of teenage life in *I Walk the Streets of Moscow* (*Ya shagayu po Moskve*, 1964) and Yuli Raizman's *But What If This Is Love?* (*A esli eto lyubov?*, 1962), in which the latter paints a touching portrait of teenage infatuation among students facing a traditional education system. The films that really shook the establishment from its feet, however, were Marlen Khutsyev's Thaw-era classics *I am Twenty* (*Mne dvadtsat let*, 1965) and *July Rain* (*Iyulskiy dozhd*, 1967), in which the Soviet filmmaker endearingly looks at a group of young people on the cusp of rebellious maturity in a Moscow facing generational changes. These films inspired Soviet directors to continue to examine the lives of elementary and high school students in the 1970s and 1980s and to debate the role of the state and state education in shaping the future of children and young adults.

In 1977, Dinara Asanova made *The Key that Can't Be Shared* (*Klyuch bez prava peredachi*), about the friendship between a female teacher and her students, which is controversial in its depiction of emotional closeness. In the same vein, albeit with a morbid twist, Eldar Ryazanov, a veteran director known primarily for classic 1970s comedies, in 1988 adapted the play *Dear Yelena Sergeyevna* (*Dorogaya Yelena Sergeyevna*), about a group of high school students who blackmail their teacher in order to gain access to their exam results. Their actions have tragic consequences for their aged teacher.

Since both Romanian and Chinese cinemas were cognizant of trends and cultural practices in the Soviet Union, despite their political animosity against the powerful rival, they picked up the Soviet challenge and delivered realistic portrayals of youth. This facilitated the emergence of a children's films industry in both cultures. Gillespie has been partially right in claiming that the foremost function of socialist filmmakers was to educate rather than entertain. This educational role, however, was not pejorative for members of society. The films' educational drive sparked interesting public debates in both Romania and China. While these sometimes were spearheaded by the Politburo, more often than not members of the general public would pick up a film's educational message and launch a public discussion about it in the popular press.

In many Romanian and Chinese films of the socialist period, children either starred in adventure films themselves, or were targeted as primary consumers for films that featured childhood-related themes. Of these, the first Romanian films screened in China were Ion Popescu Gopo's adaptation of the Hans Christian Andersen fairytale *Little Liar* (*Fetița mincinoasă*, 1956) and Gheorghe Tobias' *The Red Water Lilly* (*Nufărul roșu*, 1955), a story in which a female pioneer teaches a group of misbehaving primary school students how to protect the precious ecology of the Danube Delta. Made in 1955, this was also Romania's first color film.

A striking influence of neorealist filmmaking, *Mingea* (*The Ball*, 1958) was not strictly a children's film, but one featuring a child lead. Made by Andrei Blaier and Sinișa Ivetici, two promising fresh graduates who were to take forefront positions in the modernist movement, the film appealed to both young and adult audiences. Set during the depression of the 1930s, the movie is about a physically impaired four-year-old boy who, seduced by his peers' football games which he watches from his window in the attic, dreams of owning a soccer ball himself. Sensitive to his son's wishes, the father saves up to buy him a soccer ball but is robbed of all his money by a gang of thieves. Unable to find a job, the father finally joins the street protests of the workers' movement and is arrested. On his way home from jail, a Communist friend aware of the child's wishes sympathizes with the downtrodden father and buys the boy his coveted football. Owing to Neorealism not only an environment of brutal poverty and its dark-toned cinematography, but also a plot structure resembling *Bicycle Thieves* (*Ladri di biciclette*, Vittorio De Sica, 1948), this enjoyable melodrama would have withstood the test of time, had it not been for its ideological *parti pris*. Despite its innovative cinematic form and artistic experimentation, Popescu deemed *The Ball* a "cheap tearjerker" made by a director who did not have anything better to do with state finances (Popescu 2011, 104). The film was dubbed by the Shanghai studios and released in China in 1959, a year after its release in Romania, and it turned out to be fairly popular with the Chinese audiences.

Children's films continued to be made well into the 1960s and the 1970s, when the studios in Bucharest embarked on a series of partnerships with Western production companies. Among the most notable results were adaptations of Mark Twain classics centered on the character of Tom Sawyer. The films were coproduced with the Paris-based Franco-London Film and helmed by West German children's TV film director Walter Ulbrich. Other productions included adaptations of James Fennimore Cooper's *The Leatherstocking Tales* in four installments, which was produced in collaboration with West Germany, France and Austria. The films that emerged from these coproductions were successful in both Eastern and Western European countries and found great popularity with young audiences. Interestingly, the crews and the actors were a hodge-podge of nationalities from both Western and Eastern bloc countries.

Silent Friends (also known as *Babysitters* in English) (*Prieteni fără grai*, Paul Fritz Nemeth) was a family adventure film made in 1969. It told an educational story about a greedy criminal duo who does not shy away from murder to lay their hands on a large fortune. Their plans are frustrated by a young boy and his female companion to whose aid come a couple of endearing dogs. The film was a coproduction between the Bucharest studios and Legend Film Corporation of Canada, and in Romania it was viewed by more than two million spectators. It was released in China in 1974, only a couple of years before another Romanian delta-themed film which made good use of exotic locations, titled *Alarm in the Delta* (*Alarmă în deltă*, Gheorghe Naghi, 1975), would also be released. In an almost copycat replica of *Silent Friends*, two criminals threaten to sabotage a local water pumping station if they are not allowed to take a box of ancient artifacts over the border. Their plans are foiled by two young boys who prove more ingenious than the criminals, despite their young age. Clearly, there is an anti-capitalist component to some of these films (the criminals are connected with or working for Western networks), but more often than not the educational accent falls on bravery and promoting universal human values which (at the time) included warnings against greed and rapacity, as well as against criminal and antisocial behavior.

Interestingly, the plots of both films resemble the narrative of *Mist over Fairy Peak* (*Shen nu feng de mi wu*, Guo Baochang, 1980), in which a criminal gang intends to cross the border with a trunk full of valuable books from the Ming dynasty but is stopped in time by a female painter who alerts the authorities. The film was exported and screened in Romania in 1983. Other Chinese children-themed films of the socialist era which made it to Romania include Su Li's *Brother and Sister* (*Ge ge he mei mei*, 1956) and *Red Children* (*Hong hai zi*, 1958), possibly the most entertaining Chinese films of the genre. Although the first is a morality tale *par excellence*, in which a young boy is rude to his sister until he witnesses her performing a courageous deed, which helps change his attitude towards her and his behavior in general, *Red Children* is not only a moralizing tale. Set in the Civil War during the 1930s, the film tells the endearing story of a group of children who choose to join the Red Army in a guerilla war against the Nationalist regime in order to revenge their families. Aside from advancing courage as an admirable quality, the film is highly entertaining due to its ability to facilitate identification with the young screen heroes for child audiences.

After making his debut as a director in the war film *Guerrillas of the Plains* (*Ping yuan you ji dui*, 1955), Su Li acquired special acumen for working with children, and his films were seen as both educational and entertaining rather than ideological. Too difficult to grasp for young audiences, the political message in Su's films was left on the backburner. Instead, the Chinese director focused on cultivating positive personal attributes, such as courage, dignity and respect for the law. For this reason, his films traveled easily from one cultural context to another. As a result, compassion, respect for the elders and personal integrity became identifiable qualities in both cultures for children of an early age, leading to the creation of a transnational affective community whose solidification would later develop into socialist affect. These qualities, moreover, left a deep imprint on the lives of children growing up in China and Romania during the socialist period, as evident from their repeated appearance in various film works of both Chinese sixth-generation directors and Romanian directors of the New Wave.

The Ambassadorial Function of Socialist Film

The official mouthpiece of the Romanian Communist Party, *Scînteia*, on 30 September 1960 in a short editorial titled "Gala Night with Chinese Film *Daughter of the Party*" documented the following event:

> On the occasion of the eleventh anniversary of the founding of the People's Republic of China, the Ministry of Education and Culture organized on Thursday night at the Patria film theater a reception for the screening of the Chinese cinema production *Daughter of the Party* [...] Comrade M. Stanciu, adjunct managing director of the Cinema Institute, [...] after mentioning the struggle of the Chinese people for liberty, for bringing about a new, socialist life, spoke about the achievements of Chinese cinema in the last few years. *Daughter of the Party* presents an episode in the heroic struggle of China's youth, led by the Communists, for the liberation of the country. The audience warmly received the new production of the cinema of the People's Republic of China (Agerpress).

The Chinese film researcher Du Weijia has mentioned the following incident, this time from the vantage point of the Chinese records:

> When *The Waves of the Danube* (first dubbed and released in 1960) was re-released in 1972, workers quit their posts and flocked to remote suburbs

> to watch it; some even exchanged their furniture coupon for film tickets. The sole reason for the re-release was that as Romania had exhibited a number of Chinese films, the party leaders felt obliged to reciprocate with at least one Romanian film exhibition, and *The Waves of the Danube* was the most ideologically correct one they could come up with (Du 2015, 149).

The Romanian film *The Waves of the Danube* was directed by Liviu Ciulei, one of the country's up-and-coming and later rambunctious directors who often ran into trouble with the censors for his outspokenness. The film is about the struggle between a renegade ship captain (played by a rugged Ciulei himself) and a young communist in the last days of the war. It is based on a novella by Francisc Munteanu, a writer who himself oftentimes lived through the adventurous events about which he later wrote. Although the diegesis depicts the struggle between the two men in somewhat ideological overtones – the communist's act of sabotage determines Ciulei's character to switch sides in the film's finale. The thwarted delivery of a cargo to Nazi troops creates enough tension to make politics secondary in importance. Moreover, audiences delighted in the *Casablanca*-like love triangle, because the dramatic conflict between the two men is enhanced by their vying for the affection of one woman – the captain's wife – who also becomes the young communist's object of affection (Figure 2.3).

Figure 2.3 A scene from *The Waves of the Danube* featuring the rugged ship captain and his wife.

Unlike Romanian audiences, who were used to displays of onscreen affection, for Chinese viewers the magnetic attraction between the communist rebel and the ship captain's wife was an utter novelty. Furthermore, film historians Tan and He have noted that, although Ciulei's character did not represent the "tall, big, and perfect type of hero familiar to Chinese audiences at that time," he was nevertheless "real, and thus he [got] more emotional approval" (Tan and He 2018, 109). Spectators also appreciated the Neorealist look of the film, in which the high-contrast exterior shots alternated with the brooding darkness of the ship's hull, thus creating a mysterious and enticing ambience that placed the film at a crossroads between a thriller and a war movie.

In addition to politics being secondary in importance to romantic love, Du has mentioned the impact that this film had on Chinese audiences because the distribution of *The Waves of the Danube* came in reciprocation for the Romanian screening of "a number of Chinese films." Although it is difficult to identify which these were, the fact that *Daughter of the Party* (Lin Nong, 1958) was screened at an ambassadorial event a decade earlier illustrates the camaraderie between the two nations and clarifies the role that cinema played in fostering political ties. *Daughter of the Party* has a predictable plot that largely follows the requirements of the socialist realist aesthetics from which it hails. What makes the film memorable is the determination and zest of the beautiful young actress Tian Hua who plays a young mother compelled to abandon her baby to bloodthirsty Kuomintang troops in a scene reminiscent of the kidnapping of the daughter she had played in *The White Haired Girl* (Figure 2.4). Bonding with two other women on the run after her friends and family are killed by the Kuomintang, they put up resistance against the enemy while waiting for the Red Army to return. Caught by the antagonists in one scene, Tian Hua's character is forced to renege on her belief in Communism. Implying an almost religious creed, she defiantly replies that "abandoning one's Communism is just like losing your heart. There is no more happiness afterwards."

The virulent and effectively structured conflicts between a die-hard aristocracy and a new generation in which women were gaining increasingly more prominent roles in society made for excellent export material in the socialist world, as the issues Romania was facing *vis-à-vis* its feudal past were largely similar to Chinese ones. A Romanian work that addressed this break with the past while also propagandizing the land collectivization program of the 1950s was the noiresque, slightly formulaic but effective drama *In Our Village* (*În sat la noi*, Georgescu and Iliu, 1951). Peasants in a remote, backward region are evenly divided between those who support and those who oppose the nationalization of their land. The patriarch in the film wishes to marry his daughter to the kulak's son, even though the daughter loves someone else. Opposing collectivization and thus siding with the rightist wing, the kulak's son resorts to all forms of corruption and intimidation techniques to make the unrelenting daughter fall for him. Put off by the son's dubious behavior, however, the patriarch, previously having hesitated about

Figure 2.4 Tian Hua's character is forced to give up her baby in *Daughter of the Party*.

the collectivization issue, has a change of heart and decides to do the right thing. In the film's finale, he joins the cooperative and, understanding what his daughter's love interest means to her, allows her to marry her chosen beau rather than the kulak's son. Although reinforcing rather than undermining the power of the patriarchy, the film shows some progressiveness on the issue of forced marriage.

Liviu Ciulei, the young actor who later became famous for directing *The Waves of the Danube*, portrayed the kulak's son with a powerful and lustful gusto that added dramatic tension and gave the character credibility. Ultimately, this was a drama written "after the book" by Victor Iliu, a filmmaker trained in Moscow, and by seasoned bourgeois director Jean Georgescu. By combining progressive ideology with traditional storytelling skills, however, the cross-ideological alliance successfully spiced up what otherwise would probably have been a stale propagandistic tale.

In the context in which Chinese audiences watched *In Our Village* and Romanian audiences were treated to films such as *Daughter of the Party* and *The Red Detachment of Women*, cinema became not exactly soft power in the sense in which this expression is used today, but a means of cultural exchange. The foremost ability of film in socialism was to act as potential political mediator in a multinational performance, commanding, *à la* Levinas, the reciprocation of friendship in an ever-expanding game of diplomacy. In this exchange, film was imbued not only with political quality, but also with a performative one: it became both a site of audience contestation for a nation's political policies and a reason for the admiration of those of another. This was so even if admiration amounted to commiseration, as socialist-era critics betrayed when they exaggerated the achievements of *Daughter of the Party*.

3 Performativity

Cinema's capacity to encourage audience contestation is closely linked to its performative role. Like socialist realist films before it, 1960s cinema was performative in nature, as well as having a propagandist bent. If Romanian postsocialist critical theorists have believed that anticommunism has a performative aspect in postsocialism (Ţichindeleanu 2017, 164; Cistelecan 2019, 161) which aims to justify capitalism's domination in a country that was once Communist, then this performativity was carried over from the socialist era, when cinema also attempted to establish Communist values in society. In order to examine how performance was essential to socialist filmmaking, I shall briefly discuss the notions outlined by Siegfried Kracauer in his masterpiece "The Mass Ornament." German cultural critic Siegfried Kracauer wrote as early as in 1927 that the superficial attributes which describe a culture bespeak its inner workings more than its programmatic values. To exemplify this, Kracauer identified the "Tiller Girls" routine (visible in many Hollywood musicals of the period) as an expression of capitalist power over indentured workers, a mutual agreement in which the workers are unaware that they participate (Kracauer). In other words, the tiller girls – and the musicals by extension – in their display of ostentatious glamor help whitewash the darker sides of capitalism.

Just as what is being performed in capitalism does not necessarily bespeak the ideology of capitalism, but the auto-erotic affect of the capitalist masses coerced to become a cog in a Taylorist machine, similarly the proletariat, coerced by the nature of socialism to be its own producer of a (forced) performance, uses affect as agency to enact their rebellion and then dissolve its own newfound power. This ironically shows in the political rallies staged by both Ceauşescu and Mao, which do not signify the hypostasis of a people brainwashed by ideology, but that of performance used at its politically purest – as a weapon. Using Kracauer's theories, sociologist Slobodan Karamanić and visual artist Ivana Momčilović have claimed in their article "Cinema Antikomunisto, or How Ideology Doesn't Move Anything" that Communist rallies were not the equivalent of a tiller girls' routine. Coercive as they may be, socialist rallies, so the theorists have argued, are not so much a direct destruction of the crowd's "organisms of resistance" (as Kracauer saw the tiller girls) but a performance of the inherent *possibility* of resistance by the crowd, which is articulated via the ensuing creation of collaborative affect.

As we have seen in both Lou's and Mungiu's films, this definition agrees with my concept of "socialist affect," in that it validates the potential right to rebel as existing between socialist subjects and power. Moreover, the potentiality to rebel is validated via the outburst of both the Romanian revolution and the Tiananmen "democracy movement" protests.

It is necessary, therefore, that we complement the phrase "socialist affect" and the concept of anticommunism with the introduction of yet another concept central to this book – namely, that of "performance." Russian-American anthropologist Alexei Yurchak has contended that the main originators of binary discourses about Eastern European and Asian Communism were anticommunist dissident writers such as Vaclav Havel who in his famous essay "The Power of the Powerless" criticized Eastern European socialist citizens for their morally-reprehensible conformism derived from "act[ing] in public as if they supported ideological slogans and messages even though privately they believed them to be false" (Havel 1985–86, 17). The problem with this hypothesis for Yurchak is that "in the mask/truth models the person is first posited and then is involved in the act of wearing masks or revealing truths. By contrast, most performative theories do not posit the person completely in advance, before the acts – the person is enabled performatively in the repetition of the act" (Yurchak 2005, 22).

In contrast to Havel's reading of Communism, which saw state power allegedly forcing socialist subjects to act as automatons in an otherwise oppressive society, in the wake of anticolonial theorists such as Homi Bhabha (Bhabha 2004) one needs to ask whether the much-debated issue of agency of the socialist citizen is not in fact more on par with that of the Western subject. Does socialist agency come from hiding and lying, as posited by Vaclav Havel; mimicking, as argued by Bhabha; or from what is essentially *performing*, that is, from a stasis similar to that of the capitalist subject of false consciousness who continues to "buy into" the values of capitalism by simultaneously performing lip service to democracy and the arguable progressiveness of human rights? The question is not whether a system or a society is or is not free, but whether the subject (and subjectivity) takes part in developing a consciousness of that freedom/unfreedom – and this is exactly what the original goals of Marxism were for the New Man[1] which the Soviets wanted to create.

The current scholarly view on authoritarianism that Yurchak has sought to disprove is the bipolar Eastern totalitarian/Western freedom binary, which, so he has argued, is woven almost entirely around notions "produced either outside of, or in retrospect to, socialism, in contexts dominated by antisocialist, nonsocialist, or post-socialist political, moral, and cultural

[1] I am using the expression "New Man" as it was employed by the early Communists in reference to the utopian new society which they planned to build, and not to refer to a gendered concept. This was a society based on community, as opposed to the selfishness and individualism of the bourgeois world which they wanted to root out. Similarly, when using "Man" with capital "M," I am referring to the Enlightenment-derived concept of humanity inclusive, of course, of both men and women.

agendas and truths" (Yurchak 2005, 6). To convey a different image of the relationship between ideology and subjectivity, Yurchak has recurred to performance theory. Referring first to Judith Butler's gender performativity and later to Mikhail Bakhtin's dialogism, Yurchak has seen performance as central to the creation of a particular space in which the voice of ideology and that of the "masses" are not "self-enclosed or deaf to one another but hear each other constantly, call back and forth to each other, and are reflected in one another" (Bakhtin, quoted in Yurchak 2005, 19). The picture that Yurchak has painted is effectively one of negotiation between ideology and the masses, one in which the voices of the masses and those of state power *pretend* not to hear each other, although in fact they hear each other very well. The resulting denied dialogue between masses and power is present as subtext and ultimately lends this type of dialogue a performative character.

In order to describe Soviet realities more accurately than the "mask model," Yurchak has developed the concept of "performative shifts." Borrowed from J. L. Austin's theories of language, in which he has identified not only the contrast between constatives and performatives, but also the morphing of one into another, Yurchak has posited that the early era of Soviet socialism reflected the constatives of proletarianism, which were disseminated to the masses in order to form a dialogue via which the State literally talked to (or educated) the masses in the precepts of Marxist-Leninism. However, with the death of the leader (namely, Stalin), so Yurchak has argued, this period was succeeded by that of middle and late socialism, when the constatives became "replays" of the addresses of the leader, therefore transforming themselves into performatives. This goes as far as evidencing the validity of Mao's theory of shifting contradictions:

> ... the increasing normalization of all forms of authoritative discourse [...] does not mean that meanings simply had become unimportant, or that everyday life became a series of automatic actions devoid of meaning. Quite the contrary, the performative replication of the precise forms of authoritative representation rendered the constative meanings associated with this representation unanchored, increasingly unpredictable, and open to new interpretations, enabling the emergence of new and unanticipated meanings, relations, and lifestyles in various contexts of everyday life (59).

When applying Yurchak's theory to the socialist space in Romania and China, it becomes clear that the function of performance is not to glorify the regime univocally in chilling street rallies that reinforce the oppression of Communist ideology, but to validate both parties of a negotiation between crowds and power. Differently put, freedom or change in socialism are not enacted through personal agency, following the Western individualist paradigm, but through the ability of the socialist subject to perform – more precisely, to perform as a group.

The Korean War Films

As we have seen, *Reverberates the Valley* and *The Bridge* played a performative role strictly related to the historical context that the countries were traversing at the time. As in the pleasure derived from the shenanigans of the volunteers who recognized themselves onscreen in *Reverberates the Valley*, Chinese war films of the 1960s attempted to shake off centuries of colonial-infused anti-Chinese bias by engaging in satire, sarcasm and irony. To exemplify this, I will discuss two films made in 1960, *On the 38th Parallel* (*San Ba Xian Shang*, Shi Wenchi) and *Raid* (*Qi Xi*, Xu Youxin), with the aim to celebrate the achievements of the Chinese Volunteer Army in the Korean War, which had ended in 1953 and whose memory still lingered in people's minds. Discussed briefly by Chris Berry and Mary Farquar in *China on Screen: Cinema and Nation*, the series of late-1950s and early-1960s films made about the "War to Resist US Aggression and Aid Korea" represented more than just propaganda meant to put a favorable dent into the Chinese participation in the Korean War. In their performative nature, they were no less than a cinematic reification of Bhabha's mimicry and reaction to colonial rule (Bhabha 2004).

Shot mostly at night and favoring deep shadows in high contrast, *Raid* narrates the mission of a Chinese brigade tasked with blowing up a bridge on enemy territory during the Korean War. The noiresque photography and the predominant jungle locations make the film almost exotic; harking back to the quality of *Secret Post in Canton*, it has the features of an entertaining adventure film. What *Raid* also does is to performatize the encounter between the Chinese forces and the South Koreans and their American allies so as to shed a positive light on the PLA's ingenious unmaking of enemy plans. This cunningness of the Chinese helps them to outsmart their enemies and ultimately accomplish their mission.

Take a moment towards the beginning of the film, when the volunteer army enjoys a break from fighting. As entertainment, some soldiers decide to put on a small performance for the enjoyment of their fellow comrades, in which they stage a fictitious encounter between the PLA and the American Army (Figure 3.1). While the Chinese soldiers are sleeping, the Americans – played in the skit by Chinese actors with ostentatiously fake, protruding noses – attempt to surprise them, only to fall into their own trap. This is because one PLA soldier who was only pretending to be asleep quickly disarms them. It is a very simple, unpretentious moment; its effect is to extract a few good laughs from the recruits who are watching the skit as an audience.

If this sounds indoctrinating, Yingjin Zhang has reminded us that, "[c]onsidering the fact that many filmmakers as well as military and rural audiences had lived through years of battles and that the Korean War was raging on, it is not surprising to see the immense popularity of the war or military genre during this period" (Zhang 2004, 192).[2] While the Chinese government became increasingly vilified by Washington in the early stages of the

[2] Zhang has written about the Korean War genre film in general.

Figure 3.1 American soldier played by a Chinese with fake nose enjoying a meal before being captured by PLA troops in the sketch in *Raid*.

Cold War, one wonders if audiences did not find in the onscreen mimicry and the good-natured mocking of American omniscience the very empowerment that they needed to validate the otherwise successful outcome of the Chinese-led campaign which resounded in the entire socialist world of the 1950s.[3]

Interestingly, the satirical comedy number in *Raid* is comparable to the dénouement in *Reverberates the Valley*, where the song and dance vaudeville routine of the volunteers humorously ridicules Nikki for his laziness. As apparent in the use of theatricality and performance in both films, the employment of sarcasm and satire are common transnational devices meant to educate rather than judge. The mimicry in *Raid* has the effect of throwing the gaze back at the colonizer and of questioning the legitimacy of Hollywood's common "yellowface" portrayal of the Oriental in earlier films demeaning to Chinese sensibilities. Considering the depictions of the Asians as lazy, scheming and deceitful in movies that date back to the silent era – from

[3] Various slogans of support were used in different socialist countries in the 1950s, and older Romanians still remember the "hands off Korea" campaign. (Ironically, the slogan was also mockingly used by women at the time to fend off unwanted male courtship.) The Chinese government attempts to keep the memory of this campaign alive, via museums placed in different cities near the border with North Korea, condemning the American atrocities committed in the Korean War (on the atrocities, see Fifield 2017).

The Yellow Menace (Aubrey Kennedy, 1916), the series *Patria* (Jaccard, Wharton, Wharton, 1917) and D. W. Griffith's *Broken Blossoms* (1919) to the 1930s classics *The Good Earth* (Franklin, Fleming, Machatý, 1937) and *The Bitter Tea of General Yen* (Frank Capra, 1933) – the late socialist realism of the 1960s is a surprisingly mild, if knee-jerk reaction to Orientalism. This reaction does not demean the West by making it appear racist but acts as a performative means to help the colonized preserve a sense of identity (and empowerment), which was just in the process of being constructed.[4]

Another example comes from Shi Wenchi's *On the 38th Parallel*. The story takes place in the last weeks before the armistice that would lead to the division of Korea in 1953. What surprises the viewer in this film is the particular depiction of Americans not as villains or wrongdoers, but as the very opposite of the energetic, humanistic Chinese army. Although the film is a direct attack on American imperialism and therefore "anti-American" in tone, Americans are seen to be lounging about, generally disinterested in the surrounding Korean population. They are portrayed as superior, wearing Ray Ban sunglasses and chewing gum but, although driven by a penchant to impose their will at all costs, ultimately unaffected by the loss of North Korea. In the meantime, the Chinese, especially when helping a single grandmother living on an isolated farm defeat the American forces, understand the drama that has befallen the North Koreans, mainly by relating to it from a similar, subaltern position. It is not so much the ideological value of their "win" that the film tries to forefront, but the conditions of extreme poverty which unite the neighboring countries on a human rather than ideological level. Furthermore, the film planned to expose the wicked strategy of US forces, which supported both Rhee Syngman's regime in South Korea and Chiang Kai-shek's Kuomingtang in Taiwan, in order to establish a military foothold in the region and surround their Communist enemies. Even though undoubtedly propagandistic if regarded from this angle and highly undramatic otherwise, at the level of audience reception the film performs the dignity of the victorious subaltern.

While it is true that this strategy would help solidify the nationalism of the later socialist era, these war films can also be seen as an unaccepted Maussian gift,[5] offered in response to the West's treatment of the Far East. The refusal to accept these gifts causes both sides of the conflict to become isolated from one another and to misunderstand each other, which ultimately defines the tone of the Cold War. What we witness in the cinematic interaction between the two systems is an ineffective communication attempt. The Korean War films of the 1960s are thus a gift that the West chose not to embrace, one that might have covertly carried on the cinematic conversation between the two

[4] For a comprehensive list of early films that were used to tarnish the image of the Oriental, not only for Hollywood audiences, but also for those in Denmark and Germany, see Leyda 1972.

[5] See Mauss 1954.

philosophies of Communism and capitalism, in spite of the political breakdown in discourse.

Interestingly, Chinese cinema did not give up on its offer to communicate with the American side, even in more recent times. One example is the reiteration of motifs and themes sported in the 1960s films *On the 38th Parallel* and *Raid* in a Korean War movie made in 2021. In the three-hour production of *The Battle at Lake Changjin* (*Chang jin hu*),[6] commissioned by the propaganda arm of the CCP, the experienced directors Chen Kaige, Tsui Hark and Dante Lam tell the story of a regiment in the People's Volunteer Army which ambushes and partly destroys a regiment of the US Marine Corps. A crucial early battle in North Korea, this would help turn the tide of the war and stop the UN forces' advance towards the Chinese border.

A melodramatic story about the suffering and ingenuity of Chinese soldiers, the spectacular, fast-paced action film was considered pure propaganda by the Western press (He 2021), because never since the dystopian Hollywood-made *Red Dawn* (John Milius, 1984) have so many Americans been killed onscreen. There is nevertheless a certain Hollywood-derived amount of realistic display of wartime action – reminiscent of *Saving Private Ryan* (Steven Spielberg, 1998) and similar American war films, which is largely based on historical fact – even though there is a clear focus on Chinese bravery and patriotism. The film was an enormous success in China and after its release quickly became the most watched Chinese film of all times, despite the fact that the CGI used in action sequences seems a little cartoonish; some camera techniques such as the low angles in which General MacArthur is portrayed are invasive; and the editing moves at such a fast pace as to make some viewers queasy.

It is important to note in reference to *The Battle at Lake Changjin* that the film reiterates Chinese portrayals of Americans made famous in the clichés of the 1960s, where the Yanks were obsessed with their smoking pipes and Ray Ban sunglasses. Similar to *The Bridge*, moreover, the movie perpetuates the fairytale paradigm of using scarcity for the benefit of the underprivileged, thus making the story seem like a re-enactment of the David versus Goliath motif. This is clear in moments where Chinese soldiers bury themselves in snow to escape observation by American planes, which highlights the self-sacrificial approach that the technically weaker troops had to adopt in the face of a stronger enemy.

Having been exposed to hundreds, if not thousands, of Hollywood and Western European films that capitalized on the Allied victory in World War II, we should ask ourselves why the Chinese are still not allowed to produce a film that celebrates their meagre battle victories (in what is regarded as an inconclusive war). And why does the West rush to call such behavior propaganda? As some critics have opined, this Chinese effort is no more propagandistic than *Pearl Harbor* (Michael Bay, 2001) or *We Were Soldiers* (Randall Wallace, 2002), which overtly glorify the American side,

[6] The film is part of a franchise, the second installment of which is *Water Gate Bridge* (*Chang jin hu zhi shui men qiao*, Tsui Harkt, Chen Kaige, Dante Lam, 2022).

without making the Americans look particularly bad (Mendelson 2021). Žižek has argued that this is feasible because, despite appearances to the contrary, we live in a post-ideological age in appearance only, and the promotion of capitalism, the world's main ideology at the present, is accepted as natural rather than as propagandistic (Žižek 2001).

Despite indictments to the contrary and the Korean War's mild reaction to the US-led coalition, as Jessica Ka Yee Chan has shown, very few titles in China engaged directly in anti-American or anti-Western propaganda (Chan 2019). The situation was similar if not identical in Romania: as evidenced by *Life Triumphs* or the 1978 Romanian action film *Bus for Death* (*Acțiunea Autobuzul*), which re-enacts a real-life 1950s ambush of anticommunist partisans by the Communist forces, the few villains of the Romanian screen are the former Iron Guard sympathizers who have emigrated to the West and are constantly thwarting plots against the Communist state. In China, the quintessential enemy is, of course, the Japanese army or the Kuomintang soldiers, and their figure is quintessential to the many war movies produced in the Mao era. To claim, however, that either of these figures stood for Western civilization and that the Communist world engaged in relentless propaganda against the West is an exaggeration.

It is ironic that the sole movie promoting anti-American propaganda on behalf of socialist countries is a modern American production. *Comrade Detective* (Rhys Thomas, 2017) is a six-episode miniseries produced by Amazon that transports the tone, style and humor of late-1980s American buddy detective TV drama to late socialist Romania. The show centers on the "Bucharest PD," an aberrant version of the socialist state's militia apparatus, which fights hypothetical cocaine dealers while wearing leather jackets and quoting Lenin. It is works in the style of *Comrade Detective* alone, and not Romanian or Chinese films of the socialist or postsocialist periods, that recreate Communist history from the perspective of the poorly informed Western imaginary. Validating Verdery's observation that Communism was the least studied ideology of the modern world because of Western inaccessibility to socialist sources (Verdery 1996), it is these products, and not those about the Korean War, that perpetuate misunderstanding between the postsocialist world and the West, despite the postsocialist world's renewed efforts to find a genuine communication channel, as in *The Battle at Lake Changjin*.

The Korean War films are important on another level, namely because it is in the realm of their performative nature – the Chinese performing their image of America and, later, Hollywood performing its own image of its Cold War enemies – that the "dialogue" between the two "Others" of the former Cold War takes place. Interestingly, in the absence of any political dialogue between China and the West at the time when the Korean War movies were made – a silence which held the world in check until the emergence of the Détente in the 1970s – these films still attempted to "talk" to one another. It is also important that through these films (*On the 38th Parallel* and *Raid* representing some of the earliest Chinese examples) socialist identity was literally being constructed via a new type of empowerment negotiated at the level of the cinematic image. While it is true that this happened in contrast to an imagined – thus Occidentalized – West which has been reduced to the level of a stock character, it is also true that the West was engaged in productions that sought to achieve the very same purpose.

Lastly, these films depict China's struggle to end the aftereffects of colonial rule. In response to colonialism, China tried to achieve the international recognition which its leaders thought it deserved, in a period when the only nations giving it that kind of attention were tiny Communist states such as Romania. Similarly, Romania also clamored for world attention despite its minuscule size, and this created an inferiority complex in a country virtually absent from world affairs until then. That is why *Reverberates the Valley* as well as other Romanian films from the 1950s and 1960s, such as *Life Triumphs* and *Alarm in the Mountains*, aimed to restore a sense of national honor following the wartime humiliation that the country had endured on the battlefield and in the economy.

While for Hollywood and Western European commercial filmmakers it was important to provide continuity between past and present – as seen, for example, in Hollywood's historical films which attempted to recuperate imperial ideology from the times of ancient Rome and project them into the civilizational force of the Western present – Communism offered a break with the past, as well as a focus on the present. This Weltanschauung supported social evolution, progress, but most of all, the possibility of change; it is for this reason that the government disallowed the production of sword-and-sandal epics in China, unlike in Romania. By focusing on the unjustness of past social relations, socialist films identifying fascism as its main enemy invariably stressed the role of the working class in building the future as different. Ironically, using Western tried-and-tested cinematic formulas, they staged this opposition as a perfectly entertaining Hollywood conflict, which, as in the 2021 Chinese film example, continue to prove successful with present-day audiences.

From Socialist Realism to Social Realism

Aside from their ambassadorial functions abroad, films were meant to stimulate dialogue domestically. In the same way that children and young adult films were supposed to shape the character of the young masses and were therefore subjects of debate, Xie Tieli's *Early Spring in February* (*Zaochun Eryue*, 1964) initiated just such a dialogue. Based on a 1929 novella written by Rou Shi, a Communist executed by the nationalists in 1931, the film tells a convoluted tale of alembicated love and political persuasions that ends with Xiao Jianqiu, the hero, becoming a devout revolutionary. However, Xiao's affections waver between a young coworker at the village school and a poor widow whose husband, not unlike the author himself, was killed by nationalists. Even though Xiao decides to marry the widow, his interest in the younger woman ends up costing the widow's life. Mao saw Xiao's indecision as evidence of the hero's purported bourgeois humanitarianism, despite

Xie's attempt to teach politics to his audiences. As a result, Mao personally labeled the film "sugarcoated poison" to inflame the anti-black-line spirit of the Cultural Revolution.[7]

Film scholar Wang Zhuoyi has posited that some authors saw unwavering support for Mao's policies in the political "rituals [which] deprived individuals of their conscious minds, modifying their minds so radically that their personal identities 'dwindled to nothing'" (Wang 2014, 1). Nevertheless, Wang has also stated that these rituals cannot be generalized to represent entire societies. Furthermore, promoting such statements "contributed to a prevailing paradigm that reduces revolutionary culture to a monolith constructed by a hypnotized collective" (1) which "underestimated the historical complexities of revolutionary culture" (2).

Due to the film's innovative aesthetic freedom, which broke the strictures of the cinematic canon at the time, a chorus of critics joined Mao's call and denounced the film for distorting historical realities: instead of reflecting the "heated mass struggles" of the twenties, so a journalist has written, the director of the film turned revolutionary China into a "scenic land of peace," and therefore the film amounted to "a dose of poison for today's youth" (Bowen, quoted in Wang 2014, 163). However, some of this criticism inadvertently also legitimated the film, showing that the critics joining Mao's call were not as obedient as their actions apparently show. Although an unidentified journalist wrote the following text in order to stop the film's distribution, the effects of his words on the public amounted to quite the reverse:

> Feeling that literary and artistic works of revolutionary content are formulaic and boring, [...] should the film go public, many young students would likely welcome it and watch it passionately. They would say that this film is a true piece of "high art." [The film] would lead young people to seek a comfortable, quiet, free, and unrestricted life. [...] They would feel that today we do not have freedom to choose what subject to study or what profession to take, that we do not even have freedom of love, and that we live in an era even worse than the May Fourth Period (Wang 2014, 166).

The message is the epitome of ambivalence and, therefore, resistance: under the guise of criticizing the film, the author has offered the outrageous (and dangerous) supposition that life in Mao's China was worse than during Sun Yat Sen's republic, ultimately confirming exactly the interpretation of the film which the Party furiously denied: that of being "high art."

In tune with Communist concerns for education, there was an overt preoccupation in the press with the film's reception by the youth. Of course, the scandal caused by the criticism ensured that droves of young people flooded the cinemas and that reactions actually sympathetic to the main character began to emerge, which outweighed the patriarchal anxiety of the Party's warnings about the film's "bourgeois character": "[Students] remarked that

[7] Black liners were social subjects who were deemed rightist or counter-revolutionary during the Cultural Revolution.

the film was 'more popular than those Hong Kong imports,' that it was a 'rare wonder,' and that it was a 'must-see for having a touching plot, dramatic love, unique personalities, nowhere to find today, popular actors, rich colors, and extremely beautiful costumes, props, settings, and music" (Wang 2014, 167). A perfect example of the ambivalence of the propagandist image (here overcharged with its top-down, imposed interpretation), the film became a "hit," not necessarily because of its sly subversive message, but because the youth identified with the sexual hesitations of the star involved in a love triangle. Both through its political *and* overtly socio-sexual content, the film therefore played to its young audiences as a straightforward coming-of-age story.[8] As per Roland Barthes' analysis of cultural markers (Barthes 1972), the message of the film suffered a logical mutation in its interpretation, forcing the film to serve a different purpose altogether. This allowed audiences to project their own contemporary realities onto a film set in a different period, which then allowed the young men and women in the audience to feel empowered.[9] Moreover, if Xie Tieli's intentions cannot be doubted – and in the atmosphere of the early 1960s I believe they should not be – *Early Spring in February* personalizes Barthes' theory of the "Death of the Author" (Barthes 1986), according to which the film director's message is resignified to fit neither the intentions of the political establishment nor those of its makers, but the reading of the audiences.

The commotion that the release (and subsequent withdrawal) of *Early Spring in February* provoked at home prevented it from being screened in Romania. Nevertheless, the Chinese government did offer the movie to Romanian authorities, who bought a copy that is still in the film archives. This goes to show that the dialogue between audiences and the state in China had a significant echo beyond the country's borders, and that the film's reception went on to influence the fate of Romanian controversial productions, as shown in the next chapters. What the dialogue between the masses and power shows in the case of Xie's film is that the socialist image wove into its fabric not only the invitation to doubt it, but also the ambivalence to both validate and destroy it. In short, the image always performed a function which was imbued with a subtext – a subtext that was polysemous. At its most basic, the image represented a show of complaisance between the regime and the masses: I pretend to be your leader, you pretend to be my people, and as long as you stick to this image of authority, everything outside of this relationship is permitted. It is therefore not that some pure cinematic truth of the image had been corrupted and that late socialist realism and political films impoverished the ability to signify reality – that it was reduced to the level

[8] Zhuoyi Wang has written that some students became so enamored with the hero's demeanor that they even imitated his style of dress (168).

[9] Wen Jiang's 1994 Cultural Revolution classic, *In the Heat of the Sun*, would adapt this mutation to the screen, therefore literalizing it when it recounts how the Soviet socialist realist staple film, Mikhail Romm's *Lenin in 1918*, serves as inspiration to a gang of rebellious adolescents for both their sexual and social misadventures.

of stereotype. What the Communist regimes effectively did was to render the image immensely more powerful under the appearance that cinema was excruciatingly boring, therefore inviting audiences to decode meanings in its polysemy. In conclusion, the image was imbued with power, and this was not because it was propagandistic, but because it was ambivalent.

Socialist realism and the genres which it spawned in the 1960s served roles identifiable not with propaganda alone, but with several active spectating practices. The kind of identification shown so far – between the audience and the volunteers in *Reverberates the Valley*, as well as between the youths and the ideologically "deviational" Chinese hero in *Early Spring in February* – is based on a tacitly condoned dialogue: on one hand, the public takes away an aspect of the officially-sanctioned image which the regime does *not* support and thereby receives the gratification of having somehow cheated the regime. On the other hand – and this is evident in Mao's literal condemnation yet inability to fully control the cultural politics spawned by the film (Wang 2014, 169) – the leader, in appearance at least, puts on a show of total control of the crowds, which he knows to be totally uncontrollable.

In this, *Early Spring* represents the transition, which emerged in the 1960s in both China and Romania, from the socialist realism of the 1950s to the above-mentioned social realism that, aside from commercial cinema, would characterize the rest of the socialist period. In that sense, cinema under socialism never was indoctrinated *by itself* even at its horrid, proletkult, ideological, collaborationist worst, simply because the indoctrination was never received *ad literam* in the spectating act. As Verdery has made clear – and any socialist text no matter how ideologically neutral showed in its performative nature – the subtext of any work of art or piece of indoctrination contained an attack in disguise, a particular allusion to the West, a change in policy at the top, or a simple political development hardly noticeable to the naked eye. Indeed, the masses were too adept in "double talk,"[10] too versed in the *langue du bois* not to read between the intentionally tailored lines; too experienced in "decoding" to fall for a straightforward message.

Instead of being based on the simple idea that tyranny brainwashes its subjects, the ambivalent portrayal of ideology onscreen produced distinct communicating structures between the masses and the powers that be. Film audiences in China and Romania learned to understand these structures and to speak a complex language, because they could read messages that were multivalent. Socialist affect emerged through this vocabulary as a means of connecting with a reality different from the straightforward narrative of ideology, economics and failure that the West has come to expect from Communism. Members of the former Eastern Bloc were familiar with this type of language and this type of affect due to the same incomprehensibility that the West attached to totalitarian Communism, albeit on a different foundation. As I will discuss in the next chapter, the uneasy relationship between the masses and power throughout socialism paradoxically turned the

[10] In its Orwellian sense here but without the negative connotation.

much-maligned idea of the "Friendship of Nations" or *Druzhba Narodov* into a reality based on common experience, conduct and emotion from China to Romania. And social realism, as we will see from here on, helped spearhead that change.

Romanian Musicals and Chinese Revolutionary Operas

It may come as a surprise that Eastern Europe produced musical films under socialism. While some feel-good musicals transported the breezy atmosphere of Hollywood to Romanian shores, especially in the 1960s and early 1970s, China's musicals during Mao's era were oftentimes associated with the ethnic film genre and, of course, the revolutionary operas. In order to analyze the two national traditions of this unusual genre, largely associated with Hollywood, a brief analysis of its emergence in the Soviet Union is necessary, because Soviet cinema oftentimes influenced filmmaking style in Eastern European satellite countries and China, even though in this case its influence was less profound than usually thought.

What came to be called *kolkhoz* musicals in the Soviet Union, because of the collective farms which usually served as their backdrop, are a largely vilified series of films produced from the late 1930s into the 1960s, which glamorized the industrialization of the poor Russian countryside in the period of high Stalinism and thereafter. Sporting red tractors that dot the grain-rich background of the eternal Russian steppes, they featured smiling faces and rotund bodies involved in seemingly ecstatic agricultural pursuits and otherwise presented the Russian folk as a happy-go-lucky people with few worries other than those of fulfilling the socialist five-year plan.

Tractor Drivers (*Traktoristy*, 1939), directed by the father of the genre, Ivan Pyryev, during the tension leading to World War II in 1939, features a simple plot: protagonists Klim and Mariana start as cooperative farm rivals whose male- and female-led brigades, respectively, are engaged in a sort of healthy socialist competition vying for larger production quotas. After a series of missteps, the couple step on their personal pride and, realizing that their efforts will be more constructive in a joint cooperative, are finally married in a celebratory fest which is joined by both collectives. *Cossacks of the Kuban* (*Kubanskie kazaki*) was made exactly ten years later, in 1949. It was directed by the same Ivan Pyryev and starred the same Marina Ladynina from *Tractor Drivers* (and Pyryev's wife), this time as Galina, while her co-star was Sergei Lukyanov who played Gordei. Aside from being shot in Technicolor and featuring more songs involving larger choirs and dance numbers, the story of *Cossacks* is very similar to that of *Tractor Drivers*: two rival cooperative leaders have long been in love with each other but are too proud to confess their feelings. Gordei's temper ignites when Galina dumps prices at the annual country fair to provoke him, which causes Gordei to encourage a younger member of his team to court a girl from Galina's kolkhoz and thus destabilize Galina's production. After the usual complications are overcome, Gordei and Galina finally admit their foolishness as well as their love for each other and are in the end happily married. In both films, the Communist protagonists end up being, in fact, married not only to each other, but also to a higher ideal, which would soon come to dominate production relations and lead to the establishment of a better world based on community-driven principles. An obvious similarity between the Soviet productions and the Romanian and Chinese ones are their concern for women's liberation, and, of course, abundant optimism about a better life which both *Reverberates the Valley* and *The Bridge* later made famous in Romania and China.

Despite the fact that the film is not a documentary, the paramount argument directed against *Cossacks* by Western and Russian criticism alike is that it displays a reality very different from that of the depression in which the Soviet economy and agriculture found themselves after the war. Ironically, the sharpest indictment came from Khrushchev himself, who discussed *Cossacks* in the wake of destalinization, stressing that the fakeness of the film painted a dishonest picture of Stalin's regime (Taylor 1999). Far from being genuine film criticism, of course, the comments of the Soviet leader were a covert way of waging political war against his former mentor in order to solidify his power. It is furthermore naïve to believe that the masses followed cinema to obtain their news about the state of agriculture in the countryside. Despite this, some Western critics followed Khrushchev's lead in deploring the propaganda of *Cossacks*, disregarding both the film's proto-feminism as well as its entertainment qualities.

In contrast, film Scholar Rimgaila Salys has offered a reading of the film informed by spectatorship theory. She has dug into the Soviet press of the time to gauge a modicum of reaction to what has later been called either shameless propaganda or non-art, surfacing in the process a surprisingly honest commentary. Salys has quoted Soviet-era critic Valerii Kichin in relation to *Cossacks* and thereby repositioned the function played by the socialist realist musical genre within the context of late or "high" Stalinism: "Millions of people loved this film," has stated Kichin, "although the same millions knew, according to their own opinion, how far the country was from this magnificent cinematic abundance, this splendor at the fair. We critics made this film a symbol of falsehood in art. But it was an expression of hope" (Kichin, quoted in Salys 2003, 6).

The question that we have to ask, with spectatorship theory in mind, is not whether the film "served Stalinism" or was "escapist," but how the allegedly indoctrinating ideology was negotiated by the "millions" that have seen it. Moreover, as Salys has put it, and as film theory has long since accepted, it is not relevant whether the film "reflected" reality (Salys 2003, 4). After all, how ready are we to believe that people in love *really* sing and dance in the rain, as in Gene Kelly's iconic musical made at approximately the same time on the other side of the world (*Singin' in the Rain*, 1952), or that capitalist labor is so enamored with itself as to make scantily dressed women dance in unison, as Kracauer has intuited in reference to the Tiller Girls routine? It is therefore not relevant whether the produce displayed at the annual fair was "real," but that the film played a positive role (that of reinforcing hope) in collective memory. This perfectly illustrates what Yurchak has called "new interpretations, enabling the emergence of new and unanticipated meanings, relations, and lifestyles" (Yurchak 2005, 60).

If Romanian and Chinese films similarly impacted audiences' psyches at the time by producing collective optimism, films produced in these countries demonstrated a noticeable degree of independence from the Soviet style, bearing only a negligible trace of the Soviet kolkhoz musicals. If Romanian musicals were marginally influenced by Soviet ones, it is mainly because of the light-heartedness and romance of films featuring the well-known Russian star Lyudmila Gurchenko. Like *Carnival Night* (*Karnavalnaya noch*, Eldar Ryazanov, 1956) and *Girl with a Guitar* (*Devushka s gitaroy*, Aleksandr Faintsimmer, 1958), which could qualify as an inspiration, Romanian musicals steered largely clear of propaganda, instead showcasing the directors' somewhat negotiated interpretations of Hollywood musicals.

Rather than looking up to the kolkhoz musicals of its larger neighbor, Romania began to develop a local musical film tradition which was distinct from socialist realism, starting as early as in the late 1950s. While we briefly encountered Iurie Darie in *Alarm in the Mountains* as a border guard battling fascist infiltrators, his real breakthrough came with the 1958 film *Hello? Wrong Number* (*Alo, ați greșit numărul*), a musical comedy directed by Andrei Călărașu. A mistaken identity scenario focused on student romance in modern Bucharest, the film spoke to Darie's generation in the language of tenderness and sincerity, and audiences flocked to see the charismatic young actor onscreen. *Hello? Wrong Number* recorded the second-highest number of spectators of any Romanian film up to that time (four million), having previously only been surpassed by *The Mill of Good Luck* (*La moara cu noroc*, 1957), a dark psychological thriller with noir tendencies directed by Victor Iliu in the previous year.[11]

As his fame increased, Darie came to personify the dream of every teenager in the 1960s. He was sexy, suave and immensely popular. Besides, he could both sing and play any part that a film director required of him, from construction engineer to love-sick musician. Another Iurie Darie vehicle that came out a few years later, *Holiday at the Seaside* (*Vacanță la mare*, 1963) was Călărașu's last film but a big hit with Romanian audiences.[12] Although in *Hello? Wrong Number* characters lived in a refined, almost aristocratic world

[11] Educated under Eisenstein in Moscow, Victor Iliu is one of the unjustly overlooked Romanian directors. Because of his ideological tenets and early socialist realist productions, today he is considered a propaganda filmmaker and all but forgotten, except for his apolitical film *The Mill of Good Luck*.

[12] Of Jewish ethnicity, Andrei Călărașu was one of the few survivors of Antonescu's Jassy pogroms. After liberation by the Soviet Army, he decided to change his name from Bernard Grupper to the more Romanian-sounding surname Călărașu, in reference to the station where he disembarked the death trains in the town of Călărași. Following four years of harrowing forced labor under Romania's fascist regime, he thereafter decided to make comedy and musical films.

belonging to an older generation which was becoming passé – a world which featured classical music concerts and high-society manners – *Holiday at the Seaside* seemed to be directly adapted from a happy-go-lucky spring-break Elvis musical, the type of which were starting to play to enormous acclaim in Romanian cinemas of the 1960s.

The plot follows the accidental shenanigans of a band which mistakenly boards the wrong train and ends up at the Black Sea instead of a mountain resort. When the tourist bureau manager wants the band to play there despite their unfavorable credentials, the band leaders have to improvise a musical concert – featuring a female trio whom they recruit on the spot – which turns out to be a big success. Of course, the concert is only a small part of the band's winnings: the conductor also gets the most beautiful girl in the trio. The ending provides some spectacular aerial shots of the new Communist-built seaside hotels, but these are filmed at night, in brooding lighting, and edited to the sound of dreamy, unexpected music.

Even though little can be said to be indoctrinating in films such as *Holiday at the Seaside*, Dana Ranga, a postsocialist documentary filmmaker from Romania working in Germany in the late 1990s, has held a different view. In her interpretation of Romanian musicals, even sandy beaches were a method of mass indoctrination. In 1997, under the commercializing tagline "All Singing! All Dancing! All Marxist Musicals!" Ranga made a documentary titled *East Side Story*, which, as its tongue-in-cheek title suggests, reviews from an anticommunist perspective the musicals produced by various Communist governments of Eastern European countries and the Soviet Union. If we are to believe Ranga, all musical films made in the Eastern Bloc since the 1950s were not only propagandistic, but also an affront to the intelligence of Eastern European and Soviet audiences. Behind their cosmeticized veneer and Western-derived plotlines – as was the case with the Czechoslovak *The Hop Pickers* (*Starci na chmelu*, Ladislav Rychman, 1964), a Romeo-and-Juliet-type romance taking place in a Czechoslovak student summer camp – lurked the ostentatiously hidden and indoctrinating goals of proletarian democracy.

This reading, however, is heavy-handed and clearly abuses film texts to extort political meaning, even when such meaning is not there at all. As we shall see when discussing censorship in socialist Romania, this criticism is commonplace in postsocialism and betrays a penchant for overreaction and melodrama, not on the behalf of the socialist filmmakers, but on behalf of the postsocialist critics and documentary filmmakers. Following the regretful Romanian critic Alex Leo Șerban, who somewhat exaggeratedly considered at one point that "even [socialist] comedies were ideological!" (Șerban 2010, 17), as well as Ranga's monovalent readings, postsocialist critics indicted socialist-era cinema of propaganda, even when there was no evidence thereof whatsoever.

Sandy beaches, young students in love and teenage adventures at the seaside did not quite resonate with the political goals of international communism. Despite this, Romania in the early 1960s had already claimed its position in the Eastern Bloc as promoting a mixture of Occidentalism and Communism that seemed more original than that of the Soviet Union. This was so until the arrival of nationalism in the late 1960s and the derailment of the Communist project thereafter. Romania continued its musical film tradition until the mid-1970s. Cinema as a medium was favored for spotlighting some of the country's leading singers, like Dan Spătaru, who starred in the absurdist-experimental musical *The Songs of the Sea* (*Cîntecele mării*, 1970). Meanwhile, Elisabeta Bostan, a prolific female director whose career spanned the entire socialist period, added elements of phantasmagoria to the classic musical tradition, her youth-focused film works *Veronica* (1973) and *Ma-ma* (1976) creating bizarre fantasy worlds. While *The Songs of the Sea* featured a Soviet female singer as a co-lead, *Ma-ma* was made in coproduction with the USSR and constitutes one of the few Romanian films to find distribution (and some success) in the US at that time.

Chinese ethnic musicals found some popularity abroad as well (Zhang 2018). Featuring songs that were interspersed in the diegesis to provide a "feel-good" atmosphere, *Five Golden Flowers* showcases exotic locales and the folk traditions of the Bai's ethnic group in what is an endearing narrative of the protagonist's journey across various scenic landscapes and different regions in the Chinese Southwest. Although hailing from the spy thriller genre, *Visitors on the Icy Mountain* (*Bing shan shang de lai ke*, Xinshui Zhao, 1963) similarly features musical numbers sung by the mysterious heroine who ethnically belongs to the Xinjiang Tajik minority. Having popularized the Tajik folk song "Why are Flowers so Red?" the film enjoyed an almost cult-like success in China and continues to be well-known to this day.

Beside ethnic-themed musicals, China developed a strong tradition of revolutionary operas. Not unlike Ranga's postsocialist criticism of Romanian musical films, however, Dongning Feng has observed that Chinese revolutionary opera works have been equally vilified in postsocialism. Feng has also noticed, however, that most criticism directed at them is "disappointingly lacking in depth" and "exclusively politically predisposed" (Feng 2021, 66). He has thus combatted the position of critics who saw China as being in the grip of an unrelenting dictatorship whose citizens were subjects to state-sponsored propaganda. In order to assess the position of audiences *vis-à-vis* these allegedly indoctrinating works, it is necessary to analyze the way in which revolutionary opera films such as *The Red Detachment of Women* were spectated by the Chinese audiences themselves:

> A Western journalist traveling in China in 1967 gave the following description of a performance of revolutionary skits [...]: "I have never seen in China an audience as totally engrossed as this one. They did not applaud much, but it seemed as if they thought they shouldn't interrupt. They stared fixedly at the stage with faces completely rapt; each new scene creased their brows, wiped them smooth, furrowed them again more deeply, all in unison. Heads stretched forward so that not a single detail would escape their eyes" (McGrath 2010, 343).

The above quotation is from Louis Barcata's *China in the Throes of the Cultural Revolution*. It is used by film scholar Jason McGrath to illustrate the staging of skits illustrating quotations from Mao, which played as introductions to the longer revolutionary ballets known as *yangbanxi*, or "model works." These messages were intended to bring the message of the Communist Party to the masses, via a dramatic reworking of traditional Peking operas and certain forms of Western ballet.[13]

One is not certain at first, judging by the audience's reaction, whether to take at face value Barcata's reporting or to read into it the implication that these stage works were indoctrinating to their audiences. Over time, however, McGrath has clarified Barcata's position as meaning that totalitarian politics enacted via model operas corrupts the ideals of art. In opposition, McGrath has argued that critics such as Barcata do not understand the innovative style of revolutionary operas. Because *The White Haired Girl* or *The Legend of the Red Lantern* (*Hong deng ji*, Cheng Yin, 1971) do not always follow David Bordwell's realist mode of narration, McGrath has claimed that these works belong to a socialist type of formalism that makes them distinct from classic realism; that they are influenced by the Soviet avant-garde in that they forefront "antirealist aspects of revolutionary romanticism, including a strongly melodramatic mode of narration as well as a now almost completely formalist film style" (McGrath 2010, 335).

While McGrath has correctly identified a certain Soviet influence on revolutionary operas, it is necessary to stress that these also forefronted a mixture of traditional Chinese operatic style and homegrown legends transposed in a revolutionary key. In an attempt to rehabilitate these films, several scholars[14] have shown in their recent work that the reductive formula of "eight stage works for 800 million people (ba yi renmin ba tai xi)" (Mittler, 2010), which is supposed to demonstrate that the decay experienced by the arts during the rule of the Gang of Four, is not only a gross exaggeration, but a stereotype that intentionally denatures whatever cultural activity was going on during the Cultural Revolution. Some scholars have not only claimed that there was culture beyond the eight operas (which, as Barbara Mittler has shown, were, in fact, eighteen [Mittler 2016]) but that the experimentation and innovation that these operas adduced – by way of mixing Chinese and Western elements – created an artistic style that amounts, according to Paul Clark, to nothing short of a new aesthetics (Clark, quoted in Wang Ban 2016, 85). Furthermore, the eight operas for 800 million itself is a cliché which does not take into account the many more fictional films, documentaries and shorts made during the Cultural Revolution.

In order to understand these aesthetics better, I will examine a 2005 documentary titled *Yangbanxi*, made by the Dutch-Hong Kong director

[13] Most of these model operas existed already as narrative fiction films. These films or the stories on which they were based were then transformed into operas and refilmed as stage ballets in the 1970s.

[14] Ban Wang, Paul Clark and Barbara Mittler, among others.

Yan-Ting Yuen, who prefaces her film thus: "During the cultural revolution, which lasted from 1966 to 1976, YANG BAN XI was all that could be seen on stage or in cinemas in China" (caps in original).[15] Although Yuen has not critiqued the rule of the Gang of Four led by Mao's wife, Jiang Qing, as acerbically and authoritatively as Dana Ranga has done with the Communist system, she still has gone out of her way to paint the model operas as subsumed to the otherwise mind-numbing ideology of Communism. There is one aspect of these films that she has favored, however, and that is the performative function that yangbanxi served for Chinese audiences during and after the Cultural Revolution. To demonstrate the influence that model operas had on the people who grew up watching them, Yuen restages some of the music from *The Red Detachment of Women* and *The White Haired Girl* to modern rock tunes. The tunes were developed by musicians who remembered the operas as essential for their formative interest in music in the 1980s. By allowing the fans of these works to rewrite the music and perform it on Western instruments – as well as inviting several dancers to perform to this music in the streets of Beijing – Yuen highlights the ambiguous legacy of the yangbanxi for the generation raised during the Cultural Revolution. She also shines a valuable light on the way in which audiences utilized these works to initiate dialogue with each other, as well as to show the way in which future artists ultimately felt empowered by the transformation of propaganda into a new product. This creative process demonstrates Yurchak's thesis that the transformation of constatives into performatives *opened* rather than closed further interpretation, as well as action and, ultimately, historic development and change.

Moreover, the very orthodox story lines of yangbanxi (such as the slave girl finding emancipation in *The Red Detachment of Women*) are so simple as to act as myths and fairytales (an effect not unwanted by the Party), thus as support for further reworking these motifs into subsequent cultural products, even though they may be as basic as those produced by mimicking or reinterpretation.[16] Furthermore, as Boris Groys has shown in relation to late Soviet art, the stylization of movement and action into the innovative poses of the revolutionary operas in fact actualized the highest stage of formalism dreamed by the early Soviets. Should we still wonder, with Barcata, why for those members of the audience in 1968 each "new scene creased their brows, wiped them smooth, furrowed them again more deeply"? Should we still wonder, especially since we now know that these innovative poses represented adaptations of the traditional *liangxiang* which inspired them and which conveyed

[15] This is inaccurate. A vast number of films made in other socialist countries circulated abundantly in Chinese cinemas during the "ten years of chaos," especially as these screens were left empty by the almost total halt of cinematic production inside the country.

[16] Just as Western myths and religion have percolated to all levels of Western society and culturally transformed it. The next chapter will look at how films from the Cultural Revolution era were further transformed into cultural products in postsocialism.

messages through a slight move of a hand or the raising of an eyebrow, messages that were privy to entire audiences?

Moreover, is it not difficult to see why, when faced with the radicalness of *The Red Detachment of Women*, Western audiences did not perceive it as ideological indoctrination, but as a specific manifestation of progressiveness expressed via postmodern dramatic techniques. In fact, in a rare concession allowed by Western audiences to Chinese model operas, Liu Kang has documented the reception of *Red Detachment* in America in 1996 as having "caused post-modern audiences in Los Angeles and New York to marvel at the opera's innovative multipositionality and hybridity, in which revolutionary ideologies, exotic nativist music and dances […] and high European styles and modalities coalesce in a neo-Wagnerian Gesamtkunstwerk" (Kang 1997, 114).[17] Applying the radicalism of early feminist and revolutionary ideals to traditional bourgeois entertainment, yangbanxi arrived at such extreme stylization that the result may be considered a new form of art. In the Western reading of this material, however, the experimental audacity of radical ideologues (among whom was Madame Mao herself) was tainted by the bad name of Maoism. In a fate reverse of that which befell Leni Riefenstahl's Nazi propaganda films, the Chinese revolutionary operas lost their chance to promote their radical formalism in the West because they were too closely associated with the unfavorable politics that engendered them.

Romania was spared the virulent condemnation that China endured at the hands of the West because its socialist-era musicals were, via an over-simplistic reading, considered artistically worthless and thrown onto the garbage heap of history by her own critics. Having fallen out of favor with audiences by the mid-1970s, these musicals did not disappear altogether, however. They were replaced by adventure films, detective dramas and, of course, historical sagas. With the exception of a few films produced until the late 1980s, which drew inspiration from socialist national history, populist entertainment nearly completely replaced ideology.

[17] The author goes on: "But the political references, embodied in the rigidly designated and stylized neoclassical types, which were once deeply ingrained in the social consciousness and practice of everyday life, have been almost completely effaced in the recent restagings of these operas for profit" (Kang 1997, 114).

4 The 1970s and the 1980s

While Romania seemed committed to expand its liberalization in the 1970s, China descended into what is now referred to as the "ten years of chaos." Despite modernizing intentions as well as deep and sometimes beneficial changes that helped erase the gap between social classes, the years from 1966 to 1976 (the year of Mao's death) were marked by political infighting, the tribulations of "sent-down youth," the ill-fated experience of "barefoot doctors," and the havoc wrought by overzealous Red Guards. The negative side-effects of the Cultural Revolution were economic chaos and an atmosphere of confusion in which many neighbors turned on each other (although sometimes for the sole purpose of settling old personal scores.) Although the chaos brought about by the Red Guards[1] lasted for a much shorter time than it is generally accepted, namely from 1966 to 1968/69, it is true that during the Cultural Revolution the economy almost stagnated. Moreover, the political infighting which lingered on between Mao's school of orthodox Communism and the rightist Gang of Four, a coalition of political opponents led by Jiang Qing, who would eventually be found guilty of radicalism and succumb to Mao's authority, continued for the entire decade.

In Romania, meanwhile, because Ceaușescu did not allow Romanian troops to participate in the military operations of the Warsaw Pact, his popularity grew by leaps after his public and dramatic denunciation of the Soviet invasion of Czechoslovakia in 1968. The popularity he gained by defying the Soviets started to erode in 1971, however, when Ceaușescu embarked on a tour of state visits to Mongolia, North Korea, North Vietnam and China, at a time when the latter was entangled in the Cultural Revolution. Historians blame these visits for a shift in policy that resembled radical Chinese reforms. They also claim that these visits resulted in the "Asianization" of the country (Tismăneanu 2003, Cioroianu 2005), and that the intelligentsia never forgave Ceaușescu for this. While other historians called him the only "dissident" in the Communist Bloc (Betea, Mihai, Țiu 2018) and although he was courted by the Americans, who saw him as a reformer, in July 1971 Ceaușescu adopted a series of ideological measures that came to be known as the "July theses,"

[1] Red Guards usually were young, over-enthusiastic enablers of anti-rightist policies during the Cultural Revolution. They oftentimes beat, abused and humiliated some of their victims representing authority figures.

which according to historians represented a return to the strictures of Stalinism and the enactment of a Maoist-style "mini-cultural revolution" in Romania (Tismăneanu 2003; Verdery 1991, 107).

While 1990s anticommunism was partially predicated on Ceaușescu's alleged import of Maoist "horrors" to a Romania that was still moderately liberal in the early 1970s, this also bespeaks an Orientalist attitude. The gut reaction experienced by cultured Romanians during Ceaușescu's much-despised Asianization of the country represents the evidencing of a racist discourse at the core of Romania's purported Western culture. Seen, furthermore, in the context of Russian Narodnism and Slavophilism, as well as the Romanian Poporanism of the nineteenth century (all traditionalist movements claiming closer Asian ties for Eastern European nations, which were highly popular with twentieth-century intelligentsia), Romania's Eastward gaze in the 1970s was also a globalizing and anti-isolationist gesture. Following the first visit of an American president to a socialist state in 1969, Romania's policies at the time helped mediate the conflict between China and the US while bypassing the Soviet Union. This helped announce Nixon's equally historic visit to China in 1972. What these policies also achieved was to put Romania in both the American and the Chinese orbits and thus create a cultural context which liberated the country from the strictures of 1950s Soviet-style Stalinism.

The detraction of China in Romanian eyes therefore belongs to the same rightist revaluation of national heritage which Verdery has described, and which mirrors the quintessence of the fascist reorientation of the country starting in the 1960s. The repudiation of the forced "Asianization" and "backwardness" that Romania experienced in the 1970s, coupled with a desperate drive to "return to Europe" exposes the fascist inclinations of a culture forced to face its fraternal counterpart, and ultimately failing to do so. Despite the country's alleged loss of openness, which the July theses brought about, the Communist government in the 1970s kept the door open to bilateral exchanges with China. In this way, both the Romanian and the Chinese audiences were spared complete isolation in the Eastern Bloc and could appreciate each other's national culture onscreen.

A surefire method to increase fraternization between two subalterns of the non-capitalist world was the screening of Gheorghe Vitanidis' *Ciprian Porumbescu* in China in the 1970s. Although a mediocre biopic narrating the troubled life story of a locally famous nineteenth-century romantic composer, the movie was a hit in China because of Porumbescu's music. While few other nations would ever become acquainted with his musical creations, "Balada," a melodious aria and Porumbescu's most famous work, still rings familiar to older Chinese audiences today, not unlike the tune from *Walter Defends Sarajevo* to the Beijing taxi driver.

While classical music touched a spot in Chinese audiences' hearts, Romania would make a name for itself in China by exporting big-budget historical films. Signaling the beginning of a national franchise, Lucian Bratu's *Tudor* (1963) – a story about a revolutionary warlord who revolts against the Ottoman occupation in the eighteenth century – was released in China in 1964, where it was favorably poised to open the way for a long run of period dramas. In 1979, taking inspiration from Hollywood Westerns, Doru Năstase would make famous the figure of the adventurous gunslinger Mărgelatu in *Skeleton Road* (*Drumul oaselor*).[2] The movie uses the pretext of the failed 1848 rebellion in Wallachia – while the region was still ruled by the Ottoman Sublime Porte in Istanbul – to forefront a motley crew of characters divided into dishonest fortune-seekers and intractable freedom fighters. The "good guys" struggle for liberation as well as to come into the possession of a buried treasure that was to be put into the service of the revolution. Due to the Morricone-inspired soundtrack and Mărgelatu's discreet cool resembling an autochthonous Clint Eastwood, the franchise also enjoyed success in China where Năstase's films competed with Hollywood and Spaghetti Westerns, which had become scarce during the Cultural Revolution.

Based on the scripts of Eugen Barbu, Năstase's films were preceded by a long series of so-called *Haiduk* adventure films, in which Romanian outlaw heroes fought an exploitative and corrupt foreign-dominated elite. Directed by Dinu Cocea since 1966, when he made *The Outlaws* (*Haiducii*), the franchise endured until the early 1980s. Both the *haiduk* and the Mărgelatu series had deep nationalist substrata, evident in their rewriting of history from a Romanian supremacist perspective and ignoring the historical contributions made by cohabitating ethnicities to the development of national consciousness in modernity. At the same time, they were some of the best-attended films in the history of Romanian cinema.

If adventure franchises made the Communist government good money and attracted large domestic audiences, the prize for the highest-grossing films in Romania's history goes to Sergiu Nicolaescu. Fresh from the nationalist success that he scored with *The Dacians* (*Dacii*, 1966), which pumped up local pride by portraying the alleged ancestors of the Romanians in a positive light, Nicolaescu moved on to make *Michael the Brave* (*Mihai Viteazul*) in 1970. *Michael* is by today's standards a saccharine nationalist saga of doubtful achievement in that it glorified a not altogether objective past and aggrandized the figure of a minor-league warlord to the level of national symbol. However, the film was made following all the rules of the genre, and it rivaled Hollywood in its budget as well as its costumes, colors and classically narrated screenplay.

Ruling over Wallachia in what was then a buffer area squeezed between the Ottoman and the Habsburg possessions in Eastern Europe, and understandably frustrated with the exploitation of both, Michael sets out to expel foreign occupiers not only from Wallachia proper, which was under nominal Ottoman control, but also from Transylvania, a region of Eastern Hungary which never belonged to Romania until 1919, except in the largely nationalist

[2] The Polish translation of this film, *Droga szkieletów* or *Skeleton Road*, comes closest to the original.

Romanian imaginary. The film's combination of successfully re-enacted battle scenes and a superficial, but effective Party-censored romance, turned *Michael the Brave* into a veritable *Spartacus* of the Balkans, its entertainment value clearly verified by its attendance figures: 14.6 million people went to see the film, which in 1970 was more than half the population of Romania. By implicating a Romanian medieval ruler in the big-power game of imperial Europe, Nicolaescu sought to performatize socialist Romania's role in the complicated power dynamics of post-Soviet-dominated politics, all the while signaling the leading role of Romanian ethnicity in the makeup of what before had been a rather multiethnic population. In glorifying the eponymous warlord's fight against Ottoman despotism, the film captured the fancy of Romanian and Chinese audiences alike, even though the reinterpretation of history onscreen later contributed to the country's nationalist-fascist debacle. For this reason, it is important to point out the differing meanings of nationalism, its ambivalent effect notwithstanding, in its various Eurasian appropriations.

While equating today's nationalism with authoritarianism is valid to a point, nationalism in the past promoted local ethnic values as liberating against dominant imperialism. Well-versed in anticolonial rhetoric, Chinese audiences easily recognized in *Michael the Brave* their own "century of humiliation" which performatized the country's dignifying yet retroactive stand against West European involvement in domestic affairs going back to the British encroachment on internal affairs during the Opium Wars. Because the film referenced an anti-imperial and anti-feudal past that was easily recognizable in China, audiences in this country related to the romanticized struggle for independence by the Romanian historical heroes. Replicating the emancipatory anti-Ottoman nationalism of the Balkans in the Chinese imaginary successfully brought about the creation of an affective community, mainly predicated on the memory of national suffering, or what we today call postcolonial consciousness.[3]

Although one would expect films exchanged between Romania and China to follow ideological principles, both governments imported works with high popular appeal. These involved another genre that was to prove successful with Chinese audiences: detective films. Banking on his well-established reputation derived from historical dramas such as *Michael the Brave*, Nicolaescu developed another franchise moving forward, which would become the most popular of its kind. Adapting a script by the prolific writers Petre Sălcudeanu and Titus Popvici, the Romanian director created the famous police detectives Miclovan and Roman, good cop figures supposed to rid Bucharest's streets of its gangsters and black marketeers during the interwar period. *With Clean Hands* (1972), the first installment of the franchise, was seen by more than seven million spectators and remains one of the most popular Romanian films of all times.

---

[3] On the connection between suffering and subalternity as reified in melodrama, see Dissanayake 1993.

The narrative centers on Mihai Roman, a former rugby player and employee of a railway company who once was subjected to abuse by a fascist police officer and has since turned sympathetic to the Communist cause. He is joined in his new job on the police force by his partner Miclovan, played by Nicolaescu himself, who is unsure of his political orientation. Of the two, Miclovan imposes himself as the more experienced one. Because the wrongdoers the two men are after frequently manage to outmaneuver the dishonest legal system, Miclovan teaches Roman to fire first and ask questions later. After a string of dramatic shootouts, the two police officers eventually bust a criminal group whose unlawful activities they discover in a joint investigation. Despite the fact that Miclovan, the unscrupulous police officer, dies in the movie's climax, Roman is now clearer about his loyalties, and his actions appear to be contributing to the creation of a less dishonest, more compassionate police force.

Although the film carries a whiff of propaganda (Bujor Rîpeanu has stated that the franchise was meant to "cosmeticize the role of the Secret Police" whose "complicity and abuses in the 'personality cult' era' had become embarrassing" [Rîpeanu 2005, 51]), it is clear that Nicolaescu, in another critic's words, "hires the American gangster film school to fight against 'the old remains'" (Caranfil 2008, 212). Even if Rîpeanu is right and the film did have a propagandist agenda, Nicolaescu's franchise became a medium for empowering audiences because they loved the notion of Miclovan as a local equivalent of Humphrey Bogart. By identifying at the indexical level of the image with a strong character supposed to bring order to a semi-exoticized gone-by world, which also offered viewers a glimpse of the decadent bourgeoisie, audiences avoided the very propaganda that the character was meant to impart, choosing instead, as in the case of *Life Triumphs*, to temper the ideology while savoring the suspense. The affective community that parallel nationalisms birthed in the Eastern Bloc played an important role in developing a filmmaking style predicated on both common socialist values and similar national histories. The wide circulation of historical epics, detective dramas and films with an anti-feudal message not only spread a wave of resistance to capitalism by virtue of glorifying the nations of the Eastern Bloc, but they also placed socialism itself as second in importance to populism. In so doing, these films equally accepted and helped integrate in their countries' respective national psyches the nationalism of the surrounding nations, therefore creating a cultural web of performative difference via which, collectively, China and Romania defined their identity as distinct from that of the West, but also distinct from one another.

There is another reason why these films left a strong imprint in the socialist psyche, and that is that they harked back to the pre-modern era, which in Eurasia equally meant the presence of a dynastic and imperial past. Nationalism at that time, far from being the ugly word it has become today, served the progressive means of fighting against the tyranny of monarchy and imperialism.

Nationalism as Liberation in the Eurasian Cultural Space

Because of its cultural influences, Eastern Europe was historically as much a part of Asia as it belonged to the sphere of Western politics and culture. Being part of both the Ottoman as well as the Tsarist empires meant that Romania was particularly well-positioned to inherit Asia's cultural heritage (Boia 1997). The challenge for the researcher today is to assess whether the cultural politics that led to a forced separation between Eastern Europe and Asia, and to an equally forced reintegration of the postsocialist Eastern Bloc into the capitalist West thereafter, can be conceptualized from a standpoint that is different from that of the transnationalist project, which recently became the dominant discursive practice in cultural and postcolonial studies. In order to understand in what way correspondences between Romania and China, once members of a Eurasian continuum that shared cultural similarities, can be reconceptualized in the deceptive age of transnationalism, we need to redefine and briefly theorize the term "Eurasia." Invoking Eurasianism, rather than Europeanism, in this discourse helps to better describe the interpenetration of Asian and European traditions that ultimately impacted the development of a distinct geo-cultural space spanning from East Asia to Eastern Europe. From a historical perspective, Eastern Europe had not been considered a part of the West since long before the Communist takeover. According to Larry Wolff's convincing argumentation, the concept of Eastern Europe was put together in the patronizing minds of Enlightenment thinkers (Wolff 1994), who saw themselves as the theoretical equivalent of what Domenico Losurdo has called "master race democracy" in his caustic critique of capitalism, *Liberalism, a Counter History* (Losurdo 2011). This intellectual Western class used the Eastern European *and* the Asian Other as a negative reference against which to project their own purportedly developed humanism.

Historian Wang Hui has further made clear that the European image of "Asiatic despotism," with which both Asia and Eastern Europe have been associated, entered the European imagination through the demonization of the Eastern "barbarians" of Tatar and later Ottoman type, because these were seen as more of a direct threat to Europeans than the more distant and "racially inferior" African and South-Central American empires (Wang 2014). The image of the Eurasian as barbaric, as Wolff has equally contended, contributed to the exogenous creation of a violent Eurasian identity in the Western European imaginary.

In delineating Eurasia as a distinct space ruled by a set of politics different from that of other colonial cultures, I do not follow a Huntingtonian approach (Huntington 1996). On Marxist grounds, however, I posit that the gap in economic status between Eurasia and the West, while not the *causa belli* for a future clash, is reason for the rapprochement between the ex-members of the socialist bloc. While this gap created a homogenous cultural space running from Bucharest to Beijing, its similarities – socialist, cultural and post-imperial – are today ignored for the sake of a faster integration of the East into a Western culture dominated, not by the unifying ideology of internationalism, but by the alleged globalization predicated on Western capital.

Intra-socialist connections within Eurasia were boosted by the emergence of a cinematic movement that began in the mid-1960s in Latin America and went on to influence the way in which postcolonial cultures around the globe negotiated their colonial heritage. Although it drew inspiration from thinkers such as Frantz Fanon and Aimé Césaire, Third Cinema, as film scholar Anthony Guneratne has articulated, emerged in public consciousness as an anticolonial movement meant to combat Western European and North American neocolonialism (Guneratne 2003). The label was later applied to the anticolonial cinemas of Ousmane Sembene, for example, as well as that of other African and Asian directors.

Even though Third Cinema also came to describe Asian and Middle Eastern cultures, the anticolonialism of Eurasia – particularly in the areas where Communism formed a more or less cohesive transnational whole – originates in a different historical environment, one that, much like the anticolonial struggles of Latin America and Africa, was bathed in its own blood. While not attempting to sever ties between pan-Africanism/pan-Latino movements and their Eurasian counterparts, I argue that Eurasian cinema was born as an offspring of Eurasian Communism, which originated as distinct from the one that led to African-Latin American fraternization, in spite of what the early programs of Bandung and the Tricontinental otherwise have rightfully argued.[4] This distinctiveness is also warranted by the obsessive references of Eastern Communism not only to imperialism but also to what Wang Hui has correctly identified in Western discourse as a "despotic past" (Wang 2104) – that is, a heritage which in the eyes of the West is (still) responsible for the backwardness and underdevelopment of Asia.

It is important to also note that, while Africa and South America rightly developed their anticolonialism in response to direct external domination, which was mostly Western European, Eurasia dealt with a bifurcated heritage[5] of both direct imperialism as well as the vilified despotism and feudalism of its own past. Following the legacy of the Chinese, Russian, intra-European and Middle Eastern monarchies, Eurasia had to battle both an internal and an external enemy, who was oftentimes more difficult to pinpoint than in the

---

4 Although it cannot be detailed here, as Arif Dirlik has shown in his *Marxism in the Chinese Revolution*, Chinese Communism was inspired as much by anarcho-communism as by the revolutionary legacy of Bela Kun in Hungary, among others, and not only by what would later become Soviet Communism. It was in this form that it was later adopted by Ho Chi-Minh, the Malaysian Communist Party, as well as a majority of movements active in Southeast Asia in the second half of the twentieth century, which imbued Asian Communism at large with a local yet heterogeneous character.

5 Prasenjit Duara has discussed different but equally important 'bifurcated histories' which diverge from both official and unofficial linear narratives of the Chinese past, complicating the simplistic binary of state versus individual history (Duara 1995).

cases of overt Western European colonialism in South America and Africa. Hence, as strange as that may appear at first glance, Eurasia did battle with a "foreign aggressor" as much as with itself![6]

For Eurasian Communists, who borrowed European ideas to fit their own Asian realities, the past became therefore as much a thorn in their side as did foreign imperialism. This adduced a double-mindedness which would re-emerge as ambiguity in the national cinemas of various Eurasian cultures, including the Romanian and the Chinese. It would further infiltrate the cultural identity of the Eurasian national psyche, leading to a distinct polysemy which would later be found in the symbolism of Romanian and Chinese cinemas of the 1980s. While it is not my intention to whitewash the wrongdoings of Communist dictatorships in the Soviet Union, China and Eastern Europe, it is my belief that a clearer understanding of the region cannot be obtained without attempting an unbiased analysis of these regions' both utopian and totalitarian pasts. While most contemporary scholars of Eastern European film acknowledge the presence of older imperial colonial structures in Eastern Europe in the guise of the Austro-Hungarian, Prussian, Russian and Ottoman empires, they seem to focus uniquely on identifying the nefarious nature of Soviet imperialism alone.

In 1984, the Czech writer Milan Kundera in "The Tragedy of Central Europe" pleaded for the preservation of a pre-communist Central Europe in the face of Soviet encroachment. According to his view, the contested region could not belong to the "totalitarian Russian civilization," which, as Kundera has implied "is the radical negation of the modern West" (Kundera 1984). In demonizing and retroactively contesting the Sovietization of Eastern Europe under the pretense of defending its otherwise real multiculturalism, Kundera's plea, however, has vied for a reintegration of the region into what he has assumed are its native European values. The problem with this point of view is that it valorizes the very attributes of the older colonial powers (the intra-European and the Ottoman empires), which suddenly become less evil in comparison with the Soviet Union. This amounts to a resignification of colonialism and has the effect of simply returning Eastern Europe's cultural capital to its pre-communist past, which was almost invariably colonial and, sometimes, downright fascist.

Seen from this angle, even though Kundera's "return to Europe" was meant to foment peace, collaboration and globalization, this gesture also borders on "auto-colonialism" and self-orientalism, as Alexander Kiossev has suggested (Kiossev 2004), and it culturally marginalizes the region. Predicated on the promotion of imaginary Western values known as Occidentalism, the forced integration of Eastern Europe into Western culture led to aggressive Westernization that further fragmented the former members of the socialist camp. Compelled to compete with each other for Western investment, some postsocialist countries fell behind their postcolonial neighbors, while

[6] I do not mean the elites or bourgeois strata that existed inside these cultures, but most literally with their pasts.

awareness of each other's cultural, economic and even political similarities failed to foment any considerable and sustainable collaboration.

In the end, the breakdown of postsocialist friendship led to the internal destruction of the socialist legacy as well as to intra-bloc violence. In essence, this meant redefining national identity along fascist lines, rather than a restoration to the natural values of European liberalism. As demonstrated by the Yugoslav and the Ukrainian wars, which were fought partly in response to this heritage, reintegration adduced a deadly combination of Occidentalism and self-denial, which precipitated Eastern Europe's swift descent into an identity crisis. In contrast to Western encroachment, the possibility of reconnecting Eastern Europe to its Eurasian unacknowledged neighbors, including Far Eastern ones as remote as China should repair some of the failures to hybridize between colonizer and colonized, as discussed by Homi Bhabha (Bhabha 2004). It should also validate the correlation between the "post" in postsocialism and the "post" in postcolonialism, which has been promoted by Katherine Verdery and Sharad Chari, in which the two anthropologists advance the alternative of a partnership between postsocialism and postcolonialism that is based on economic and affective commonality (Verdery and Chari 2009).

Such a pluri-perspectival approach is necessary because in our attempts to hybridize, as Walter Mignolo has warned (Mignolo 2006), we seem to continuously territorialize – that is, we forget that the locus of discourse always influences the process of hybridization. Despite our subscription to postmodernity, hybridization cannot take place following a postmodern recipe, as in a worldwide application of the American melting pot model, which works not so much because it is a melting pot but because it is American. To make hybridization work in Eurasia, we need to consider the critical amalgamation of identities instituted by political regimes born out of utopian constructivism, a bipolar view of the world and cultural nationalism, all the while remembering "Asiatic despotism" (Wang 2014), and an otherwise real divide between the First and the homogenous Second and Third Worlds in existence, at least since the intervention of colonialism.

What I argue is that the difference between the East and the West has to be *made* first before it can be *unmade*. While it is farthest from my intentions to reaccentuate a new "split," or let another Iron Curtain fall between the East and the West, I claim that no progress can be made in our understanding of the relationship between the postsocialist and the Western worlds by simply willing away history, or by erasing Cold-War-era ideological differences. A factor that could help evidence the homogenous character of Eurasia is that these erstwhile ideological differences survived in postsocialism in the guise of socialist affect, which continues to play an important role in the way in which postsocialism and the West interact with each other and construe their identities. An alternative to Westernization therefore is the common exploring of objective local histories – socialist-era and even nationalist histories included – from a perspective that does not encourage the vilification of the past. I posit that historical transcultural influences interpenetrated each other and traveled from Bucharest to Beijing, as it were, and even farther, giving the socio-historical Eastern European space a Eurasian rather than a uniquely European makeup. Furthermore, the fact that Communism had the same goal in its ideal of adducing fraternization among the nations of postcolonial Eurasia proves that the socialist past can be separated from its dictatorial character.

Communist Role Models

One way of building national pride via cinema was that of creating contemporaneous characters who could be emulated or hailed as commanding respect from one socialist country to the next. Although a propagandist effort at its core, the process had the interesting side-effect of suggesting progressiveness, even though this was oftentimes read incorrectly in different cultural contexts.

Aside from his warlords and police detectives, Sergiu Nicolaescu in the 1970s created yet another character who would go on to empower audiences. However, that empowerment did not occur in Romania, but all the way on the other side of the world, where – much like the ship captain from *The Waves of the Danube* did in the 1960s – Engineer Coman would become a Chinese celebrity. When *Hot Days* (*Zile fierbinți*, Nicolaescu, 1975) was shown in China a few years after it came out in Romania, it crowned Nicolaescu's already blossoming international career.[7] The film tells the story of an overzealous manager of a naval shipyard in the Black Sea port of Constanța, who chooses to reject an imported Japanese propeller in favor of a locally made model that, despite questions about its effectiveness, ends up serving its purpose on a new ship. Unfazed by the lack of raw materials and skills that socialist Romania was facing at the time, Coman is convinced that Romanian engineering is superior, and he even defies Party orders to prove so, firmly believing that his rather authoritative actions will benefit the factory and its workers. By doing so, Nicolaescu (playing the main character once again) makes the very provocative claim that mid-level managers occasionally know more than the Party bosses in Bucharest.

The engineer's autocratic, even monomaniacal managerial style and his preference for making decisions based on what seem to be irrational, personal whims have been the subject of criticism regarding the movie. Interpreters went so far as to claim that Nicolaescu's conceited behavior furthered the Romanian Party's isolation and self-sufficiency, with Popescu

[7] Because Nicolaescu became involved in politics as a social democrat in the 1990s, and because he attempted to turn the fascist figure of Antonescu into that of a nationalist hero, his prestige dwindled in postsocialism. In an environment fraught with political infighting where even the social democrats had to embrace the dominant anticommunist line, politically motivated accusations of collaboration with Ceaușescu's regime started to pour in. Because Nicolaescu also chaired the National Cinema Center and received state support for his films, his figure is considered the epitome of collaborationist filmmaking today.

likening Coman to the erstwhile engineer from *Life Triumphs* who, in the author's view, was as dictatorial as Ceaușescu himself (Popescu 2011, 222). Even though the film failed to impress Romanian audiences, the Chinese ones loved Coman's challenging of Party authority via his non-conformist managerial style and outspoken rejection of directives originating "from the top." In the eyes of the Chinese, the protagonist infused a healthy dose of enthusiastic individualism into the mandatory system of a planned economy, following a cinematic model that resembled a Hollywood production more closely than a late socialist realist and early social realist one.

Ironically, the Chinese audiences' interpretation of Coman also brings to light some of his more ambivalent traits, resulting in a more positive reception for the picture in China than in its home country. Hailed as the epitome of a Communist hero, Coman came to represent the prosperous factory self-management style modeled on Tito's moderately liberal Yugoslavia, which at the time was experimenting with various industrial reforms. The film's 1977 release also marked the end of China's "ten years of chaos" and was seen as especially pertinent to the country's industry as it approached restructuring in Deng Xiaoping's new era of the "Four Modernizations" – namely those of the agriculture, industry, defense and the science and technology sectors. Moreover, in his reading by the Chinese, Coman's uncompromising management style reflected a particular willingness to modernize based on a local understanding of Communism, one that took account of Chinese topographic and economic realities that differed considerably from those of the Western cultures in which most of the modernizing technology originated. The fact that the imported propeller in the film was made in Japan, China's longtime enemy, furthermore added Chinese audience support for the engineer's decision. Because of this, Coman's passion and commitment were seen in China as a form of working-class empowerment that lacked the phony logocentrism and language structures to which Yurchak has referred as the performative Marxist ideology of late socialism. *Hot Days*, or *Boiling Life* (*Feiteng de shenghuo*), as it was translated, is still remembered in China today as a symbol of brave leadership and is regarded as exemplary behavior in an institutional setting.

Coman's model harks back to the enthusiasm of Su Li's forgotten late socialist realist masterpiece, *Youth in Our Village* (*Women cunli de nianqing ren*), produced in 1963. In addition to supporting grassroots leadership required to construct a power plant, this movie promoted local entrepreneurship as a response to the Communist Party's rigid bureaucracy, putting rural China on the path to modernity during the Great Leap Forward. Despite its political message, the film won over the hearts of some Western critics (Leyda 1972), because it portrayed a realistic 1950s Chinese society where the resistance of old-timers clashed with the youthful exuberance of newcomers in what was then a very sensitive and pressing matter: the development of rural areas. In addition to a lesson in regional economics and an essay on ideology, the movie also served as a compelling and captivating drama.

Chinese filmmaker Li Wenhua would likewise address the irksome disparity between the Chinese and Western economic realities in *Breaking with Old*

Ideas (*Jue lie*), a 1975 film released in 1977, in the same year *Hot Days* was shown in China. Li's film served as a metaphor for the ongoing power struggle between the Gang of Four and the faction of the Party controlled by Mao Zedong, and it tackles the insufficient attention that the Chinese Communist cadres paid to education in rural areas. Despite being mostly propaganda for Mao's side and defending the decision to "send down" cadres to the countryside during the Cultural Revolution, the movie is also ambivalent because, as its progressive characters assert, it advocates for nothing less than a complete revolution in education.

The film depicts the founding of the Jiangxi Communist Labor University in 1958, during the time of the Great Leap Forward. It primarily focuses on the fossilized teaching methods used at that time in rural agricultural colleges, which were still using European (and Soviet) textbooks that were "divorced from reality" in the countryside. Following a formulaic plot pitting the new principal Lung (formerly a cowherd and veteran of the anti-Japanese war) against the old Dean Sun (a methodical professional with a bourgeois upbringing), the film gives voice to the disempowered students hailing from poor backgrounds who, in the beginning of the film, are denied the chance of taking an entrance exam due to their insufficient education. Claiming that the callouses on their palms are enough to qualify the underprivileged students, Lung admits a new batch of young women and men demanding admission. Among them is Li Chin Fing, the mother of a small child, whom the dean has previously rejected and who turns out to be a hard-working and capable student. However, when her duties in the rice fields prevent her and others like her from taking an important exam, the old management expels them. Li interprets this decision as a return to the exploitative ways of the Kuomintang, in which students were used by the bourgeoisie to serve their masters' needs for enrichment. Her dismissal from the univerity, so she charges, proves that the old management is determined to bring about the return of capitalism. In an act of rebellion, the students rise against the red academic bourgeoisie, as well as against the old Chinese educational system, and condone the reform proposed by Principal Lung and endorsed by students such as Li.

At a time when China was in the throes of a very dangerous ideological debate between liberalization and traditionalism, the film was of utmost importance for the outcome of political infighting. Although it was disconsidered in both Romania and Western Europe for promoting the "wrong" ideology, Li Wenhua's film received somewhat positive reviews in the US, by none other than *Washington Post*'s Gary Arnold, who called it "inspirational indoctrination" (Arnold 1976). At the same time, William Johnson has written for *Film Quarterly* that Li's film "is as accessible, as ingratiating, as high Hollywood," and that, "whatever the truth of the sweeping charges against the 'gang of four', *Breaking with Old Ideas* itself offers little supporting evidence for them" (Johnson 1978). Even though he has agreed that for American critics "no possible blend of aesthetic and political criteria seems satisfactory" (Johnson 1978), both Johnson and Arnold have appreciated the message of the film and seemed to go as far as to admit, albeit not at face value, that there is potential for social change even in the starkest examples of Communist propaganda.

This potential is captured in a memorable scene in the film in which Dean Sun teaches a class on the uses of a horse's tail. This causes a courageous young student to suggest that Sun change the syllabus, because horses were entirely absent in the geographical area in which they lived, and that Sun should focus instead on buffaloes and pigs, which were the animals with which the students had to work. The scene brings to mind Bhabha's exemplification of contestatory anticolonialism in the context of the teaching of Wordsworth in India (daffodils do not grow in that country, as the critical theorist has reminded us [Bhabha 2004]), thus furthering parallels between the anticolonial and the intra-bloc anti-hegemonic movements of subaltern nations. Making oblique references to Soviet hegemony in the Eastern Bloc, Li Wenhua's film constitutes a subtle exploration of the contradictory relationship between nationalism and socialist internationalism. As in Nicolaescu's *Hot Days*, nationalism gains a privileged position because it exposes the hegemonic power of a giant such as the USSR. This also makes clear why Romanian censorship did not oppose Nicolaescu's film, while the subtler nuances of this ambiguous work were otherwise lost on both leadership and postsocialist critics.

As seen in this context, Nicolaescu's disparaged work not only landed on already familiar ground in 1970s China, but it also demonstrated that ideological films could be tense dramas centered around character studies that, ultimately, were also dramaturgically appealing. For audiences familiar with Hollywood characters such as Sylvester Stallone's Rambo from the bootleg VHS tapes which had started to penetrate China's black market since the 1970s, the powerful socialist character offered by *Hot Days* became a comparable role model who was closer in style and behavior to the Eurasian mindset and reflected the audiences' social and economic realities more intimately than did his North American counterparts.[8]

Coman from *Hot Days* and Lung from *Breaking with Old Ideas* act as onscreen synonyms for reform. Although they hail from different cultures, they represent a concomitant need to modernize and re-technologize the system in two countries at the opposite ends of Eurasia. The call was heeded by Deng Xiaoping in China but fell more or less on deaf ears in Romania, leading to the stagnation of the 1980s in the latter country. This stagnation, however, would inspire a new generation of Romanian directors to redouble their criticism of those systemic failures that needed reconsideration. This inaugurated a new filmmaking style that can only be described as social realism.

Will We Listen to You, or Will You Listen to Us?

Before engaging in a discussion of the 1980s, however, I will consider two other Romanian and Chinese films that reified this need for change, even if

[8] For an in-depth discussion of Coman's character, see Tion 2022a.

they were made more than a decade apart. *Hot Days* may have served as an inspiration for Huang Jianxin's *The Black Cannon Incident* (*Hei pao shi jian*) made in 1985. The first political satire to come out of China, Huang's film introduces the figure of Zhao Shuxin, a mousey forty-something translator in a mining company whose only hobby is playing chess. When Zhao loses one of his chess figures during a business trip, he sends a telegram to a friend, asking him to locate the missing piece in the hotel room where the two had stayed. The political leadership becomes suspicious of Zhao's laconic telegram ("Lost Black Cannon. Look 301") and interprets the message as connoting a possible conspiracy. Consequently, Zhao is investigated by the inefficient bureaucracy of the state apparatus.

The Party is additionally unsettled by Zhao's professional relationship with Hans, a German delegate who delivers equipment to the Chinese factory. This ultimately becomes grounds for Zhao's dismissal and replacement by an inexperienced translator who botches the professional relationship that Zhao had maintained with Hans. In one scene where Hans asks for help in setting up the equipment which the Chinese bought from Germany for a substantial sum of money, the translator gives Hans a bullet instead of the wheel-bearing for which the latter asked. This leads to a series of errors, which highlights the inadequacy of excessive regulations. Although Hans finally gets Zhao back to translate for him after considerable effort, it is already too late to fix the broken machinery.

Along with offering situational black humor, the film criticizes the state's unfounded misgivings about political opening to the West. In one of the film's memorable scenes, Hans brings Zhao a pair of all-white sneakers as a gift, but the Party apparatus frowns on the act, believing the practice of receiving gifts from foreigners to be unsuitable and dangerous. In his treatment of Party cadres in the scene, Huang ridicules the restrictions concerning Chinese interactions with foreigners. To be clear, it is not Communist ideology that becomes the target of Huang's criticism but the inefficient bureaucratic practices of a state which is inexperienced in conducting business with the West while in the process of modernizing its industry. Huang makes this clear in his use of color in the film. The washed-out, dominantly monochrome color palette punctuated by splashed-out reds emphasizes certain objects such as tables and walls to create a sense of discomfort and alienation. In one scene shot in monochrome white, Huang focuses on a gigantic clock that decorates the back wall of a meeting room, drawing attention to the stiffness and uselessness of factory meetings.

In line with Nicolaescu's indictment of rigidity in factory planning and his vying for the reconstruction of a fossilized state system under new principles, *The Black Cannon Incident* delivers a poignant commentary on economic restructuring. In Romania, these principles, which involved more power to the workers, were never implemented and entirely ditched after the anticommunist revolution, in favor of the so-called "shock therapy" that sought to dismantle the country's industrial base built during socialism and to replace it with Western capital. China, however, insisted on improving the ineffective economic bureaucracy that Huang criticized in *The Black Cannon Incident*, and on continuing to build its socialist-era industrial infrastructure to develop its economic dominance.

The works of Nicolaescu and Huang were made possible by a new trend that began to take shape in the 1970s. Because the Stalinist 1950s were beset by abuses which led to show trials and executions as well as life sentences for many members of the Communist Party who fell into disfavor with their former comrades, this period came to be known in Romania as "the obsessive decade." As in other Eastern European countries at the time, films denouncing the abuses of this decade reshaped, if only momentarily, the direction in which socialism appeared to be headed. For example, *The Power and the Truth* (*Puterea și adevărul*, 1972) is a three-hour-long film, directed by Manole Marcus, which chronicles the internal power struggles that occurred among members of the erstwhile Communist underground during the period that followed their seizure of power. The film's central question is not so much who among the Politburo members is trustworthy; rather, it is the question as to who is prepared to genuinely dedicate their life to improving the lot of the people in spite of the hardships and seemingly insurmountable obstacles that became apparent in the 1950s. Stalinism, which sometimes figured in films made during the first socialist decade, appears less significant here than the management of resources intended for national reconstruction.

Although surprisingly critical of Dej's strong personality type, the film is structured as both a character study and a conflict-based drama. While the conflict is, for the most part, over-intellectualized and over-ideological, the revisiting of the past gives screenwriter Titus Popovici – probably the most prolific screenwriter of the socialist era – the opportunity to show Dej in a human light. In a daring scene, Popovici goes so far as to paint the Securitate in a negative light, while in another scene Dej himself is treated as a simple citizen when attempting to enter a state institution, which works to downgrade his former iconic status. Even though Dej is portrayed as a lonesome fellow working virtually alone on the reconstruction of the country, he is sometimes supported in his work by Duma, a character supposed to represent a young Ceaușescu, who comes across as sincere when he holds no punches in denouncing Dej's aberrant behavior. The two clash especially harshly over the treatment of Petre Petrescu, a Communist engineer who believes that the procedural and technical goals of the Romanian industry are unachievable and stands against the development of a hydropower plant intended to provide electricity for the new nation – at least until the country accumulates enough resources to move at its own speed, that is. Reversing the scenarios of *Reverberates the Valley* and *The Bridge*, engineer Petrescu seems to speak with the very voice of the bourgeois engineer in *The Bridge*, echoing the latter's concerns about the lack of materials, education and equipment. The film thus questions the blind volunteerism of the 1950s, advancing a form of economic maturity that ironically validates historical realities, while it surprisingly validates the figures of the former bourgeois film characters.

Approving the depiction of his own onscreen persona as Duma, Ceaușescu himself allowed *The Power and the Truth* to discuss for the first time in Romanian cinema the abuses of the obsessive decade. In order to accentuate these abuses, Popovici made certain to portray Petrescu as an *alter ego* of Communist activist and public leftist intellectual Lucrețiu Pătrășcanu. A tragic victim of the purges, Pătrășcanu was executed in prison after a six-year-long trial ending in a death sentence. Mirroring the similar trials of László Rajk in Hungary and Rudolf Slánský in Czechoslovakia, Pătrășcanu was rehabilitated posthumously immediately after Ceaușescu came to power in 1965. Meant to reflect the change in political leadership from Dej's personality cult to Ceaușescu's initial liberalism, Petrescu's figure in the film condemns the show trials and political assassinations of early communists who did not walk Dej's line. However, these abuses serve as contrast to the more lenient period emerging under Ceaușescu's liberalism.

Writing on Chinese revolutionary cinema, film critic Ying Zhu has stated that those "films typically sublimated style to narrative in privileging a linear narrative trajectory with emphasis on a clear and intensified central conflict" (Zhu 2001, 453). Because style in the film pales in comparison to its subject-matter, the same applies to *The Power and the Truth*. In contrast to his earlier innovative camera work, Marcus uses basic techniques, zooms and cliché framing to depict a rather straightforward story. He only deviates from this standard practice in the scenes that follow Petrescu's apprehension and arrest. In these scenes, Petrescu and his interrogator are depicted as being divided by a lamp's shadow, which gives Marcus' creative camera some effectiveness and provokes contemplation about Pătrășcanu's actual destiny. In an honest admission, the way in which Marcus sets up his *mise-en-scène* casts Petrescu/Pătrășcanu as a scapegoat – that is, as someone whom the early Communists wrongfully blame in a desperate attempt to escape the economic deadlock in which they found themselves when faced with the enormous burden of rebuilding the terribly impoverished nation.

The terse style does not take away from the film's achievements, however. Marcus' effort was unthinkably honest for its time, reflecting the hopeful moment of the Thaw, when Romania was enjoying unimaginable liberty from Moscow as well as an opening towards the West. In a scene in which Petrescu alludes to the tortures that he suffered at the hands of the secret police, Duma urges him to speak up so that such abuses will never happen again. Although this is highly optimistic for 1971, it describes a decade or so of relative freedom which, given the dire economic context of the 1980s, the country would never again enjoy until postsocialism.

The film's humanism is also reflected by certain on-set props. Office wall banners, which evoke the sentimental optimism of the early Communist movement, impart non-ideological messages, such as "Treasure every minute," instead of reiterating the Stalinist narrative. If some of the dialogue is overly hackneyed, it is not because Popovici is a poor writer; rather, it is because he tried to temper the Communists' unwavering dedication to politics. This makes Duma's statement to his lovely wife (meant to be an idealized version of Elena Ceaușescu), that "without love the notion of Communism is a caricature," seem more genuine than it sounds when spoken onscreen. Remembering the words of Tian Hua's character in *Daughter of the Party*, Popovici tried to give Communism a humanist quality instead of a logocentric and sententious one. For this reason, he made an effort to soften the faith of the erstwhile Communists, which their obstinate militancy was made to sound stilted.

Another line with a prophetic ring is the question that Dej asks of an unyielding, reticent Pătrășcanu: "Will we listen to you, or will you listen to us?" In an effort to convince the latter to join the new government, the phrase alludes to a moment in the history of the new state when the lack of resources and technology made the fate of the country momentarily hang in the balance. Making use of such dichotomist language, the script effectively conveys the ambiguity and bewilderment that pervaded the time-period, even among the Politburo's upper echelons. This makes the film seem more authentic, even though the script reimagines a highly politicized conflict from recent history that otherwise could have come off as contrived.

Despite these achievements, *The Power and the Truth* has been regarded by film theorist Claudiu Turcuș as adhering to the canons of propaganda, which work to synchronize Romanian cinema with Ceaușescu's cultural revolution imported from China (Turcuș 2017, 199). Similarly, film historian Bogdan Jitea has thought that the movie orchestrates the dictator's first attempt at political propaganda so as to establish his authority and set himself apart from the Dej administration (Jitea 2021, 278). Jitea has concurred with Cristian Tudor Popescu when the latter has claimed that *The Power and the Truth* validates the Communist system by criticizing and rejecting the wrongdoings of its own beginnings (Popescu 2011, 213). Despite agreeing that the film manipulates history and instrumentalizes the Stalinist period to make Ceaușescu look good, Popescu has admitted that "*The Power and the Truth* is the film providing the highest amount of political and philosophical debate in Romanian cinema" (214).

The Power and the Masses: Dialogue in Romania

Marcus' work was made possible by a film that had garnered accolades on the international film circuit only a few years prior. Partly because Lucian Pintilie's *Reenactment* (*Reconstituirea*) was completed in 1969, released in 1970 and withdrawn from the main distribution outlets of the country's cinemas following a controversial brawl involving Ceaușescu himself a few months later, today the film is almost unanimously considered by Romanian film critics as the apex of dissident filmmaking and one of the best films ever made in the country.

As evident from Vaclav Havel's reading of socialism, dissidents in the Eastern Bloc were those persons who shed the metaphorical masks under which a majority of the populace hid their disapproval of socialism. Havel's own anti-governmental activity in socialist Czechoslovakia attracted the attention of the secret police, and he spent approximately four years in jail for subversive politics. His writings and career represent the standard of dissidence in the socialist bloc and became a model that was partially followed in other countries east of the Iron Curtain.

Although it does not mirror Havel's political career in Czechoslovakia exactly, as it concerns cultural rather than political matters, Lucian Pintilie's dissidence[9] in Romania was brought about by work on his second feature film, *Reenactment*. Considered a "tragic farce" by leading film historian Bujor Rîpeanu (Rîpeanu 2005, 170), the film re-enacts an episode of disorderly conduct among youth, and it stars two adolescents who vandalize and destroy state property following a night of drunken reveling. Recalling the educational streak of the state's earlier interventions in public life via cinema, the rather patriarchal militia – or the socialist state police – conditions their release from arrest on their restaging of the violent incident for an educational film. This is to be shot on location in the riverside country tavern in which the initial fight occurred, but the shooting is constantly interrupted by village residents and intruders who bespeak a society in the throes of poverty and backwardness. In a scene halfway through the movie, the crew, alongside the militiamen and the two youths, are literally sent on a wild goose chase, as an old woman who arrives on the set demands that the prosecutor find the geese which the two youths had scared away. Commenting on the futility of the re-enactment, and thus on the inefficacy of the party-state that dictated it via its militia apparatus, after the shooting is concluded and the prosecutor leaves the scene in a car that is being pushed out of the mud by a crowd of fans returning from a football game, one of the two young men tragically dies an accidental death while hitting his head on a stone after an inadvertent fall.

Using a variety of descriptive long shots and powerful close-ups, Pintilie presents an eclectic fresco of realistic character studies. Aside from the vibrant portrayal of the two youths played with gusto by two of Romania's up-and-coming talents of the late 1960s, George Mihăiță and Vladimir Găitan, the character who surprises audiences is the boys' elderly, drunken professor who evidently hails from a bourgeois background. Visibly distressed by the events he is forced to witness, which he sees as a reflection of the precarious social reality, he is tormented by the national political drama and feels guilty for holding ideological views that diverge from those which the regime demands of him. In an attempt to expiate this guilt, he even makes the pointless gesture of surrendering to the prosecutor, only to be benevolently waved off by the latter. The scene illustrates the pressure that intellectuals in the new regime felt from having Communist ideology imposed on a nation which the intellectuals did not believe ready for such radicalism. In a vicarious gesture of identification with the professor, Pintilie tacitly shows that he empathizes with the suffering of intellectuals and relates to their concerns as a disgruntled social class.

---

[9] Opposition would be a better phrase to describe Pintilie's career, but since many critics refer to it as "dissidence," I am using the same term here.

This class contrasts sharply with the masses, who are shown as a disorderly crowd of football fans returning from the stadium in the film's finale. Pintilie's scathing portrait of the working class as backward and wild shows that his allegiance metonymically lies with the old professor, not with the disorderly crowd. This identification hardly made the film palatable to a state which pronounced the dictatorship of the proletariat, following class struggle and a long string of hard-won victories, and it probably played a leading role in the film's partial withdrawal.

Although Romanian criticism severely condemned the government for its limited censorship of the film, Bogdan Jitea in his research has shown that Ceaușescu, in an unexpected display of liberalism, approved rather than condemned it: "About this film, *Reenactment*, I think that reactions are a bit exaggerated. It criticises some militiamen. So what? In capitalist countries the police are criticised every day… [The filmmakers] can go ahead and criticize the militia because we have lots of idiots serving in it" (Ceaușescu, quoted in Jitea 2021, 153). Romania's *Reenactment*, in that sense, is China's *Early Spring in February* because the film's release engendered dialogue reminiscent of state interference in Xie's film in China. While Ceaușescu disagreed with the misrepresentation of the working class and the rebellious youth – although he sincerely supported the condemnation of the militia – he invited rather than stifled criticism about the production.

Shifting focus from Ceaușescu's alleged misconduct to the way in which the director depicted social realities, film theorist Bogdan Popa has seen the film as iconic for the unsympathetic treatment of the working class in Romanian filmmaking and believed that this treatment favored the spreading of a pervading and long-standing classism which differentiated between white middle-class Romanians and the uneducated poor (Popa 2018). Such treatment naturally would not escape the Politburo, which would lead an almost direct attack on Pintilie. The director, who had the backing of Cannes where *Reenactment* was surprisingly screened that year, decried the partial withdrawal of the film as an authoritarian gesture. Because he saw in the character of the bourgeois professor an *alter ego* for Pintilie himself, Ceaușescu considered the director a descendant of the grumbling intellectual class.

The setting in which *Reenactment* takes place, moreover, is the same Jiu Valley where the earlier *Reverberates the Valley* had been filmed. The paradigm shift enacted in the period from the early 1950s to the late 1960s and onwards betrays an increasingly vilified portrayal of workers in Pintilie's career, which would continue in his postsocialist films. From the heroic pathfinders of the early days of Communism, the working class became "an ignorant and violent agent to discipline those who seek freedom" (Popa 2018, 93); moving on to postsocialism, they transformed from defenders of the "cult of labor" into distrustful and cynical human beings (Andreescu 2013, 99).

Describing the militiamen's attitude as over-traditional and patriarchal as well as the state's apparatus (in the prosecutor's persona) as inactive and perfunctory was one thing. Denigrating the working class and moreover vying for a tacit reactionary return to bourgeois principles in education amounted to a cardinal sin. In the years preceding World War II, Ceaușescu had battled valiantly and been repeatedly imprisoned to ensure that the false ideals of the bourgeois age would never be restored. The other Communist members of the Politburo, who had experienced a similar treatment during the interwar fascist regime, genuinely agreed with him on that point.

In a sense, the film did glorify interwar fascist values, which the state in the late 1960s was not yet prepared to condone, even if later it would end up doing so by means of morphing interwar fascist ideals into nationalism. As Katherine Verdery's analysis has shown, the dialogue between Marxism and nationalism, which spanned the entire socialist period, in fact equaled a dialogue between Communism and right-wing values. As a result, the Communist Party was pulling the country left while "the masses" were going right. It was these ideologically unsanctioned masses that Ceaușescu abhorred in *Reenactment*, and Verdery, using the general cultural context of the country in that era, has explained why this was so:

> To understand [the national] speech as simply a manipulation of popular support impoverishes what was in fact a much more urgent and consequential project: to constitute, through discourse, wholeness for a reality that was in fragments and sovereignty for a vassal – to constitute a wholeness and a sovereignty that were imaginary. Years of trying to build up a state resting on a teleology of progressive change and an ideology of internationalism (with the acceptance of internal diversity) had ended in the realization that the state could adequately construct itself only in terms of what it had at first denied: a teleology of *national continuity* and an *ideology of national values*, premised on internal uniformity (Verdery 1991, 131, emphasis added).

This explains the peculiar equilibrium between fascism and communism in Romania. Although Verdery has refrained from equating the obsessive discourse on the Nation with fascism, the case can be made that neo-Stalinist Romania – as Verdery has called the second age of socialism – resorted to the *interbellum*/war-time fascist discourse to court the country's otherwise marginalized intellectuals to join the new ideology of Romania's own so-called mini-cultural revolution epitomized by the July theses.

If the socialist world was far from monolithic and the interactions between the Party's control and the artists' resistance engendered a semblance of continuous dialogue (Verdery 1991, 116), then Pintilie offended the leadership's willingness to participate in that dialogue. While the rule of thumb had previously and subsequently been that divergences between intellectuals and power would be resolved via negotiations and compromises – an image which disagrees with that of abject totalitarianism – *Reenactment* asked that that procedure be put to an end and that total democracy be restored.

This, however, was not the direction that the Romanian Communists wanted to pursue. As Yurchak's analysis has shown when he has described the transformation of constative values into performative slogans in the Soviet Union (Yurchak 2005), Marxism ironically spoke through the language of nationalism, and sometimes even through that of fascism in Romania. For that reason, the party-state considered that public discourse in the cultural arena had hitherto been polysemous. Verdery has eloquently captured this polysemy extant in Romanian culture at the time: "Nearly all Romanians I have met, regardless of social position, are deeply attached to the values of the Nation, whereas the values of Marxism-Leninism have enjoyed the respect of almost none" (Verdery 1991, 139). Pintilie distorted those Marxist-Leninist ideals with his crude and uncouth portrayal of the masses. Even if Pintilie's portrayal was realistic, because at the time the country was still under-developed and under-educated, this amounted to something of a personal attack on the leadership, which perceived its own valiant efforts to modernize and to improve the lot of the poor as futile, and the film as ignoring these efforts while legitimizing rightist goals.

As we have seen in the case of spy thrillers such as *Life Triumphs*, the performative nature of such films served as both a legitimization for the goals of the Party and a contestation thereof via audience identification with the villains. Because real-existing socialism held the seeds for both subordination and dissidence – because it was indeed dialectical in its nature – socialism never ceased to invite dialogue. In that way, cultural life in socialism resembles the polysemous universe of Bakhtin's heteroglossia, where various entities of several political persuasions could enter a dialogue with one another in a carnivalesque scenario in which the identities of these factions were never described at face value (Bakhtin 1995).

Far from thinking that it would corrupt audiences, the movie's partial distribution withdrawal should therefore be seen as the result of an almost personal affair. Film critic Mihai Fulger has believed that the movie's Cannes premiere and its partial ban are the only events in the film's history that helped to generate excitement for the film in the years that followed, and he has pointed out that Romanian dissidents constructed a mythical narrative around *Reenactment* mostly as a result of the film's partial disappearance from theaters. This narrative holds that *Reenactment* was officially outlawed and that its fate was sealed until 1989, despite the fact that, as Fulger has argued, the film was actually occasionally revived and exhibited in certain selected locations throughout the socialist period, until the fall of the communist regime in 1989 (Fulger 2020).

Because it rarely happened (only four pictures were irrevocably banned from Romanian screens over the entire socialist period), dissidence in socialism is exaggerated since most of the directors who faced censorship issues resorted to negotiations with their censors or "studio gatekeepers," as film scholar Radu Toderici has called them, and favored a relationship that was oftentimes marked by compromise (Toderici 2017, 197). Moreover, some directors approached delicate subjects by way of employing symbolic or roundabout discussions of sensitive issues. Yet, although this circuitous discourse sometimes brought directors in conflict with censorship, this did not mean, as film theorist Gabriela Filippi has articulated, that all films sanctioned by censorship were automatically masterpieces:

> … film critics and journalists still find "hidden gems" where there aren't any. The reflex interpretation of pre-1989 cinema is to consider a film a masterpiece if, at the time of its production, it had problems with censorship, this being considered proof of the intellectual narrowness of the former regime. However, this sometimes simply wasn't the case (Filippi 2017, 21).

A film did not have to be dissident to express the will of the people, and many social realist films in Romania, as I shall discuss shortly, strongly criticized the outcome of Communist labor policies, in the same way in which *The Black Cannon Incident* did in China. It is one thing to criticize the products of Communist labor, however, and quite another to attack the idealism of Communism, which in time acquired something of a religious zest. As Florentina Andreescu has put it, "the cult of labor was one of the most elaborated regimes of worker symbolism in the socialist world" (Andreescu 2013, 56). This is an important distinction that led authorities to institute a partial ban on *Reenactment* and to affirm that they, in fact, did not oppose creative people from staging their opposition to the regime.

Revisiting the Cultural Revolution

The portrayal of the working class as vitiated in Romanian cinema stands in contrast to the consistently benign treatment of workers in Chinese cinema. Although there is a tendency to question the collective intelligence of industrial plant employees in *The Black Cannon Incident*, for instance, and while there is an observable shift from the early lionization of the working class in *The Bridge* to its more realistic portrayal in *Old Well* (*Lao jing*, Wu Tainming, 1987) and, moving forward, *Still Life* (*San xia hao ren*, Jia Zhangke, 2006), their treatment is less swayed by the subjectivity of the director, as in Pintilie's case. This shows that Chinese cinema tends to look at the working class more realistically, no matter the political era, and to make less organicist comments on the inherent nature of workers' personalities.

This description applies even to films made during the time when Chinese history started to look back at the traumatic personal experiences of those authors who had experienced the Cultural Revolution. While *Breaking with Old Ideas* goes back in time to discuss the tribulations of the 1950s, it was not until the early 1980s that China engaged in serious criticism of recent history. Because Mao died in 1977 and Deng Xiaoping was struggling to enforce his rule in the 1980s, the Chinese films made at that time indulged in a restrained contestation of past abuses. For that reason, Chinese films of the 1980s made by the so-called fourth generation directors can be seen as something of an equivalent to the trend launched by *The Power and the Truth* in Romania.

Because the abuses of the Mao era during the Cultural Revolution personally marked the destinies of a larger number of people than Stalinism did in Romania during the "obsessive decade," criticism of the past in China took a slightly different form. Moreover, in the 1980s China's wounds were fresher.

For that reason, and because some of the films made at that time were adapted from similarly themed literary works, which referenced the debilitating violence of the Cultural Revolution, these films came to be known as a cinematic version of "scar literature." In his research of the period, Chris Berry has noted that "[s]tarting as early as 1977 but concentrated between 1978 and 1981, mainland Chinese cinema was taken over by a brief but intense episode of national self-examination" (Berry 1995, 87). Even though the market was flooded by "scar literature," films of this era attempted to take a truthful, non-retaliatory look at the past. These included the works meant to "speak bitterness" over the abuses committed in the name of equality. Berry has written that the "scar films" made between 1978 and 1981 "initiated in the cinema what has since become a new pattern of unstable authority and polyvocality constituting the Deng Xiaoping era as postsocialist" (88), and he has identified that no less than sixty-six movies portraying the Cultural Revolution were made in this period.

Troubled Laughter (Ku nao ren de xiao) made in 1981 by Yanjin Yang and Yimin Deng[10] is one of many such films that make use of radical techniques and innovative film style to comment on the recent past, using a narrative format that departs from the style of Mao's era. Bold and experimental, Yanjin Yang's debut feature explores Fu Bin's post-Cultural Revolution return to civilian life in a nearly slice-of-life manner. A sensitive journalist, Bin is shocked to discover a world he does not recognize upon returning to his workplace. When a famous former surgeon and dean of a medical school – who during the Cultural Revolution had been demoted to the institution's janitor – is cruelly treated and humiliated by an incompetent group of young cadres during a self-criticism meeting, Bin realizes the hypocrisy, cold-heartedness and conformism of his peers. Although he asks to be moved to another assignment, Bin is still forced to report on the case. Despite pressure from the Party Secretary Song, his conscience dictates that he writes truthfully on the events he has witnessed, but this plunges Bin into conflict with his bosses, former mentor and his wife, who, in line with the societal norms of the time, are afraid to stand for their beliefs. Undeterred, Bin writes an article condemning incompetence and injustice, and, although he does not have the courage to print it, it still leads to his downfall.

With *Troubled Laughter*, Yang changes the style that had been predominant in Chinese cinema until that point. Laying a brooding and disquieting drum beat and electronic score on top of scenes that are otherwise realistic, and alternating rapid editing with more traditional techniques, the director plunges audiences into Fu Bin's subjective experience. In order to accentuate Bin's perceived distress at the sight of his peers, in one scene Yang recurs to metaphor to trace a parallel between the political Party bosses and the bygone world of Chinese monarchy, depicting the Party secretary in charge of his case as an emperor. The German shepherds who share the table with

---

[10] It was customary in China from the beginning of the socialist era onwards for two directors to work jointly on a film. *Troubled Laughter*, however, is mostly the directorial product of Yanjin Yang.

powerful aristocrats feasting on grotesque human skeletons while mist and smoke surround the confused protagonist remind one of Pier Paolo Pasolini's *Salò, or the 120 Days of Sodom* (*Salò o le 120 giornate di Sodoma*, 1975) and the oneiric dreamlike sequences of Federico Fellini's *8 ½* (1963). Using skewed camera movements and Dutch angles to portray characters wearing swastikas and using the Nazi salute to greet the emperor, Yang intentionally creates anachronisms to liken China's late Communist leadership to a corrupt elite, thereby communicating the unease and disquiet that his protagonist experiences when encountering the state's power structures (Figure 4.1).

The combination of high and low angles in the dream sequences and the frequent montages of freeze frames mirrors the use of overlapping and sometimes conflicting voice-overs to portray Fu Bin's internal struggle. Staging most scenes in dilapidated interiors which contrast with the uprightness of his protagonist, Yang delivers a powerful tirade on what it means to be honest in a world where professionals have become psychotic from the fear and inability to speak up for the people. In a scene once again reminiscent of Fellini, Yang uses the visual metaphor of the circus to describe Fu Bin's tightrope-walk between truth and conformity, as he is being coerced by the secretary to uphold the tenets of the Gang of Four. Although Bin realizes that these tenets were conducive to abusive treatment of authority figures who ended up being punished out of revenge, he does not have the support of his peers to condemn such fallacies. His wife, moreover, although fully aware of Bin's predicament, chooses to ally herself with the conformist winds of the time,

Figure 4.1 Oneiric scene from *Troubled Laughter.*

Figure 4.2 The domestic dispute between Bin and his wife in *Troubled Laughter*.

advising him to think of their daughter before printing the article. Her attitude sends Bin into a tailspin, as he realizes that his values are being trampled on by the people closest to him. In a disturbing quarrel that the couple have in their bedroom, Bin blames his wife for betraying their past together and even regrets having a child with her. The powerful scene adds a realist substratum to the dream sequences, strengthening the overall narrative and making both characters realistic (Figure 4.2).

This is also Chris Berry's assessment of the scar films in which protagonists do not appear as self-assured as the Party officials of the Mao era. Instead, characters like Fu Bin "vacillate and make mistakes" (Berry 1995, 93). Although the film slips into melodrama at the end, when the *mise-en-scène* of the fairytale re-encounter between Bin and his wife compensate on the oneiric level for the unjustness of his arrest,[11] the film is a dire critique of political and humanistic ideals betrayed by conformism and constitutes an ode to the innocence of friendship and honesty. Even if some of the film's reverberation effects and frequent zooms appear naïve by today's standards, the film stands out as a stylistic marker of the period, as its innovative form helps condemn the animalistic side of the human condition in favor of preserving humanity in the face of chaos. As we will see shortly, in line with the Romanian directors

[11] Chris Berry has proposed that the ending, as in Nicolaescu's *Hot Days*, suffered changes required by the censors, which altered an otherwise too pessimistic finale (Berry 1995, 94).

of the 1980s, Yang does not criticize Communist ideology *in toto*, but the betrayal of Communist political goals by the second and third generations of politicians who should have, according to the director, improved the lives of the populace and delivered the fruits of Communist labor.

If the preservation of humanism in the face of antagonism was the central message in *Troubled Laughter*, Yang returns to the theme of the dualism of human nature in his second film discussing the Cultural Revolution, a more in-depth character study. *Narrow Street* (*Xiao Jie*, 1981) is a story told in flashbacks, which focuses on the unlikely friendship between Xia, a youthful truck driver, and Yu, an innocent-looking girl whom the protagonist meets by chance and confuses for a boy because of her short hair and slim physique. Xia feels a confusing attraction for Yu, which he nevertheless ignores, deciding to think of their relationship as one between brothers. The narrative moves at a leisurely pace, which allows for lengthy dialogues to take place on board of Xia's truck or by the side of a lake. These initially innocent conversations soon take a serious turn as the protagonists try to figure out what good and evil mean in the aftermath of the "ten years of chaos." Despite the innocent mood that describes their friendship in the beginning, dark recollections start to emerge, revealing that Yu was mistreated during the Cultural Revolution on account of her mother, a former teacher, who had been deemed a rightist.[12]

Several scenes portray Yu pursued by her tormentors. These scenes depict her hair being cut short and herself being humiliated and abused. In a particularly painful scene shot in grainy black and white, Yu is treated with disdain by two men wearing Red Guard uniforms. A critique of both misplaced political authority and sexism, Yu is filmed at a high angle, from the perspective of the guards looking slightly down at her. Framed by the backs of the guards' heads and squeezed in the center of the shot, Yu appears even more innocent and frail than usual (Figure 4.3). Although we never see the guards' faces, their sententious voices drown out Yu's high-pitched whimpers, and she is forced to run and take refuge in the corner of the room where she cowers against the wall, agonizingly repeating the same phrase: "Why do you insult me?" The scene conveys the defenselessness of oppressed victims more effectively than any of the more violent scenes that follow.

Yu confesses that she had to hide her true identity in order to guard her safety. The bucolic scenes from the present are continuously interspersed with black-and-white footage from the past, tinted in various hues. This makes us wonder, alongside the protagonists, why Yu's innocent playmates have turned evil and why humans generally succumb to their lower instincts when placed in a position of authority. When Xie finds out that Yu is, in fact, a girl, he wants to help her regain her good looks. In a move meant to restore her self-respect, Xia steals a wig from a traveling Chinese opera troupe but is caught and blinded by the owners in a muffled display of onscreen violence.

---

[12] Teachers, landlords, rich farmers and rightists were categorized as belonging to the so-called "black line," which in the eyes of orthodox leftists opposed the Cultural Revolution.

Figure 4.3 Yu framed by the silhouettes of the guards in *Narrow Street*.

Despite medical treatment, Xie remains partially blind and is unable to find Yu again, who in the meantime has moved house. The blinding is a subconsciously twisted Oedipal reference in which the director punishes himself for sexually desiring what was up to that moment an innocent playmate. The fact that Xia confuses Yu for a boy seems to express an innate desire to return to an idealized period in early human development, when feelings were based on innocence rather than sexual gratification and when gender apparently was inconsequential. Reflecting austere traditionalist norms, this half-incestuous infringement of societal taboos causes a type of self-flagellation that also marks an evident authorial sadness *vis-à-vis* the passage of childhood.

In an attempt to turn his story about Yu into a script, Xie recounts it to a friend who is a film director. Hence the plot's postmodern framework, which in fact is a reflection of Lyotard's belief that fragmentation, not unity, governs forms of literary expression in the wake of modernism. Since the director (played by Yang himself) does not believe that the script has the proper ending, he and Xie discuss several possible scenarios, which Yang plays out as potential finales. Chris Berry has found in this narrating style a certain similarity to Godard (Berry 1995, 94), and the comparison is not too far-fetched: in one of the endings, Xie is a taxi driver who once again encounters Yu at a party and takes her home in his cab. In this version, Yu is an exceedingly materialistic woman living a frivolous life, despite having a boring factory job. Yu confesses to Xie that she chose the glamorous lifestyle in order to compensate for her past suffering. Their reserved conversation in the car is contrasted via a quick flashback to the exhilarated exchanges that they shared in Xie's truck. Due to the rain falling outside, Yang chooses to shoot the car interior in a blue tint, which gives the scene a certain coldness, reminiscent of Godardian ennui.

As Yu bolts from the cab, Xie follows her to the portico of a giant edifice, where she describes her mother's funeral while her face stays close to the marble colonnades. The high-angle shot of the couple on the entrance steps evokes the insurmountable emotional distance that has come between the characters since they have lost touch with each other. Although Xie opposes her decision to live the good life, Yu prophetically warns him that they are both products of their own generation; that the effect of the Cultural Revolution cannot be effaced by ignoring the past; and that they are indeed victims of their own histories. "The world needs us," laments Xie to a reluctant Yu upon hearing this, but she disapprovingly pontificates as she blows the ash off her cigarette: "No, nobody needs us. We are a completely unwanted generation."

Characters who feel victimized and lost are also recurrent in Romanian films about young adulthood, such as the two young men portrayed in Pintilie's *Reenactment*. Although self-victimization would become more visible in Romania in the 1990s and early 2000s, both cultures portray the 1980s generation as afflicted by traumas, thus featuring a similar transnational inclination for melodrama. In both the Romanian and the Chinese films, the characters find themselves unable to change what appear to be their doomed destinies. The re-emergence of these themes in the 1980s demonstrates an almost incapacitating lack of the ability to deal with adult life and a continuous penchant for taking refuge in an idealized notion of childhood. As the narrative of *Narrow Street* progresses, for example, both Xie and Yu repeatedly lament that children have to grow up and are increasingly aware that, sadly, their relationship anticipates the end of their childhood. Yu's child-like appearance and general jolliness also testify to this effect. Although she is oftentimes seen playing like a child or enjoying innocent pleasures, such as laughing at Xia's missteps, she is continuously reminded of the pains of growing up in a world that would turn out to be evil, a world in which she lacks parental or authoritative support. Like the blinding episode which changes Xie's life forever, this is a wake-up call to a reality that is more complicated than the simplicity of infancy, about which the characters reminisce with nostalgia. Finally, the inability to overcome their innocence keeps characters fixated on what appear to be naïve or unrealistic goals. This also resembles Yang's other protagonist, Fu Bin from *Troubled Laughter*, who, although torn between walking the political line and telling the truth, chooses to stand up for an ideal that may well be infantile or inappropriate for his situation – namely, that of preserving his honesty.

Scar films continued to be produced in China in the early 1980s, and *River without Buoys* (Mei you hang biao de he liu, Wu Tianming, 1983) serves as a perfect example. The film starts with a melancholy camera gliding over still waters, while a voice-over introduces us to a story that is "not as old as the river" but as important as its source of life and nourishment. It is important because it is about three raft pilots who are getting away not only from the places that they have left behind upstream, but also from their own memories. These memories have to do with their traumatic experiences of the past. Try as hard as they may, neither Lao Pan, who is older, wiser and more hardened-looking, nor Shi Gu, the young and restless type, can somehow forget the injustices that they experienced at the hand of various administrators of revolutionary policies. Because they cannot put the past behind them, the two men cannot put aside their animosity for one another, either, and if it were not for Zhao Liang, a calmer and more practical man who usually stays out of other people's business, the two would be at each other's throats every day. Unbeknownst to them, however, they each lost their girlfriend to the tribulations of the Cultural Revolution and are now back to claim what was theirs. This shared experience, in fact, is what makes them more similar rather than different from one another, and it helps them overcome the difficult traumas of the past.

What makes this otherwise lackadaisical story noteworthy is the fact that, instead of blaming Communist policies for their misfortunes, the protagonists are clearly out to get the people, not the ideology, that wronged them. In other words, Lao Pan does not condemn the government for instituting the anti-rightist campaign but the particular figure of his nemesis who dares to call him a rightist. Even less implicated in politics than his older peer, Shi Gu uniquely bemoans the loss of his girlfriend to a local Party chief. This common injustice is enough to make both men ask for retribution, even when faced with the inflexible orders of the Red Guards who come on board the raft to require them to watch a revolutionary model opera in the film's climax. More concerned with the wellbeing of an older friend who is dying than with following orders, the men instigate a minor scandal implicating their girlfriends in order to deliver some ginseng to the dying friend.

Reminiscent of Polanski's *Knife in the Water* (*Nóż w wodzie*, 1962) because of the conflict between the older and the younger man, but also of *The Waves of the Danube* because of the claustrophobic space of the raft, the film discusses politics as secondary in importance to human character. It is the passions and the way in which they are controlled or mismanaged – the same way in which a pilot may steer his raft away from danger – that brings wellbeing or misfortune in people's lives, and the film is very conscientious of this premise. In the film's finale, although the rafters are caught in a storm by surprise and although Lao Pan disappears, he may have just swum to a place upriver, so the same voice-over that opened the film tells us. As in Yang's dramas about personal inner conflict, Wu's message is that man is the measure of all things, no matter what the political winds. It is therefore up to each person's private conscience to act humanely in respect to his or her fellow peers and to avoid the tragedies that befell Chinese society because over-enthusiastic Red Guards, as in *Narrow Street*, at that time abused the state's calls to action.

Wu Tianming's film also stands out as an achievement in realism. Unlike in Mao-era cinema, he uses close-ups not only to convey importance to a character, but also to communicate the pain or joy that a character is experiencing. In the fight between Lao Pan and Shi Gu, the sweat on their bodies gives a clear indication of the men's force and determination, as well as their backgrounds and character. Similarly, in the scene where the men go ashore, the discussions that they spontaneously start with the farmers while they are surrounded in the morning mist on the fields convey some of the endurance and resilience that Chinese peasants experienced during and after the "ten years of chaos." This makes Wu's film vivacious and true to the reality which it sets off to depict, despite the somewhat staged dramatics of the storm in the film's finale.

Wu Tianming and Yanjin Yang are both Chinese directors that can be assigned to the fourth generation, because they promoted a new language to discuss the confusion which the country was experiencing as leadership was progressively changing course in the 1908s. Referring to this exciting time, film historian Zhu Ying has called this...

> ... a transitional period when new cinematic ideas competed with old ones for legitimacy. Indeed the turn of the 1980s was the period of cinematic confusion and confrontation between the cinematic legacy of the surviving third generation and the new cinematic aspiration of the fourth generation. [...] Yet the fourth generation film's ideological and formal ambiguities not only reflected the unsettled transition in the Post Cultural Revolution China, but also linked Chinese cinema's art wave with a international modernist cinema, providing a theoretical topology for the positioning of the Chinese art wave within the realm of film modernism (Zhu 2001, 457).

This transition reflected the cinematic transformations taking place in other socialist countries, such as Romania, where the same confusion would pop up in the social realism of the 1980s, in a period prefiguring the transition to the new postsocialist regime. The realistic tone of the fourth generation furthermore prepared the ground for the fifth generation, with which Wu Tianming himself is sometimes associated for making stark portrayals of survival in China's rural environment, such as *Old Well.* This style would also make possible the realism of Zhang Junzhao's *One and Eight* (*Yi ge he ba ge*, 1984), the film that would signal the fifth generation's rise to international fame.

1980s Social Realism

In the 1980s, the socialist realist goals of early Communism came under criticism for failing the citizens who labored intensely to transform the world into the visionary one promised by that ideology. Films made during this decade criticized the shortcomings of socialist leadership and, in a manner reminiscent of *Breaking with Old Ideas*, revealed the nefarious side-effects of state policy. Criticism of socialist realism thus birthed a *social* realist style, which in turn was influenced by the advent of the co-called *film de actualitate* genre in 1960s Romania.

I have briefly discussed above "actuality films" as productions that sought to describe the lives of the working class in a realistic manner. Moreover, some early actuality films were concerned with the tribulations that young people experienced after high school graduation or when faced with a significant career change. In that sense, they were also slice-of-life films that captured a particular aspect of everyday reality in the life of a person, an institution, or a collective. In doing so, they bear a striking resemblance with the Chinese *Gongnongbing* genre, or the peasant-soldier-worker-style developed in that country in the early 1950s. If the previously discussed *Charming Girl* belongs to this genre, it is worth looking briefly at other productions made in the 1960s to understand the development of the genre in the last decade of socialism.

The Last Night of Childhood (*Ultima noapte a copilăriei*) is a film made in 1968 by Savel Știopul, a director with a perceptive eye for psychological dramas, who had previously directed poetical character studies in his triptych *Seasons* (*Anotimpuri*, 1966). Heavily marked by Michelangelo Antonioni's style and modernism in general and shot in black-and-white in order to contrast the predominantly white interiors with the poetic nocturnal landscapes of a young city, *The Last Night* paints a fairly accurate portrayal of teenager confusion as it focuses on a protagonist who is mystified by life's choices after his high school graduation. His predicament is further complicated by a tightly woven friendship with a male classmate as well as his romantic involvement with a temperamental girlfriend. Despite its honest portrayal of teenage crisis and its modernism, postsocialist critics largely ignored the film.

They instead focused on *Mornings of a Sensible Youth* (*Diminețile unui băiat cuminte*, Blaier, 1967). Almost a decade after making *The Ball* in 1959, Andrei Blaier demonstrated increased maturity and an ability to skillfully adapt Western modernist techniques in a reasonably powerful film which follows another high school graduate as he meanders emotionally between various life choices. Unable to get into college, Vive (whose name connotes exuberance) is violently confronted by an authoritarian father who forces him to question his chaotic lifestyle and find a stable job. Crushing his rebellious spirit, the traditionalist father persuades Vive to join a young team of like-minded youth on a new construction site. If Vive previously could not decide which road to follow in life and if his new job offers him temporary stability, the conflicting advice of the people whom he meets at work only make him unable to commit either to his newfound love interest or to the tediousness of his position as a work safety inspector. The film ends with Vive having a nervous breakdown and suffering an accident at work because, ironically, he refuses to use protective equipment to ensure his safety.

Although the script is simplistic in its dénouement and although the brutality of the paternal character is artificially constructed to contrast with Vive's emancipated spirit, Blaier made a provocative film about choices while managing to skillfully avoid the cliché of the new battling the old. Hemmed in between the father and a benevolent older boss who complains of not having made the right choices in his youth, Vive is realistically portrayed as a confused teenager whose ramblings appeared relatable to young audiences faced with similar difficulties in a society undergoing massive changes in the liberal 1960s. Furthermore, Blaier's reasonably innovative cinematography put a personal touch on Vive's story. The scene in which he arrives on the construction site for the first time conveys his confusion and anxiety via a quick montage of alternating high- and low-angle shots edited together to the dissonant sounds of industrial machinery. This not only avoided the alleged pomposity of earlier films such as *Life Triumphs*, whose clear-cut good guys/bad guys Manicheism sounded preachy to the ears of postsocialist film critics, but it also prefigured postmodern techniques in which industrial landscapes deepen the emotional lives of characters, as in Antonioni's use of backgrounds to reflect on the intensity of a character's state of mind. Shot in black-and-white, *Mornings of a Sensible Youth* recalls the contrasting play between lights and shadows of Antonioni's earlier *L'avventura* (1960), in which a deceptively sunny landscape is used to conceal the characters' angst and confusion.

Despite its accurate portrayal of teenage confusion, Blaier's exploratory essay under postsocialism was accused of being yet another propaganda piece for the 1960s socialist regime. Jitea has thought that the film advertises the construction site as the only panacea for Vive's alienation, thus promoting this stereotype as the ultimate solution to life's problems in general (Jitea 2021, 268), while Popescu has found Blaier's film even more nefarious than earlier propaganda, because it promotes the anti-intellectualism of the working class – via the character of Vive's father (Popescu 2011, 163). One critic who comments positively on the film is the Belgian-Romanian film scholar Dominique Nasta. Despite calling it yet another "worksite stereotype film," Nasta has argued that Blaier avoided the propagandist nature of earlier movies of its kind. She has further stated that, even though Romanian cinema missed the opportunity to renew itself (as that of other Eastern European countries, such as Czechoslovakia, did in the 1960s), *Mornings of a Sensible Youth* is clearly influenced by the Czech New Wave, and it is remarkable for bringing to the screen for the first time "violent quarrels between old-fashioned parents and their emancipated children, suicide attempts and even the death of an old factory worker addicted to alcohol" (Nasta 2013, 25). Despite this, she has failed to identify the influence of *film de actualitate* on the Romanian New Wave and largely considered other manifestations of the genre as indoctrinating.

In spite of the mainly negative assessments that *film de actualitate* garnered in postsocialism, *Mornings of a Sensible Youth* helped prepare the ground for the 1980s generation, which focused on portraying the questionable side-effects of state socialism using restraint in their criticism of working and living conditions. In that sense, Romanian films of the 1980s – such as Ada Pistiner's *Snapshot around the Family Table* (*Stop cadru la masa*, 1980) and Aurel Mihele̦ș's *Too Young for Wrinkles* (*Prea tineri pentru riduri*, 1982) – are similar to the productions of China's fourth generation, which also treated the past with respect and moderation.

Made by a female director coming from the documentary tradition, Pistiner's slice-of-life *Snapshot around the Family Table* describes an adultery that a married man in his forties commits with a younger woman. Played by

Russian actor Aleksandr Kalyagin, who became famous for his part in Nikita Mikhalkov's *Unfinished Piece for Mechanical Piano* (*Neokonchennaya pyesa dlya mekhanicheskogo pianino*, 1977), the protagonist is an architect with a beer belly and a receding hair line, who has grown tired of the routine that his wife and daughter demand of him. His mistress, however, is a vivacious young singer clearly in need of the material support that an older man like him could provide. The brief romance between the two is characterized by genuine conversations that center on the singer's life decisions, in contrast to the man's exclusive focus on their physical relationship. Although things return to normal in the film's finale and although the husband goes back to his wife, the film is the poignant character study of a man who evades responsibility towards his family to indulge in his own pleasures. Pointing her camera onto the characters in such a way as to reveal their most intimate sides in a manner that looks thoroughly natural, Pistiner portrays the husband's adultery with an honesty that is neither moralistic nor intrusive, and this makes her style appear as a precursor to the minimalism later employed by Romanian New Wave directors. Endorsing a feminist point of view that clearly ascribes the guilt in the relationship to the philandering husband, the film was allowed to pass censorship despite the anti-patriarchal (and therefore anti-authoritarian) views it espoused.

Although Dominique Nasta has briefly summarized Pistiner's film in her monograph on Romanian cinema, she has not made the connection between Pistiner and the New Wave, content to call this film made by a woman filmmaker "an exception" and to note that the London National Film Theatre program called it "superb" as early as in 1981 (Nasta 2013, 44). Nasta has, however, compared Pistiner's sensibility to that of "shelved" Soviet female auteur Kira Muratova and opined that "[h]eavy censorship seems to have been applied to the film, as apart from two or three kisses, no sex is shown" (44). In other words, the concern of postsocialist critics is mainly about the amount of material that socialist-era directors could "sneak" past the censors and less with the relationship between ideology and cinema, which is central to the debate on socialist-era filmmaking.

This relationship is evident in the way in which the film comments on the ideals of socialism, but also on the achievements that state-run Communism was supposed to have made a few decades after its implementation. For Pistiner, the most important of these is the state's promise to reduce and eventually eradicate differences between men and women, while offering both equal chances for advancement in social and economic life. Because the film clearly shows the advantage that men enjoy in relation to women in a society that is still clearly patriarchal (the protagonist flatly abandons his mistress when he becomes bored with her), the film raises concerns about a social system that has not fully lived up to its promises to society. Although cinematic critiques of the social and legal aspects of Communism became much more common in postsocialism, it is important to remember that the first films mounting concerns *vis-à-vis* state socialism were the socialist-era films themselves.

This is also the case with *Too Hot for the Month of May* (*Prea cald pentru luna mai*, 1984), directed by Maria Callas Dinescu. Adapted from a formulaic novel, the film was criticized immediately after its release for its schematic plot and cliché situations (Ulieriu 1984). Despite its structural flaws, however, the film dared to take stock of the red bourgeoisie – that is, with those members of the intelligentsia who held important functions in the higher echelons of the industrial and judicial establishment. In the story, the son of an important newspaper manager, while behaving in a sexist fashion towards his girlfriend, accidentally hurts a passerby and is indicted for manslaughter. The boy's father intervenes on behalf of his child but is prevented from meddling in the case by an incorruptible prosecutor who also happens to be the father's friend. An excellent student who risks being expelled from school, the adolescent does not welcome his father's interference, accusing the latter of being over-protective. Whatever was left of an already distant relationship is finally destroyed by the father's intrusiveness, which in the end favors the son's departure from home, as well as his estrangement from his girlfriend.

Although not particularly inventive at the level of cinematic language, the film condemns both the son's machismo and the father's favoritism. Furthermore, the parental intervention in his child's life ironically prefigures the meddlesome father in Mungiu's *Graduation* (*Bacalaureat*, 2016), in which an overbearing parent intervenes in his daughter's graduation exam, thereby endangering her future. What we see in both socialist-era and postsocialist films is a critique of powerful individuals whose status and prestige in society makes them prone to favoritism. Reminiscent of Vive's father in *Mornings of a Sensible Youth*, who is played by the same actor, the father in Callas Dinescu's film, like Pistiner's protagonist, is unconcerned by moral conduct. Their behavior contrasts with that of Yang's protagonist in *Troubled Laughter*, who, unlike his Romanian counterparts, takes the high road when faced with a moral dilemma. Despite differences, both Romanian and Chinese directors in their films demonstrate a pressing concern for ethics, which reflects the Zeitgeist in both societies of the time.

Another film that shows the betrayed ideals of Communist social policy and its unfortunate failures in creating a fair society is Aurel Miheleș's *Too Young for Wrinkles*. The film describes the disillusions that three teenagers experience when they break out of an orphanage to search for their parents. The premise that imbues the plot with suspense is that the parents are alive and well, and it is they who have abandoned their kids in the orphanage in the first place. Although their absence causes the teenagers intense suffering, the parents do not wish to be found at all. Following a short teenage romance with a girl who similarly lives away from her family – and therefore can better understand the boy's suffering – the final meeting with the parents comes as a huge disappointment: not only do the parents reject their offspring once again, but they refuse to even admit to their wrongdoing. This forces the teenagers to return to the orphanage, only to be met by tragedy on the way home when one of the boys dies in an accident in the film's finale.

One boy's return to his mother's apartment to ask whether she would take him back is a scene that builds empathy for the young protagonists. After he and his friend brush against a man who leaves the apartment in a hurry, the mother opens the door in a revealing negligée and lies about her lover's identity, insisting that the man they just saw was her cousin. After recognizing her son and showing some surprise at how much he has grown, the mother indifferently invites the boys inside for a sandwich. When she inquires about the reason for their visit, the boys sarcastically tell the mother that they were on leave, much like the mother's cousin. The scene ends with the mother rushing to the toilet to arrange her bathrobe while humming a catchy tune, too concerned with her appearance to catch the sarcasm of the boys' remark. Despite its light-hearted tone, the scene persuasively portrays the lack of intimacy between mother and son. This lack relates the emotional distance experienced by children growing up with neglectful or absent parents, particularly the despondency experienced by the many orphans resulting from the 1966 decree, either because of maternal mortality at birth or because of parental abandonment.

The washed-out colors of the slightly over-exposed film stock and the predominant cloudy settings that Mihele chooses for his exteriors give the film a desolate feel. The shoddy apartment buildings and the dilapidated suburban landscapes that the director favors for most *mise-en-scène*s intensify the endearing portrayal of teenage romance and give the aimless wanderings of its characters a melancholic touch. In that sense, the film also served as criticism of a broad-based socialist practice whereby parents too busy working left their children in the care of grandparents and other relatives, which then negatively impacted their emotional development. The results of this practice became even more problematic in postsocialism, when parents moving abroad for work trusted relatives to look after their children, which often had dire consequences for the children's wellbeing. Undergirding the similarity of the socialist and the postsocialist eras, rather than the rupture between them, this is also the subject of *When I Want to Whistle, I Whistle* (*Eu când vreau să fluier, fluier*, Șerban, 2010): a mother who leaves for Italy for an extended period of time abandons her children in her relatives' home, only to face the wrath of her elder son who ends up in a reform school.

While *Too Young for Wrinkles* was clearly conceived to make Ceaușescu's anti-abortion decree more palatable to the public, the director also mounts a scathing critique of dysfunctional behavior in socialist families *in toto*. Another interesting effect of parental abandonment is the type of relationships that the boys in the film develop with one another. The pain that the children feel as a result of neglect increases the intimacy that they experience in each other's presence and makes them distrust the adults around them. The friendships that these characters build outside their families, moreover, prepare the ground for the emergence of the socialist affect attributable to small communities and student collectives, such as those portrayed in Mungiu's and Lou's films discussed above.

Even though not a popular movie with audiences at the time due to its unattractive subject-matter, the charming portrayals of youthful love and the naturalistic acting of the child performers contributed to making the film compelling in its display of affect for the young public. In the same manner in which Yang Yanjin's fourth-generation Chinese films condemned the immorality and irresponsible behavior of his authoritative characters and thus prepared the way for Chen Kaige and Zhang Yimou, Mihele̦s's film prefigures the realism of Mungiu's *4, 3, 2*. Going further, without explicitly condemning the government for its otherwise mistaken decision to control the lives of its citizens, Mihele̦s upstages the implicit criticism of the state in Mungiu's work, by presenting a more comprehensive existential conundrum regarding the actions of parents and caretakers following the passage of the anti-abortion law.

A common theme emerging in a side-by-side comparison of Mihele̦s's and Yang's *Narrow Street* is the treatment of filial piety. In both films, characters present an almost eerie inability to overcome the past, which is predicated on what appear to be unnaturally powerful bonds between children and parents, bonds which seem to characterize both cultures. While Yu is strongly attached to her dying mother in *Narrow Street*, for example, the parents who have betrayed their children in Mihele̦s's film command a different kind of retributive response from their offspring – something which can be seen as a reversal of the filial piety principle, this time born out of revenge and resentment against authority figures who have fallen into disrepute. Reflecting concerns about education and the role of parents in the lives of children and young adults, *Narrow Street* and *Too Young for Wrinkles* are similar in that both films discuss the conspicuous absence of authority figures from children's lives, be these parents, governmental institutions, or important functionaries of the regime. For example, although Yu's mother is central to the plot in Yang's film and although her abuse has significantly impacted Yu's life, the mother never appears in the film. Comparably, we see the despicable parents in Mihele̦s's film, as well as the teachers who do their best to replace the parents at the orphanage school, as transitory and perfunctory presences.

The figure of the absent parent becomes literal in *The Herdsman* (*Mu ma ren*, 1982), made by veteran Chinese director Xie Jin, in which a son and his father are reunited after a long absence. Although equally present in Yigong Wu's *Evening rain* (*Ba shan ye yu*, 1980), one of the first memorable films to unreservedly discuss the Cultural Revolution, the motif of the search for the absent father in *The Herdsman* is important because it opens up lines of questioning, not about the political but about the familial past. This is because the repeat encounter in Xie Jin's film takes place after the father had voluntarily left his family behind to emigrate to the US. Sporting familiar themes of integrity and honesty in the face of vicissitude like its earlier counterparts, *The Herdsman* also anticipates themes featured in Romanian films, such as the mother-son conflict in *If I Want to Whistle, I Whistle*. The fact that the Chinese and Romanian films made during the 1980s reflect similar concerns associated with a troubled past and reminiscence about an innocent childhood while discussing the problematic relationship between children and parental figures leads us to identify the existence of a common sensibility associated with the 1980s generation in both cultures. This sensibility is predicated on a similar affective response to societal stimuli that affected, as we have seen in the historical development of political trends, Chinese and Romanian cultures while birthing the same socialist affect.

In conclusion, social realist dramas demonstrate that Romanian cinema's critique of power structures made possible by the industrialization of the country, the slackening of rigid traditionalist morals and the modernization of the workforce was well underway in the 1980s. If postsocialist theorists pushed the dissident agendas of film directors such as Pintilie, who dared to protest openly the rigidity of socialist censorship rules, this does not lower the social, technical, aesthetic and artistic merit of the otherwise accomplished 1980s social realist films, even though these may have been less popular with audiences than their so-called dissident counterparts. However, it would be a mistake to see in social realism a desperate attempt to turn the socialist realist values of the 1950s upside down, as Dominique Nasta has done, only in order to reveal the dark side of utopia. Various film scholars have extolled the contestatory qualities of Mircea Daneliuc's *Microphone Test* (*Proba de microfon*, 1980), for example, because the film dares to present the bleak reality of the working class in a faithful manner (Nasta 2013, 62). *Microphone Test* is about the relationship between a news cameraman and a down-and-out factory worker who is unsure of her affection for him. While the protagonist blames his monotonous lifestyle on impoverishment combined with middle-age socialism, his depression most clearly originates in his unsuccessful attempt to keep the girl. For that reason, the film is primarily about the instability of human feelings – and an expressive one at that – while the political message, if present at all, is secondary.

What most Romanian critics have ignored is that, like Poland's *Cinema of Moral Anxiety* with which it is related, this type of 1980s cinema focused on social criticism more than politics. Unlike Daneliuc, whose rambunctiousness got him in trouble with the authorities, much like Pintilie before him, directors of social realist cinema did not call for the abandonment of Communist ideology, but for an honest appraisal of its downsides. Without offending the original goals of the Communist revolution, as Pintilie did, the films of Pistiner, Callas Dinescu and Miheleș criticized only the long-lasting effects of that revolution. In doing so, they can be considered *avant-la-lettre* manifestoes for social change, ultimately opening the road for the themes and aesthetics of New Romanian Cinema.

As we will see shortly, film critics in postsocialism endorsed a Manichean reading of socialist-era filmmaking, separating dissident cinema – as illustrated by *Reenactment* and even *Microphone Test* – from the works of allegedly "collaborationist" filmmakers, such as Sergiu Nicolaescu's *Hot Days*. This film and those of Pistiner and Miheleș, however, command a different interpretation. If raising the Iron Curtain in 1989 permitted filmmakers to finally expose all that lay hidden behind the propagandist façade of socialism, it does not mean that socialist productions were propagandistic and postsocialist ones honest in their portrayal of socialist-era realities. Disparaging socialist-era cinema for not promoting uniquely anticommunist goals, as film critics have demanded retroactively in postsocialism, only created an artificial rupture between two allegedly contrasting ages: one dark, the other luminous. This contrast, however, was as artificial as the propaganda that the critics decried in socialist-era filmmaking.

Symbolism

The same sacrifices that China made in the late 1950s and 1970s Romania would experience in the 1980s. The heavy blow that the oil crisis imparted on the economy and the country's increased isolation in this period forced Ceaușescu to turn away from the goals of Marxism-Leninism and to promote a fierce form of nationalism via an increasingly totalitarian rule. Literary critic Mihai Iovănel has believed that the regime's use of nationalism in the last socialist decade was a desperate attempt to make up for economic stagnation (Iovănel 2021, 72). Iovănel has also claimed that, as a result of the country's economic failure in the 1980s, Ceaușescu was essentially compelled to replay his role as a protector against Soviet aggression, which accounts for the increasingly frequent and meticulous parades that promoted his personality cult.

The personality-cult-era favored certain types of expression over others, and the most effective of them all was symbolism. While Pistiner, Callas Dinescu and Miheleș explicitly tackled issues of adultery, teenage orphan culture and middle-class favoritism in the last age of socialism, other directors chose to comment on related issues using allegory and metaphor. Because they thought poetry was richer and more polysemous than realism, 1980s filmmakers developed a visual language riddled with symbolism and adopted a communicative technique demonstrating ambivalence. Like many other films of the decade, Mircea Daneliuc's *Glissando* (1982) and Dan Pița's *The Contest* (*Concurs*, 1982) took a Bakhtinian approach, choosing to speak allegorically to their audiences, not only as a way to subvert authoritarianism, but also as a way to mirror the confusion that the regime itself was beginning to experience during the decade that would ultimately lead to its downfall.

Furthermore, as in Dan Pița's film discussed below, directors combined symbolism and magic realism to express the discomfort, confusion and alienation of the populace in the face of economic turbulence and nationalist excess. As Aga Skrodzka has shown in her study of Eastern European cinema, magic realism had been a homestay of Hungarian, Bulgarian and Polish filmmakers since the 1930s; thus, Romanian directors only had to tap an artistic vein already present in the region to "communicate an anxiety over the status of locality and, perhaps more significantly, over one's relationship with the locality that is being inadvertently changed and often severed by the workings of […] 'mosaic modernity'" (Skrodzka 2012, 24). This added further importance to the language that artists used in order to engage in dialogue with the regime and rendered the communication between the party and audiences – but also that between filmmakers and audiences – inherently polysemous.[13]

Stuart Hall has claimed that meaning structures at the level of production are not the same as meaning structures at the level of reception (Hall 2019, 54). I shall further explore this in relation to encoding/decoding during the real-existing socialism of the 1980s, where meaning structures were infiltrated with expectations and anticipations, which affected the way in which the material was both produced and spectated. The fact that the creative capacity of the Party did not actually belong to the Party but to film directors who technically belonged to the "masses" makes this doubly ambivalent, because the clear delineation Party/Masses existed in theory only. This is simply because the Party is made up of the masses, and therefore some contestation to power exists within power itself. The reverse is also true: the masses did not contest the Party directly, because they needed the Party to supply factories, homes and industries with basic resources that only the Party itself could provide (Verdery 1993, 183). The relationship between the masses and the Party was therefore symbiotic, and this type of relationship also described the creative process.

In *Glissando*, Daneliuc illustrates this symbiosis by equating the authoritarianism of the 1980s with the fascism of the 1930s, rather than explicitly condemning dictatorship. Using dimly lit interiors and chiaroscuro lighting, the film portrays the downfall of an art collector and inveterate card-player who ends up attempting suicide while confined to a sanatorium. The greenish tint of exterior shots filmed almost exclusively on overcast days, coupled with the backlit interiors of the protagonist's apartment, cause the audience to experience a sense of unending claustrophobia and frustration. While brightly lit scenes describing the love affair between him and his future wife are few, most of the narrative detailing his descent into addiction is unnervingly gloomy. The pessimism of the film is enhanced by the absurdist behavior of sanatorium convalescents who recall the unjust treatment of prisoners in Pasolini's *Salò* or the lacerative medical experiments tried on inpatients in Miloš Forman's *One Flew over the Cuckoo's Nest* (1975).

The most obvious similarity between *Glissando* and Chinese surrealism is the comparable style used by Yanjing Yang in *Troubled Laughter*. Made only two years apart, although probably unaware of each other, both films used expressionistic techniques that startled their audiences at the time. Considered bold and provocative, the films constituted strong indictments of a leadership that had lost touch with the populace. In Danliuc's film, symbolism prevails over diegesis to condemn authoritarianism (Jitea 2021, 194); this is evident in the final scene where the director's nervous camera observes

[13] Popescu has spoken of a veritable excess at the level of interpretation of late-socialist era Romanian films, where audiences were expected to read various subversive meanings into the most minute gestures that a character made because the directors "wrote it deep." As such, the mania surrounding certain films went so far as to seek meanings in the *ecriture*, even if in fact there were none (Popescu 2011).

the collective movements of an inpatient crowd as they are led through their morning exercises. While some of the fascist-related imagery, such as the use of swastikas and the steamy interiors of the sanatorium baths remind one of Yang's oneiric sequences in *Troubled Laughter*, there is less in the way of enabling agency in Daneliuc's film than in that of his Chinese counterpart. Unlike Fu Bin, Daneliuc's hero appears downtrodden and defeated by a world which he has long given up trying to change. Moreover, the constant sense of foreboding and self-indulgence that accompanies the main character reflects on the director, who uses his opus to raise a plea for deliverance from a crippling sense of depression.

If Bogdan Jitea has informed us that the subversive message of the film and its allusions were not lost on Daneliuc's contemporaries (Jitea 2021, 194), he has also agreed, however, that this "baroque, metaphorical and sometimes confusing film is tantamount to a failure, which does not have the coherence of Daneliuc's earlier work" (185). Popescu has seen the film as a straightforward anti-Ceaușescu allegory, in which wannabe swastikas stand for the hammer and sickle while the head doctor in the sanatorium is none other than Ceaușescu himself (Popescu 2011, 252–54). As potent as Stuart Hall's call to abandon authorial intent may be, such interpretations are based solely on speculation. The film remains primarily the work of an auteur slightly out of his comfort zone, working in a difficult new genre.

This is because Daneliuc hails from the *film de actualitate* tradition, and because he was one of the first Romanian directors who, before Pistiner, engaged in descriptive realistic tableaux describing a disgruntled working class that appeared dissatisfied with the results of socialist policies. In his 1980 film *Microphone Test* (*Proba de microfon*), as well as in his earlier *The Ride* (*Cursa*, 1975), the director conveys this exhaustion with socialist ideals via flesh-and-bone characters who, unlike their socialist realist counterparts, behave onscreen as naturally as they do in everyday life. Daneliuc's decision to change registers and try his hand at surrealism is a choice that reflects broader changes in artistic and cultural expression in late socialism. These tendencies traveled extensively in the region, including to and from the Soviet Union, as the hegemon of the Eastern Bloc itself was feeling the brunt of exhaustion and preparing to experience the changes of the oncoming Perestroika. Thus, parallels can easily be drawn between such Soviet 1980s films as Roman Balayan's *Flights in Dream and Reality* (*Polyoty vo sne i nayavu*, 1983) and Daneliuc's *Glissando*.

The same changes are evident in *The Contest* (*Concurs*, 1982), a film appearing to admit that the enthusiasm of the working class, after three decades of sustained effort to fulfill work quotas, has finally run out of steam. What takes the place of this enthusiasm in Dan Pița's oneiric work is confusion, disorientation and anxiety. The plot describes a forest-orienteering contest organized by an unspecified state institution, featuring three rival teams of mostly middle-aged contestants. None of them is very interested in getting a prize, their attitudes to the race being somewhat blasé and nonchalant. We follow the members of the first team, which is led by an excessively ponderous man in his late forties. He is despondent because his attractive young wife has skipped the contest and stayed behind in the bus, offering as excuse a headache. In fact, she is having an affair with the bus driver.

Gliding over wet roads and panning to take in the lush green of the forest to the sound of a meditative electronic soundtrack, Pița's camera follows with excitement the shenanigans of the group. Instead of pursuing their goals, the contestants get sidetracked by minute details. In one scene, they help jump-start a chicken transport truck which is stuck in the mud of a forest road; at other times they fight over resources and go off searching for water. When a contestant finally finds a brook, the others immediately wonder whether the water is poisoned; they get into an argument over whether someone perchance is trying to poison them. Most of the contestants are unreasonably edgy, jumping at each other's throats (sometimes literally) over the smallest comments and innuendos. There is enough suspicion going about the group to divide its members and to keep them from crossing the finish line, and enough anxiety to make them alarmed at the smallest sound that reverberates through the mysterious forest. The only time they seem to support each other is when the team comes across a ridiculously shallow ditch over which they all have to jump. For unknown reasons, they become unnecessarily motivated and cheer each other on, even though objectively this does not mean much progress for the race.

The anxiety and mutual suspicion that the contestants feel points to the late-socialist-era disintegration of the collective. No longer the determined group of combattive citizens who oppose the exploitation of the bourgeoisie as in *Reverberates the Valley*, this particular group seems more interested in sabotaging itself and its own objectives rather than looking for class enemies. In that sense, *Contest* resembles the overlooked work of Soviet director Vadim Abdrashitov, such as *Parade of the Planets* (*Parad planet*, 1984) or *The Train Has Stopped* (*Ostanovilsya poezd*, 1982), which combine surrealism with alembicated, oftentimes confusing plotlines, endowing his films with a tinge of the fantastic.

Although Pița's contest is most probably a metaphor alluding to the Party-sponsored programs seeking to stimulate socialist labor via competition while referencing the erstwhile Stakhanovism of the 1950s, which was celebrated in films like *The Bridge*, the characters in *The Contest* show utmost disinterest in competition, confirming the corruption of earlier lofty ideals. To show this, Pița's characters mostly pursue their mundane pleasures and only pay lip service to the collectivist goals. These pleasures involve an older man having sex in the forest with an attractive young woman, and the bus driver presumably engaging in sexual activity with the group leader's wife. As in *River without Buoys*, there is also a conflict between old and new. When a twenty-something-year-old joins the group, he is asked by the older contestants to carry out all the tasks which they themselves are too lazy or too complacent to perform. Contrasting with the lassitude of the group, the young man's energy stands for the willingness of the youngest generation to revert to the ethical morals of an earlier age and to uphold the rules of the collective. It is the devious collective, however, that ends up corrupting him instead.

A relevant scene in this sense is the one where the contestants hear a woman's desperate screams for help coming from somewhere deep within the forest. Instead of heeding ethical laws and responding to the screams, the older contestants pretend that they have not heard anything, reasoning that, even if they had heard something, the woman in distress should be the problem of the militia, and not their own. Such lack of solidarity was rarely shown in Romanian cinema until the 1980s, and when it finally occurred, it rang the death knell of the proletarian ideals of the 1950s. The awakening to a reality darker and more somber than that of Communist ideals is made even clearer in the film's finale, when the young man by accident discovers the body of a woman who has been raped in the forest. This finding has a both cathartic and disquieting effect, making the bickering among the group members pale in comparison with the approaching specter of death. The prescient metaphor relates to the death of the collective and, of course, to the future disintegration of the socialist affect that up to that point managed to hold the members of society together.

Part Two

5 The 1990s and Postsocialism

Postsocialism in Romania and Socialism with Chinese Characteristics

The post-revolutionary years in Romania witnessed economic and social shockwaves that ranged from massive downscaling of the workforce to the closing of factories, and from economic precarity to emigration, all of which had a profound effect on the country's postsocialist social fabric. Romanian economist Florin Georgescu has argued that the country chose to enact the transition to capitalism following a top-down formula which was devised and implemented outside the country's national borders by the World Bank and the IMF (Georgescu 2018, 28), following oftentimes immoral and illegal paths enacted in a legislative vacuum and guided by corruption, favoritism and nepotism (65). Drawing on the work of the Romanian sociologist Vladimir Pasti, he has stated that capitalization led to the collapse of the state's authority and control mechanisms, so much so that everyone "in the first years after the revolution did pretty much whatever they pleased" (Pasti, quoted in Georgescu 2018, 32). This, in turn, led to the violent collapse of the legal and administrative systems, which birthed not so much a liberal, but a *libertine* economy and style of doing business – an economy and style that describe Romanian economic and administrative practices to this day, according to Georgescu.

Hungry for cash, successive post-revolutionary center-right governments dismantled and sold the country's industrial base for scrap. Reversing the message of films such as *Hot Days*, which took exaggerated pride in promoting the national industry, within a few years after 1989 the government would sanction the dismantling of 60 percent of the Communist-built industry, which would lead to an inflation of 250 percent and a 23-percent drop in industrial output (Ban 2014, 126). One economist has estimated that the quantity of iron that the Romanian government sold abroad after 1989 in a desperate attempt to close down Communist-era industries equals, if it were so shaped, a train circumscribing the entire globe along the Equator, and then some.

Political economist Cornel Ban has argued that this was possible because of the toxic neo-developmentalist episode of the early 1990s and the unrealistic experiment following 2004, in which Western doctrines were artificially and ineffectively transposed to the nationalist-Stalinist realities via the fundamentalist and overzealous application of neoliberal formulae. Ana Bazac has thought that the transition to capitalism was managed by incompetent intellectuals who were not even economists and who "repeated slogans about the superiority of capitalism while motivated by the mantra of consumption and liberal political democracy," even though they did not know what these meant (Bazac 2017, 37). Finally, unlike the organic buildup of capital in Western democracies, Eyal et al. have stipulated that Eastern European capitalism was built by technocratic elites in a reckless and speedy process, which most authors refer to as "shock therapy" (Eyal et al. 1998). The effects of low economic performativity worked to put the country in the early 2000s on par with some of the poorest economies in the Third World, insuring peripheral treatment by the European community. Although a left-wing government successfully stemmed the neoliberal collapse at the beginning of the 2000s, the results of shock therapy would unequivocally place the country in neoliberal hands and transform it into a dependency on foreign capital until the present (Ban 2014).

The current picture of the postsocialist economy closely mirrors the country's interwar period. According to most economists and social scientists, the postsocialist economy is currently dominated by Austrian, German, Dutch and British capital, with approximately 80 percent of banks in Austrian and Greek hands (Ban 2014). Compared to the 2,102 industrial factories and cooperatives built under socialism and extant in 1990 (Comisia națională pentru statistică 1990, 420), Romania in 2015 counted the smallest number of small and medium-sized businesses in the European Union, which is astounding for a country whose population of almost 20 million ranks sixth in the Union (Georgescu 2018, 84). As result, Ban has posited that the country currently serves primarily as an assembly line for products made in the West, rightfully earning Romania its *maquiladora* name in reference to the Mexican-style outsource-based industry (Ban 2014).

When it left behind Maoism in 1978, "China had no foreign debt and received virtually no foreign investment" (Maddison 2006, 19). While Romania's economy in the first postsocialist decade faltered, that of China after Mao's death took a decided turn for the better. This is because restructuring started in China two years after Mao's death (MacFarquar and Schoenhals 2008, 2), with the so-called Reform and Opening Up movement under the leadership of Deng Xiaoping. Even though it created inequalities almost instantly, Deng's so-called "Four Modernizations" program was allowed to continue with the view that it would ultimately lead to common prosperity (Dunford 2022, 36). This allowed Deng to establish his historic Special Economic Zones starting in Shenzhen, Zhuhai, Shantou and Xiamen in 1980, an action that bore the fruits of capitalization and modernization as early as a decade later.

This came at a double cost for China: prioritizing growth from 1979 onwards meant that "some people and places [got] rich first," while others trailed behind (Dunford 2022, 39). However, unlike postsocialist Romania, redistribution of state income was prominent, favoring a more equal development of all economic areas. As in neoliberal Romania, privatization also contributed to massive lay-offs of millions of workers and their mass migration from the countryside to the cities. However, some of these lay-offs were offset by government initiative, and they ultimately contributed to the consolidation of competitiveness for state-owned enterprises (Dunford 44). Unlike in Romania, where an anti-corruption campaign mainly prompted the arrest of a few important business and political figures, the tough intervention of the state in the crackdown on financial crime and real-estate speculation assured that Chinese reforms did not lead to the societal violence and severe inequality that they produced in Romania. That the CCP intervened despite the criticism of economic experts, who had deemed these measures suicidal, is proof not only of the continuing authoritarianism of the Party, but also of the more humane and balanced control of the ongoing developmental process.

Postsocialist Transnationalism

Because in this book I have so far followed a comparative approach between two national cinemas that, I argue, should be culturally and theoretically linked, it is vital to parallel the "return to Europe" argument advanced by scholars of Romanian cinema to the "transnationalism" promulgated in the new school of Chinese-language cinema. Film scholars Gina Marchetti and David Bordwell have certainly held very distinct theoretical positions when it comes to their stance on Chinese cinema. However, there is a common thread running through their theorizing practices – namely, that of seeing Chinese film originating in the People's Republic of China as well as in the Pacific Rim enclaves of Hong Kong, Taiwan and Singapore as sharing similarities that make them ultimately products of an overarching Sinophone culture.[1]

No argument there. However, in a vein similar to the tendency of Europeanizing Romanian cinema, these scholars then proceeded to integrate both the fifth- and the sixth-generation mainland Chinese directors into the rejuvenation drives that birthed both the Taiwan and the Hong Kong New Waves of the mid-1990s and early 1980s, respectively.[2] As such, Gina Marchetti has argued that Chinese-language cinema *in toto* should not only be regarded as cohesive across the ideological divides splitting the mainland from the Pacific Rim, but that it also should be seen as the linchpin that could unhinge Hollywood from its dominant position in film studies. Under this

[1] Chris Berry is one of the few scholars of Chinese cinema who has taken a more cautious approach towards the homogenizing drive of all Chinese-language film. In his comprehensive *China on Screen* (co-authored with Mary Farquhar), the authors have claimed that nationalism, particularly that of mainland cinema, is not as dead as partisans of transnationalism would like it to be.

[2] There exists some confusion as to whether the New Wave identifies with the fifth or the sixth generation of Chinese directors. In this book, the New Wave indicates the generation of directors whose work reached its apex in the 1990s, while the subsequent one will be referred to as the sixth generation.

banner, she has promoted transculturalism for its otherwise perfectly honorable mission of upholding an interstitial identity that is different from that of Western film. She has identified this amorphous identity particularly in dramas of Asian immigration to the West, naming as representative for this subgenre the films of Clara Law, Stanley Kwan, Evans Chan and even Ann Hui, among others (Marchetti 1998).[3]

While this subgenre undoubtedly exists and while a proliferation of immigration films in the 1990s endorses such a categorization,[4] it is problematic to include this cinema under the heading of transnationalism. Even though Marchetti's arguments are that transnationalism stems from what she has called "uncertain and fluctuating" identities (Marchetti 1998), it does not take into account that all flux and flow of identitary politics migrates in one direction only – from the Third towards the First World, therefore legitimating the power of transnational capital more than that of identity. Finally, this leaves a major question unanswered, one which this book takes up: what is the fate – in the transnational framework – of the project of Eurasian socialism, that Big Other of postsocialist politics (which formerly was tied to its own network of transcultural ideological partners), other than its relegation, under the banner of propaganda, to the dustbin of history?

If the above theorists have not answered this question, David Bordwell has done so even less. While attempting to knock (for good or bad reasons) cultural studies off their pedestal for their preference to assert that subjectivity and locality can challenge universality in audience reception, Bordwell has succeeded in ultimately preserving the Eurocentrism of what he has proudly called 1975 Film Theory (Bordwell 1996). The Bordwellian position has been reinforced by what the American film scholar has identified as a common Hong Kong *and* Western narratological style, in which Hong Kong filmmakers follow rather than boycott or resist Hollywood (Bordwell 2000). This position implies that mainland Chinese cinema would follow the course of Hong Kong and, subsequently, that of Hollywood.

If other Sinophone cinemas tend to follow the Hong Kong mode of narration, this is possible only because Hollywood is taken as the standard against which all Sinophone cinema is measured. For a narratology built on the tripartite structure of character/plot/dialogue, which is fundamental to Bordwell's theory commonly referred to in film studies as cognitivism (Bordwell 1996), never could Hollywood be seen as one genre among many; and never shall Hollywood be challenged by non-Hollywood. Thus, under the noble goal of pointing to what makes us all the same – which is my watered-down version of Bordwell's cognitivism – the American theorist reinstates the legitimacy

---

[3] Evans Chan's films, particularly *To Liv(e)*, are an exception. However, in negotiating a particular Hong Kong identity, so Marchetti has argued, they equally stand for a way of countering Hollywood's hegemony.

[4] I particularly refer to films that Marchetti has held important for redefining Sinophone cinemas from the late 1980s onwards, such as *Full Moon in New York* (Stanley Kwan, 1989) and *Song of Exile* (Ann Hui, 1990).

of what ultimately is a capitalist way of both production and reception being perpetuated on a global scale.

In the current condition of the Eurasian postsocialist Other having been banished by the leveling discourse of capitalism, the question that seems relevant is the following: how can we talk of difference, of cultural discontinuity, of alternative Otherness in a post-Said, postethnic-informed context? And although, incidentally, postmodern postcolonial discourse does have an answer to this question – as evident in tropes such as "diversity," "multiculturalism," and, more theoretically, "hybridity" – I argue that such a solution is no solution at all and, as we have seen from socialist film examples, definitely not for the postsocialist world, which is confronted with its own specific problems. By subsuming the East/West reintegration project to the bigger one of postmodern fragmentation originating in Western academia, we are faced with more monolithic thinking than its opposite and desirous plurimorphism. In other words, by leaving out the specificity of postsocialism, Marchetti's transculturalism forces us to apply methods of assimilating Eurasia to a geography and chronology that are otherwise forcefully modernized following a "First World" model. Critical theorist Fredric Jameson has made clear, from an assumed American perspective, that national literature cannot be assimilated to some vague transnationalist project, because "I don't see how a first-world intellectual can avoid this operation without falling back into some general liberal and humanistic universalism: it seems to me that one of our basic political tasks lies precisely in the ceaseless effort to remind the American public of the radical difference of other national situations" (Jameson 1986, 77).

Since the inability to theorize the Other from a specific postsocialist position has forced academia to capitulate to the (barely theorized) hegemon of plurality, yet another binary was unwillingly created – that of accepting or rejecting plurality and fragmentation, with the First World perpetuating the binary of an enlightened versus traditional worldview. This discourse further robs the subaltern of speech, even though it belongs to the transnationalist philosophy which seeks to incorporate the Other into a particular schema of thought propagated by the West. And since this binary eschews the problem of difference, what follows for the Other, yet again, is either self-Orientalization, cultural nationalism, or fascism – outcomes that are only too familiar at the close of a convoluted postcolonial twentieth century.

To invoke Marcel Mauss' paradigm, despite their allegedly propagandistic messages and uneven representation of reality, in their performative way socialist realist films represented an offer that led to a *real* exchange between masses and leader. As long as the authoritative symbols (constative in the first period, performative in the second) were accepted by the masses, then the masses were literally unaffected by ideology, so much so that personal life could be entirely divorced from politics, as seen in Mungiu's *4, 3, 2*. If performing socialism represented Romania's or China's external validation of their newfound dignity in the socialist-era films of the 1960s, then their lack of dignity in postsocialism becomes a cry for the validation of their subaltern status.

This is particularly relevant in China, where the former performative function of film was shifted from negotiating the polemics between leader and masses (think of the impassioned exchanges in the press pertaining to *Early Spring in February*) to performing a vision of China for Western audiences, as most of the writers critical of the fifth generation have pointed out (Grossman 2009, Kaplan 1993, Jinhua 1995). In other words, the former ambassadorial role of film in China and Romania under postsocialism became that of selling Eastern subalternity to Western audiences. From this angle, it would be hard not to subsume the Romanian and Chinese films to be discussed in the following two chapters under an altogether distinct universe of marginalization and subordination. In this case, Jameson's warning could apply not only to specific "national situations," but to Eurasian subalternity *tout court*, whether one talks about film or literature.

The Fifth Generation in China

In the long aftermath of the Cultural Revolution – namely, in the Deng Xiaoping era of Reform and Opening Up – the films of fifth-generation Chinese directors epitomized by the 1982 graduating class of Zhang Yimou, Chen Kaige and Tian Zhuangzhuang undoubtedly achieved world acclaim. A lot of ink has been spilled (both in China and elsewhere) to pinpoint whether these Chinese directors, following what David Bordwell has promoted as cognitivism, ran counter to or followed the basic Hollywood formulaic plot structure and mode of narration. Although questions as to whether *Farewell My Concubine* (*Ba wang bie ji*, Chen Kaige, 1992), *The Blue Kite* (*Lan feng zheng*, Tian Zhuangzhuang, 1993), or *To Live* (*Huo zhe*, Zhang Yimou, 1994) orientalized China for the West are perfectly appropriate and entirely pertinent, few people have asked whether the very themes that these films' directors employed are not equally problematic. It seems that the question one should ask is not whether these groundbreaking films used Western methods to advance their own goals, or whether they were really truthful to Chinese sensibilities, but whether these films are new or old – that is, whether they are as innovative in their proposed thematic offer as they purport to be. The relevant question is therefore: how do these films compare not to the West, but to their revolutionary-era precursors, which filled Maoist screens to the brim with alleged propaganda and didacticism?

From the many examples that the New Wave of fifth-generation directors put at our disposal, I will restrict the following discussion to two of Zhang Yimou's so-called historical trilogy films, which the up-and-coming director made in the early 1990s: *Ju Dou* (1990) and *Raise the Red Lantern* (*Da hong denglong gaogao gua*, 1991).[5] I will compare these films' themes with Jun Li's *Serfs* (*Nong nu*, 1963) and Wang Bin's *The White Haired Girl* (1950), which are but two of the many instances of propaganda that Maoist cinema produced between 1949 and the Cultural Revolution. Both *Ju Dou* and *Raise the Red*

[5] The third film of the trilogy is *The Story of Qiu Ju* (*Qiu ju da guansi*, 1992).

Lantern take place in the still feudal China of the republican era,[6] and in their otherwise complex plots they condemn the old remains of the social system in place since the Qing dynasty. In that sense, they not only reprove the blatant encroachments on the rights of women, but also resemble a long list of feminist films promoted by Mao's government in the mid-1950s and early 1960s.

In *Ju Dou*, Zhang Yimou describes the tribulations of the eponymous heroine (played by a sensual Gong Li) who, unable to hide an illicit affair with the nephew of her leprosy-ridden husband, is led to destruction by the stringencies of an unjust, misogynistic and male-centered social system. The cruel chains of patriarchy also feature as a main theme in *Raise the Red Lantern*, a film in which the same director (once again employing Gong Li in the main role) champions the emancipation of women. Set in a household of surviving aristocracy and at a time when sexual practices hailing from a patriarchal past continue to rule the behavior of the characters, the plot better evidences the constrictions and inhumanity of the concubine system while condemning polygamy and abuse.

Following the analyses of cultural theorist Rey Chow and film scholar Gina Marchetti, the approximate critical consensus is that, in Marchetti's words, "Zhang Yimou's films cross borders because of their ability to shift gears as they circulate on different screens globally" (Marchetti 2006, 4). She has further quoted Chow as stating that Zhang Yimou's films "wish to liberate Chinese women, which seems to be the content shift into the liberation of China which shifts into the liberation of the image of China on film, which shifts into the liberation of China on film in the international culture market, and so on" (Chow, quoted in Marchetti 2006, 4). In a discourse resembling Nasta's take on New Wave Romanian films, the implied statement in both theories seems to be that socialism has oppressed women, and that the political system during Mao's reign did not allow directors to express their repressed claims for justice and equality. Only the innovative fifth generation was finally able to do so by condemning the values of socialism.

A cursory look at the motifs employed in Zhang's trilogy allows one to observe that the alleged goals of the liberation of women onscreen have, not surprisingly, been a mainstay of the entire period of socialist cinema. Indeed, it seems that in Zhang's films the socialist realist and revolutionary romanticist eras were cosmeticized to agree with the aesthetics of what Bordwell has called cognitivism. Moreover, it seems that these films resignified the very values that socialism has vigorously and relentlessly pursued since the 1949 revolution. The question is: were these films internationally successful because of their message? Because of their Westernized look? Or, in fact, because they were equated with the gradual abandonment of the Communist political ideology that accompanied the transition to a market economy in Deng Xiaoping's era of Reform and Opening Up?

---

[6] Although China was supposed to modernize after the republican revolution led by Sun Yat Sen, which toppled the Qing dynasty in 1911, feudal values remained strongly imbricated in society until the Communist revolution of 1949.

A movie that several authors have closely associated with the liberating ideology of socialism (Berry and Farquhar 2006, Lu 2007, Chenaktshang 2003), yet inextricable from the propaganda of the CCP, *Serfs* is a captivity narrative of sorts, which focuses on the life story of a male slave. The film describes the Communist annexation of Tibet, which is portrayed as a brutal, class-based society where those at the bottom of the social hierarchy suffer from abuse and even die from mistreatment – that is, until the liberating Red Army arrives. Although the film clearly has a propagandist message, the political element is subdued by placing the issue of slavery at the center of the story. Framing the male slave Champa as the victim of a cruel social system via close-ups and camera angles meant to reflect his suffering, Jun accentuates the inhumane treatment of slaves and focuses the narrative on the progressive changes brought about by the modernization of the strict hierarchical structures of the Buddhist kingdom.

This is the reason why Tian Zhuangzhuang, after a full two decades, chose to film his much-celebrated *Horse Thief (Dao ma zei*, 1986) as a replay of *Serfs*, without however offering the rather optimistic ending provided by its earlier "propagandist" counterpart. By focusing on the details and subjective experiences of his slave protagonist, Tian revalidates Jun Li's 1963 film while extracting the propaganda from one side of the equation (the annexation) and leaving the other intact (the social issue). Tian's use of dreamlike camerawork and extreme long shots to underscore the vastness of the Tibetan plateau in proportion to the diminutive condition of the characters constitute an essential difference between the earlier version and that of the fifth-generation director, and it brings out Tian's distinctly personal style that would henceforth become his signature.

The White Haired Girl, a mainstay of Communist "propaganda," was filmed in two different formats: a simple narrative in 1950 and a revolutionary ballet in 1971, at the time of Jiang Qing's monopoly of the arts during the Cultural Revolution. As discussed above, it depicts the forced separation of Xier, a young girl, from her family in a feudal era plagued by infant mortality, disease and slavery. Deciding to run away from her feudal master as well as her fiancé, Xier hides in a mountain temple where, after her hair turns gray from lack of light, she is transformed into a ghost-like apparition of her former self. When many years later her fiancé turns up at the head of a small PLA detachment looking for her, Xier comes to understand the liberatory power of Communism, after a transformative experience. A centerpiece of Maoist cinema, the story had deep reverberations which alluded to the cruelty of class relations extant in the pre-communist era.

Early Chinese Communist writers and modernists such as Lu Xun frequently criticized feudal times, and their portrayals were never too far from the truth, even though, as in Wang's film, the sheer brutality yet realistic aspect of the events described – a father selling his daughter into prostitution and slavery – seem preposterous in the modern era. While these films have been closely associated with both socialist realism and Communist propaganda by a large number of Western scholars and thereafter stigmatized for their ideological underpinnings, fifth-generation cinema promoted essentially the same themes (and, in Tian's case, almost the same plot) as their predecessors. Moreover, while both movements promoted the universal values of human rights and the emancipation of women, Zhang Yimou and the New Wave have been critically acclaimed in the West while socialist realism has remained vilified.

An interesting coda to *Serfs* is that in many ways the film redoubles the aesthetics of Romanian socialist realism. Jun's use of classic *mise-en-scène* and effective camera angles to highlight the suffering of the protagonist Champa brings to mind the narrative and cinematography of the Romanian film *The Thistles of the Baragan* (*Ciulinii Bărăganului*, Vitanidis and Daquin, 1958) (Figures 5.1 and 5.2). Based on the novel of prominent leftist writer Panait Istrati, who is known to have said to Stalin while visiting the Soviet Union that he could see the broken eggs necessary for building socialism but not yet his famous omelet, the film recounts the tragic destiny of a family who strives for a better life in an inhospitable and arid region of the country, which ultimately puts them in conflict with their feudal masters who then proceed to massacre them. Reflecting the cruel historical realities of the 1907 peasant revolt in Romania (which itself was styled on Russia's 1905 revolution), the film effectively combines the classic *mise-en-scènes* of the earthen peasant houses' dark interiors with extreme long shots of the deserted area to show the sad fate of the protagonists and to denounce the murder of over 10,000 peasants at the hands of the bourgeois government.

Analyzing the way in which New Wave films compare to their pre-revolutionary and Maoist counterparts in the way in which *Horse Thief* compares to *Serfs*, Chris Berry and Mary Farquhar have focused on three ideologies, three ages and three actresses: Ruang Lingyu, Xie Fang and Gong Li, representing leftist utopianism, revolutionary romanticism and sexual liberation, respectively. In discussing the contemporary figure of Gong Li – Zhang's favorite choice of heroine in all films of the trilogy – Farquhar and Berry have arrived at the conclusion that, "[i]n fact, there is nothing new at all in this rebelliousness itself, and by the late twentieth century the trope that

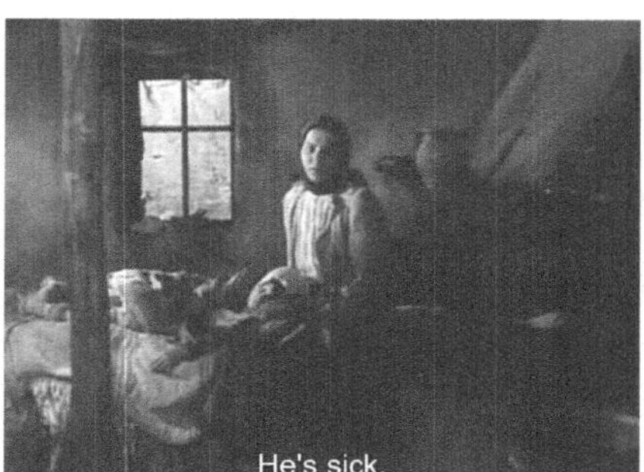

Figures 5.1 and 5.2 Similar compositions in Jun Li's *Serfs* and Vitanidis's and Daquin's *The Thistles of the Baragan*.

Gong Li cites here was already hackneyed" (Berry and Farquhar 2006, 125). The authors then go on to argue that Gong Li's manifestation of a brand of feminism stronger than that of her predecessors' is reified through Zhang's liberty to portray the liberation of sexuality onscreen, particularly of feminine sexuality – an action totally absent in Ruang Lingyu's and Xie Fang's earlier sublimation of sexuality into utopian or revolutionary zeal. While agreeing with this reading, the question I ask is: how empowering is it for an audience (this time the Chinese, not the Western) to find its lasciviousness satisfied by Gong Li's sexual screen liberation; by the fact that, as Berry and Farquhar have put it, "in each film she seeks out another male sexual partner to help liberate her from these patriarchs?" (126). Does this translate into the post-socialist sexual liberation of Chinese women? Or does it simply attract the attention of Western capital, which could finally reel in the rewards of universal cognitivism by allowing that Chinese women, too – Communist as they may be – have sex, and that they can be seductive *à la* Gong Li while doing it?[7]

Berry and Farquhar have not made it a secret that the sexual liberation of Chinese women that these films allegedly capture uses the dubious trope of the (re)sexualization of post-Maoist women. Using Laura Mulvey's famous *cri-du-guerre* against the exploitation of the feminine presence onscreen, which is treated ambiguously in the films, the authors have recognized the objectification of Gong Li. This amounts to nothing but a paradox of which the authors are very well aware, particularly when citing the many instances of accusation brought against Zhang's objectification of Gong (126–27). However, citing Rey Chow, the authors have defended Gong Li's screen persona as empowered through the reverse gaze that she employs to continuously challenge patriarchy and, therefore, have rejected Mulvey's pinning of women as objects of the gaze as applicable in this case. Moreover, they imply that Gong's return of the gaze – her looking into the camera – represents a defiant act against the Communist Party itself. Despite their argument, the question remains: do audiences (Chinese audiences, and primarily Chinese women) identify with this return of the gaze? Do they derive empowerment from it, or does the gaze simply notify the West that postsocialist Chinese women are now, for all intents and purposes, sexually free at last? And are they free of traditional patriarchy or free of Communism?

Of course, it is not Chinese women whom these films wish to liberate, nor China as a cultural-political trope, but Chinese capitalism redoubling the acceptable message of Western feminism applied to Chinese women, or soon-to-be *ex-Communist* Chinese women. If it were women alone who mattered for international audiences, Jiang Qing's model operas should be even more passionately defended than fifth-generation films, as the messages of both *The Red Detachment of Women* as well as *The White Haired Girl* were not only more revolutionary than Western feminism, but also strongly egalitarian at that.

[7] See also Andrew Grossman for a criticism of Zhang Yimou's 'selling' of cosmeticized suffering for Western audiences (Grossman 2009). Other authors who have engaged in this debate are E. Ann Kaplan and Dai Jinhua.

Had the works of the red screen not been so deeply politicized, had they not been read solely in an anti-Communist key, some of these works might have found an appropriate place in the history of (non-)Western cinema.

As this brief analysis has shown, fifth-generation Chinese films paradoxically reiterate the liberatory message of socialism by employing the same narrative structures on which socialist realism itself was based, finding in the cliché antagonism between conservatives and progressives (or in Gong Li's case, her opposition to patriarchy) the power to renew the voice of film after the "ten years of chaos." Only the dubiousness of this renewal needs to be brought into question as the socialist-era equation of "despicable old" versus "progressive new" is *de facto* replaced by the fifth generation with the antagonisms "despicable old" versus "sex," or, even more literally, "no more Party in films" versus "sex." And this only leads to an adjacent question to be debated in a very different context – namely, one which objectively evaluates the superiority of performed sexual liberation as that of performed social equality.

In conclusion, the empowerment that fifth-generation films purportedly promoted is not necessarily deceptive, but not as innovative as it may seem. As evident from the analysis of socialist realist films in Romania and the early production of *The Bridge* in Mao's China, Communist audiences equally participated in a *critical* reception of socialist films, and they did so even more when *contesting* what they saw, or privately rejecting the propaganda while retaining the enjoyment of the drama. Additionally, with the legitimation that directors such as Zhang Yimou received from the West, fifth-generation films ended up reinforcing not necessarily the villainy of feudalism, but the ability of film to act as a weapon against social injustice. This was a trope that both capitalism and Communism had long used. For that reason, Chinese New Wave films not so much empower audiences, as they forcibly shift the position of the audience from that of critical assessors of the "propagandistic" image to that of "brainwashed consumers" of this image, sexualized for emancipatory purposes as this image may be. Paradoxically, if there is any "brainwashing" in socialism, it seems to arrive in *post-* rather than *high* Maoist China.

Reprising the tone of "scar literature" from their predecessors in the 1980s, fifth-generation directors would go on to produce *Farewell my Concubine*, *To Live* and *The Blue Kite*, which go beyond the mere condemnation of feudalism and mount a courageous criticism of the Cultural Revolution, as well as of the Maoist period in general. However, this does not represent a complete novelty, either, because *Farewell my Concubine* reprises certain themes and the narrative style of Jin Xie's *Two Stage Sisters* (1964), while *The Blue Kite* borrows its melodramatic panache from the pre-Maoist-era classic *Spring River Flows East* (*Yi jiang chun shui xiang dong liu*, Cai Chusheng, Zheng Junli, 1947). The fifth-generation films are also very much indebted to the Lao She adaptation of the three-generation saga *Teahouse* (*Cha guan*), filmed by Maoist-era director Tian Xie in 1982, while *To Live* derives its epic structure from *Life of a Beijing Policeman* (*Wo zhe yi bei* zi, Hui Shi, 1950). What a side-by-side comparison of these films reveals, as the fifth-generation directors themselves have agreed,[8] is that China's New Wave *redoubles* rather than *counters* the history of socialist film, by recycling the antagonism of earlier dramas contesting monarchic or nationalist injustice, and by directing it – albeit in a veiled way – against the asperities of the communist regime.

Rather than "freeing" the image of China, as Marchetti and Chow have claimed, Chinese New Wave films uphold rather than condemn the ideals of Communism. Fifth-generation directors wittily repackaged these ideals and made them more palatable for Western audiences while adapting them to the aesthetic of Hollywood, without however abandoning – as Boris Groys has prophesied for postsocialism – the premise of socialist realism. Let us examine whether this reiteration is a phenomenon strictly pertinent to Chinese postsocialist realities, or whether this constitutes a paradigmatic shift describing postsocialist Romanian cinema as well.

The Anticommunist Fiction Film

Even though they are roughly ten years apart, the Romanian cinema of the 1990s is comparable not to China's fifth generation, but to the films made in China in the 1980s, by directors belonging to the fourth generation. While Chinese directors spoke all the bitterness they could as they revisited the Cultural Revolution, it is only in the postsocialist 1990s that Romanian filmmakers started to "talk back" at Communism, and they did so immediately after the 1989 revolution, by severely condemning the "obsessive decade" of the 1950s and its aftermath in a brooding, dark filmmaking style.

However, unlike their Chinese counterparts, who were using the liberties of Deng's Reform and Opening Up era to vent their frustration against the misuse of public policy, under the anticommunist star, most 1990s Romanian directors virulently condemned the country's past overall, while overlooking all the economic and social progress that Romania had made in forty years of socialism. Therefore, at a time when Zhang Yimou and Chen Kaige were breaking world-records for Chinese cinema by finding distribution abroad, Romanian cinema was caught in the quagmire of self-victimization. The most blatant and relevant example of this occurrence can best be seen in Nicolae Mărgineanu's *Somewhere in the East* (*Undeva în est*, 1991), one of the first productions to be filmed after the 1989 revolution and the forerunner of anticommunist films *par excellence*.

Somewhere in the East (*Undeva în est*, 1991) is an adaptation of Augustin Buzura's socialist-era 1970s novel *Faces of Silence* (*Fețele tăcerii*), by the poster child of anticommunist cinema, Nicolae Mărgineanu. If the novel is about the nationalization of a mountain village in the 1950s, in which both party cadres and laymen come across as complex characters who oftentimes engage in theoretical polemics predicated on their opposing social and ideological

[8] A most useful source allowing us to hear the fifth-generation directors themselves speak of their choice of themes is Tony Rayns's documentary *New Chinese Cinema*, made in 1989.

backgrounds, the film simplifies the conflict between the two sides, turning complexity into caricature and demonizing Communism via cliché characterizations. Although the film was an abandoned socialist-era project, which ran into trouble with censorship (Toderici 2017, 187), in the postsocialist revival of the shelved film the Communist characters are rendered exaggeratedly abject, being portrayed either as drinking without measure or eating copious amounts of food while speaking with a drunken slur, or as unnecessarily devious and cunning. Furthermore, they are seen engaging in violent rape onscreen, just like Crețu in *Reverberates the Valley*, despite the fact that, naturally, none such scenes were present in the book published under socialism. Female characters are similarly transformed: despite being a militant and a feminist in the novel, a female Communist Party member is turned into a downright slut in the film, when she is depicted as seducing and having sex with a soldier, just as a military ambush is about to take place on the lionized Iron Guard sympathizers. It appears that, alongside rewriting socialist history, Mărgineanu also wiped out whatever progress forty years of socialism had brought for women's liberation in Romania.

Reversing the 1950s trend, *Somewhere in the East* turned the models of socialist realism upside down. If the bourgeois engineer in *The Bridge* or Nikki and Crețu in *Reverberates the Valley* lacked proper characterization and appeared sketchy and superficial, the same treatment was applied to Party officials and sympathizers in anticommunist films. Lacking complexity and depth, the communists overnight were turned into the bourgeois villains of the socialist realist period.

Other aspects of the 1970s novel also fell victim to this trend. For example, Buzura's intellectual debate about the viability of implementing Communist ideology in an impoverished country such as Romania – which had center-stage in the novel – is forgotten and replaced with an assumption that Communism is an evil ideology. This is taken for granted by all the characters in the film, to such a degree that even the Communists themselves appear unconvinced of their beliefs and only perfunctorily engaged in their duties. Needless to say, the obverse happens with Iron Guard sympathizers: focusing solely on the juicy conflict between rightists and leftists (not unlike the Communist filmmakers did in *Alarm in the Mountains* from the opposite angle), Mărgineanu whitewashes the fascist sympathies of anticommunist fighters, to the point of glamorizing their characters.

While the exteriors in *Somewhere in the East* are slightly over-exposed for dramatic effect, the interiors are usually dark, gloomy and lit by dim light sources. For instance, in a scene in which a legionnaire's son is hidden in the basement by his father so as to escape the fury of the Communists, a single beacon of light protrudes through a miniscule window above him, to crudely symbolize his family's religious belief in salvation. In fact, Mărgineanu acquired something of a renown for making popular religious-themed films in postsocialism, such as *Bless You, Prison* (*Binecuvântată fii închisoare*, 2002), about a female dissident of the early Communist regime who has a religious awakening while incarcerated, and the biopic *The Cardinal* (*Cardinalul*, 2019), about the arrest of Catholic priests who refused conversion to the Christian Orthodox faith.

Whereas the detail of a single source of light in dark interiors is a direct inheritance from socialist realist films, the overall gloomy ambiance in anti-communist films is an influence not only from the above-mentioned social realist dramas of the 1980s, but also from a new artistic current emerging during the Perestroika period in the Soviet Union. Dubbed *Chernukha Cinema* for the overall gloominess of its cinematography, as well as for the dilapidated interiors and cityscapes that signaled the widespread poverty of the 1980s, this style was made famous, among others, by Sergei Solovyov's *Assa* (1987), Vasili Pichul's *Little Vera* (*Malenkaya Vera*, 1988) and even Sergei Bodrov's *Freedom is Paradise* (*Svoboda eto rai*, 1989), some of which were received to popular acclaim in Romania during the time (Ţion 2020). This style was adopted by Romanian directors because they could easily verify that Communist policies in the Soviet Union of the mid-1980s had engendered a society and type of affect easily recognizable across the entire Eastern Bloc. While the Soviet *Chernukha* equally influenced the Romanian New Wave that would emerge in the 2000s, anticommunist films of the 1990s would only inherit from *Chernukha* their penchant for using a dark ambience while being less realistic and minimalist than their late-Soviet predecessors.

The legacy of *Somewhere in the East* for subsequent political films is primarily a mode of narration in which Communists would continue to be depicted in the style intoned by Mărgineanu – as whores, villains and drunken scum. This is applicable to anticommunist productions ranging from the older *The Oak* (Balanţa, 1992), directed by the helmer of *Reenactment*, Lucian Pintilie, to the more recent *Portrait of the Fighter as a Young Man* (*Portretul luptătorui la tinereţe*, Popescu, 2010), which goes as far as to indirectly glamorize anti-Semitism. Not unlike the anticommunist partisans glorified in *Somewhere in the East*, Constantin Popescu, the director of *Portrait* had to contend with the correlation between the partisans' anticommunism and their pro-fascist sympathies inherited from the Iron Guard. Popescu aimed to shoot a realist film which faithfully portrayed the lifestyle of militants who scuffled with Communist authorities in the remote mountain areas where they found refuge from the law. However, the film ended up contrasting the purported bravery of the fighters to the despicable behavior of the people's militia who, after being in hot pursuit of the outlaws, eventually capture them at its conclusion. Stressing the religious behavior of the partisans in contrast to the atheism and purported anti-humanism of the militia, the film not merely reprises Mărgineanu's religious propaganda from *Somewhere in the East*, but, more importantly, it introduces subtextual fascist propaganda by way of glorifying figures such as Gavrilă Ogoranu, the film's hero, who was an overt sympathizer of the Third Reich. Falling barely short of exoticizing the country's fascist past in order to sell anticommunism to the West, when he submitted *Portrait* to compete at the Berlin International Film Festival, Popescu came under fire for whitewashing the rightist tendencies of his partisans, thus promoting an anti-Semitic and racist organization (Blaga 2010). Although the film was supposed to have a sequel centered on a female anticommunist fighter, that sequel never was made after the controversy.

Somewhere in the East was quickly followed by *The Oak*, yet another adaptation of a socialist-era novel produced in 1992. Having been criticized for *Reenactment* and for having made yet another picture deemed subversive by the censorship in the 1980s, Lucian Pintilie felt particularly in the right to "speak bitterness" about the old regime. Although the novel that he adapted steered mostly clear of political implications, *The Oak* was suffused with anticommunist whoopla from the very first scene, in which we are introduced to Nela, a no-nonsense woman in her thirties, who watches a home movie with her sick father in bed. What first appears to be a nostalgic act spent in voluntary withdrawal turns out to be an ambivalent mixture of pride and resentment which Nela feels for her father, who literally dies onscreen from a medical condition. The forbidding interiors littered with cigarette butts and dotted with dilapidated appliances make Nela's depression worse when we understand that her father was a hero in the early Communist movement, and his specter is there to haunt her for the remainder of the film. This proves to be accurate because the regime which her father helped put in power seems to only bring her suffering and misfortune. As Nela moves to take a job in a highly polluting chemical plant far away from home, she experiences rape at the hand of a group of miners and is hospitalized. In the hospital she meets an energetic young doctor whose resolution is to change the inefficient medical system, and Nela indulges in an amorous if chaotic relationship with him. Apart from making us witnesses to an unsuccessful operation that the doctor performs on a terminally ill patient, their relationship is mostly a pretext for Pintilie to show the couple roaming the country from one location to the next without apparent rhyme or reason, while the events they experience grow in intensity, from mildly distressing to highly disturbing.

The last of these overly dramatic events is a full-scale assault staged by the Securitate on a group of fascists who sequester a bus. Similar to the ambush against the Iron Guards in *Somewhere in the East*, even though the fascistic allegiance of the criminals is not clearly shown and even though, more importantly, they take a group of small children hostage, the secret police and the army massacre the captives in cold blood, the children included, in what appears to be an unmotivated act of pure evil. This leads to a confusing denouement in which Nela, now manic and exasperated, finds refuge under a magnificent oak tree that, in counterpoint to her feelings, is filmed in the romantic shades of sundown. There she uses a pistol taken from one of the victims to threaten her partner, only to nervously decide at the last moment that she in fact wants to have a child with him. A symbolic death-and-rebirth motif among pessimism and chaos, this is too little too late to alter the doomsday scenario that defines an otherwise onerous plot.

While following the couple as they travel the countryside, Pintilie's camerawork is highly conventional. What shocked audiences in the third year of democracy was not the film's style but its use of vulgarities such as onscreen vomiting, urinating and foul language, a practice that would become familiar to many postsocialist productions thereafter. What made the film memorable for the critics, however, was the nervous, almost exaggerated acting style of the two leads, who used their adrenaline-powered momentum to credibly portray an unconventional relationship. It is also noteworthy that Pintilie, following his denunciation of the proletariat's decline in *Reenactment*, does not hold back when painting yet another unsympathetic portrayal of the working class. The novel features a scene describing the difficult conditions of travel on an overcrowded train filled with refugees fleeing the floods that took the country by surprise in the 1970s. Referencing the 1990 events in which miners were called upon to violently suppress anti-government protests against the socialist regime that had survived the revolution, Pintilie imagines a scene in which the same train is being assaulted by miners who show their savagery by breaking windows and destroying furniture. An after-effect of what Popa has identified as the demonized working class of Pintitlie's *Reenactment*, the scene directly connects the debased masses produced by Communist ideology to the decreased standard of living in the country, thus contributing to a bourgeois reading of Romanian culture.

Film scholars have praised the film for its novelties, seeing how it counterbalanced the socialist-era discourse that glamorized Communist characters, even if not all socialist-era films idealized Communists, as visible in *The Power and the Truth*, for example. Despite this, Andreescu has considered that the film's task was that of "healing the social and traumatic scars" of socialism (Andreescu 2013, 116), while Nasta has praised the film's anticommunist intent, which percolates, according to her, to the minutest aspects of the *mise-en-scène*. Concerning the banal opening in which Nela watches home movies of her family with her father next to her, Nasta has believed that "the heroine is subjectively re-infusing her hate and disgust for the Communist regime into reinvented images from her childhood" (Nasta 2013, 100). It is not clear why these images are reinvented, since they play on the screen in front of Nela, nor why she infuses them with hate, since they seem to reference a commonplace nostalgia. Other critics, however, have condemned the simplicity of treating the past in a monovalent key. Turcuş, for example, has called the bus scene "a gratuitous expression of Communist evil" (Turcuş 2017, 169), while Iulia Popovici has criticized the rape scene, correctly pointing out that, instead of focusing on the sufferings of the heroine, Pintilie lionizes the doctor who comes to Nela's rescue (Popovici 2017, 139).

Ironically, there exists an earlier version of *The Oak*, made by an iconic director of the socialist period who also opposed the regime, albeit tacitly. Alexandru Tatos adapted *Red Apples* (*Mere roşii*, 1976) from an earlier draft of the story,[9] which focused on the character of the young doctor, instead of that of his girlfriend, and on the conflict between him and an older hospital manager. The plot is centered on the medical operation which the doctor

[9] In fact, Ion Băieşu, a prolific writer, adapted the screenplay for *Mere roşii* from his own novella *Thirty-Eight Degrees Point Two* in the 1960s and then in the 1980s developed it into the novel *Balanţa*, which narrates a similar story.

insists he perform on a cancer patient (the only aspect that Pintilie chose to retain in his later adaptation), but he runs into conflict with the career-oriented manager, who also is a rigid man of traditional persuasion. The conflict between old and new and the call for change in the workplace makes *Red Apples* similar to *Breaking with Old Ideas*. Much like Li's students, the enthusiastic doctor asks that the medical profession renew itself according to up-to-date research findings in the field, and that the medical staff be less apathetic in their work. The fact that the patient dies at the end curbs some of the doctor's enthusiasm but does not prove him entirely wrong. The premise that hospitals were in need of retechnologization, and that medical staff was unprofessional is surprisingly honest and truthfully reflects the day-to-day reality of the 1970s. While it opposes blind volunteerism, much like *The Power and the Truth*, the film accepts the need for change voiced by the younger generation and agrees that technology is not up to par with the required professional standards.

In comparison to its postsocialist counterpart, *Red Apples* is more ambivalent than *The Oak*. Instead of deploring Communism *in toto*, Tatos' debut makes a dialectical claim about socialist reality, which balances the advantages and disadvantages of the government's successes in establishing new institutional structures in the country. For this reason, *Red Apples* reinforces the Hegelian thesis according to which progress results from an active negotiation between a thesis – the young doctor's intent to carry out a difficult operation – and its antithesis – the negation that such an operation is possible, as enunciated by the traditionalist manager. While *Red Apples* is different from its 1992 remake, *The Oak* is also a far cry from Chinese films adapted from scar literature. Despite having been tainted by painful memories, the directors of *River without Buoys*, and even the more formulaic *Hibiscus Town* (*Fu rong zhen*, Xie Jin, 1987), for example, portray anti-rightist characters and their victims realistically, making the historical situation appear true to the complexity of ideological beliefs battling for prominence in those troubling times.

Unlike *Horse Thief*, which complemented rather than opposed the message of the earlier and more propagandistic *Serfs*, *The Oak* almost entirely ignored the positive thrust of *Red Apples*. Although both *Horse Thief* and *The Oak* are based on a certain form of "scar literature" inspired by the recent past, the transformations of early leftist films into their 1990s successors in China and Romania took very different paths. While the power of fifth-generation directors in China partially came from improving the material that was made available to them by their predecessors, Romanian postsocialist cinema chose to negate its prior history. This practice, as Poenaru has warned, disallowed audiences from accessing the complexity of the past in favor of promoting historical accounts rewritten and resignified solely from an anticommunist perspective (Poenaru 2017).

Another film from the early 1990s which continued to promote the demonical treatment of the past with minimal concessions to objectivity is *The Earth's Most Beloved Son* (*Cel mai iubit dintre pământeni*, Marinescu, 1993). An adaptation from Marin Preda, one of the most prodigious and talented novelists of the socialist period, the movie continued to use shocking imagery such as that of degrading homosexual rape, public urinating and vomiting to promote the desolation that Mărgineanu made famous in *Somewhere in the East*. The film is about a philosopher arrested on trumped-up charges and convicted to ten years of hard labor. Upon release from prison, the main character finds out that his wife has dumped him in order to marry someone else, and shortly after he meets another woman, he discovers that she is cheating on him. Since Preda did not oppose Communist ideology and even started out as a socialist realist in his first novella written in 1952 (Goldiș 2018), the book, not unlike some of the material that the fourth generation's work was based on, is a philosophical reflection that questions the durability of friendship and the sincerity of human relationships in times of political upheaval, injustice and conformism. Vaguely recalling the thesis from *Narrow Street* according to which innocence turns to evil when beleaguered by unjust authority, the lyrical portrayals of love and friendship were however lost in the filmic adaptation, and the film lacks the nuance and the ambiguity of the novel. As Claudiu Turcuș has agreed, the film "flattens differences in order to make obvious the fact that the communist regime obliterates the individual and creates a repulsive society" (Turcuș 2017, 169). In a way, this is a pessimistic version of *Troubled Laughter*, in that it shows the aggressive way in which unscrupulous individuals profited from political change. The Romanian and Chinese directors, however, chose to describe this unscrupulousness in very different ways: while Yang concentrated on the sensitive lead who does not feel empowered to contest the injustice he suffers as a result of his subjective vision of the surrounding human environment, Marinescu, although working in the realist register, portrays the human milieu in exaggeratedly evil colors that only remotely reflect reality. Furthermore, characters are portrayed in a one-sided manner. Individuals holding administrative functions in the early Communist government, for instance, are happy to abuse their power, and guardians continue to be shown as uneducated, asinine and despicable. At the same time, the film preserves a minimum iota of ambivalence toward the early socialist regime, showing the gradual liberalization that occurred from the 1950s to the 1960s somewhat realistically.

The depiction of early socialism in unsympathetic colors did not stop in the 1990s. Titus Muntean's *Kino Caravan* (*Caravana cinematografica*), made in 2009, is about the projectionist of a mobile film unit who roams the countryside propagandizing Communist ideology in the early 1950s. Shot in a brownish tint that accentuates the darks to show the director's lack of sympathy with the main character and filmed in the muddy alleys of a remote village flooded by rains and covered by perpetually gray skies, Muntean's film feels as propagandizing as the very propaganda he reneges. The actors playing Communist characters, including the protagonist, indulge in overacting, while the villagers deliver their lines in a stilted manner, which makes them appear false. While the dramatic structure is formulaic, the singular goal of the film is that of establishing the animalistic nature of the Communist projectionist. Film historian Marian Țuțui correctly observes that the protagonist's attempt at masturbation during the screening of a war movie for the benefit of the villagers is as unnecessary and grossly exaggerated as the film's ending in which, after constantly teaching the female librarian the benefits of the new ideology, the projectionist suddenly rapes her (Țuțui 2011, 342). Like the antecedents of its genre, *Kino Caravan* suffers from the same indoctrination of which critics accused socialist realism in the 1950s.

This is to be contrasted with the way in which Chinese directors remember the socialist period. Unlike the highly pessimistic *Kino Caravan*, with which it shares thematic resemblances, *Electric Shadows* (*Dianying Wangshi*, Xiao Jiang, 2004) goes back to the 1970s to recapture the "golden age of the movies," when, in the protagonist's words, "the images and voices of the people onscreen brought us all together – breathing as one, dreaming as one." This is because the film reproduces the community built around the open-air screenings made possible by a traveling projectionist who would frequently visit a small mining town to introduce the locals there to the magic of cinema. Attended by working class audiences who breathlessly gathered around an impromptu screen hanging from a wooden frame every night, these audiences are not portrayed as indoctrinated by socialist-era films but rather in love with the spectating act.

In the images flickering on the open-air screen, we summarily recognize Xie's and Yu's faces from *Narrow Street*; we see the dramatic struggle for survival of two female resistance fighters in a popular Albanian film; and we witness nostalgic reruns of 1950s Chinese films such as *Railway Guerillas* (*Tie dao you ji dui*, Ming Zhao, 1956), a very popular war drama of the 1950s, as well as *Sparkling Red Star* (*Shan shan de hong xinga*, Ang Li, Jun Li, 1974), an ode to childhood and child heroes resembling Su Li's *Red Children*. Furthermore, we even hear about Michelangelo Antonioni's Italian documentary *Chung Kuo*, which I will discuss in the conclusion.

Electric Shadows, which moves backward in time via flashbacks and begins in the first decade of the twenty-first century, narrates the story of a deaf and dumb woman who isolates herself in her apartment, where she is surrounded by film projectors, posters and other movie memorabilia, as if in an effort to keep out the over-commercialized China of the 2000s (Figure 5.3). In eerie similarity to Nela's surroundings at the beginning of *The Oak*, the protagonist Lingling is intent to exact revenge on a certain figure from her past, who apparently did her wrong. Unlike in Pintilie's film, however, this figure is the slow-witted but heartily likeable Mao Xiaobin, a boy whom Lingling used to know in her childhood.

As the film progresses, it becomes obvious that the two were inseparable friends when they were little, and their lives revolved around Lingling's parents, both of whom were involved in the open-air screenings at the factory. Tragically, Mao Xiaobin's macho behavior halfway through the film compels Lingling to momentarily abandon her little brother, whom she was supposed to chaperone. Left alone, the boy falls to his death from the top of a building that Lingling used as a hideout for watching the films screened below. Lingling's long-overdue revenge on Mao Xiaobin therefore occurs

Figure 5.3 Lingling's mother waiting for her husband in front of posters of old Chinese film titles in *Electric Shadows*.

not for some unresolved political reason, as in the Romanian film, but out of understandable personal resentment. This allows the otherwise melodramatic tale to end on a happy note. In the final scene, Lingling is reunited with her parents, from which she had been separated before, as well as with Mao Xiaobin. Their affective relationship is validated via yet another film that they all watch together as a family.

Literally translated as "the past of electric shadows,"[10] the film is an ode to the magic time of the 1970s, which are not remembered for the hardships spawned by inclement social policies, but by the affective community woven around working-class characters who shared the joy of watching movies together. Recalling Giuseppe Tornatore's nostalgic look at the past in *Cinema Paradiso* (1988), Jiang portrays film spectatorship as a generator of affective affinity, which ultimately helps strengthen interpersonal relationships and facilitate the socialization of groups hailing from diverse and contrasting backgrounds. Movies, in other words, worked as community-builders.

Because it closely relates to a community that included distant Eastern European films, if only affectively, an important scene in the film is that in which workers and villagers in the impromptu open-air cinema are shown an Albanian movie. Called *Victory over Death* (*Ngadhnjim mbi vdekjen*, 1967) and made by Gëzim Erebara and Piro Milkani, the film memorializes the appalling treatment that Albanian women received from the Nazis and their Italian fascist allies during their occupation of Albania in World War II. Based on a true story, the film ntells ofarrates the resilience of two female militants who resort to their beautiful memories of the past so as to withstand

[10] The film is also known in Chinese as *Meng ying tong nian*. In Chinese, the phrase "electric shadows" refers to motion pictures in general.

torture and ultimately execution. A very popular film in Albania, where it was seen by three-quarters of the country's two million inhabitants when it was released, the tinge of melodrama that the story possessed appealed to Chinese audiences in the 1960s, where the film, not unlike *The Waves of the Danube*, became an immense success.

Jiang Hongbo, who plays Lingling's mother in *Electric Shadows*, herself used to be something of a sensation on Chinese screens. Despite this, Hongbo's character is never sexualized. Wearing mostly loose-fitting sweaters and the drab military green uniforms usually worn by men and women alike during the Maoist period (uniforms which were universally condemned in Western culture for engendering uniformity and boredom), Hongbo's screen persona is the opposite of Gong Li's sexualized character in Zhang Yimou's *Ju Dou* and *Raise the Red Lantern*. Although this desexualized portrayal did not bring the director Xiao Jiang any fame (she would go on to make only one more film, in 2008), *Electric Shadows* sacrificed glamor for verisimilitude to accurately yet nostalgically describe the communities extant during socialism. As in *4, 3, 2* and *Summer Palace*, which take place in the late 1980s, Jiang's film demonstrates that the type of affective collectives created during the socialist era endured throughout the entire period and onwards in postsocialism, and that watching socialist-era films considered indoctrinating today is the very reason why this happened.

Why did Romanian audiences turn judgmental about a majority of films from the 1950s onwards until 1989, while Chinese audiences were able to appreciate their aftereffects, as it were, until the present? Unlike theorists who have posited the socialist period as unreservedly traumatic, I argue that the trauma experienced by Romanian social actors was predicated on the generalized angst emerging not during forty years of socialism but during the abrupt arrival of capitalism in the early 1990s. The shocking effect of this collective angst, as we shall see in *The Death of Mr. Lăzărescu*, to be discussed in the next chapter, forced Romanians to look back in anger, in a way that unrealistically contrasted their undesirable past with a coveted Occidentalist imaginary. Unlike the fifth-generation Chinese directors who built their work on the effective scaffolding of the Mao era, as *River without Buoys*, *The Herdsman* and *The Black Cannon Incident* all show, Romanian directors of the 1990s felt compelled to negate what their predecessors had built and to overcompensate for the shortcomings of the past by recreating the past's screen version whose pessimism was contrasted to a hopeful capitalist future. Romanian cinema would have to wait until the early 2000s for a more balanced view of the past to emerge in the guise of the New Wave.

6 The Romanian New Wave and China's Sixth Generation

In Romanian criticism of the New Wave, there is a prevailing disposition which holds that the films of Cristian Mungiu, Corneliu Porumboiu and Cristi Puiu condemn the socialist past in a way similar to 1990s Romanian cinema. In this chapter, by reading the 2000s films of the above-mentioned directors in a key that makes them comparable to their sixth-generation Chinese counterparts, I will show why this is an overstatement.

In Chinese director Feng Xiaogang's 2003 film *Cellphone* (*Shouji*), the highly technologized, digitally interconnected China of the twenty-first century stands in contrast to the desperately poor China of the Great Leap Forward. To underline this contrast, the camera follows Yan Shouyi as a child riding several kilometers with his girlfriend on the back of a bike to reach the nearest village in order to make a phone call. Mountains line the roads partially covered in snow before the couple make it to a bustling village where a large vociferous crowd lines up outside a decrepit old building. Farmers await their turn to gain access to the only crank telephone around in order to make a call to their relatives.

The physical interconnectedness within which the villagers are portrayed in 1969 is contrasted to the way in which the characters in Feng's film rely on telephones in the present day to make only superficial contact, even to cheat on each other. The fact that Yan Shouyi betrays his wife and engages in an adulterous relationship maintained via his cellphone reveals the ironic side-effects of technology and brings the viewer back to a time when human contact via interpersonal affect was stronger than that enabled by technology. This is not only a point that Cristian Mungiu and Cristi Puiu will make (in subtler ways) in Romanian New Wave cinema, but also evidence suggesting that the socialist and the postsocialist ages are separated in the mental collective by an affective rupture. Some contemporary film scholars have instrumentalized this rupture to differentiate between films made before and after the new millennium, claiming that the films of the 2000s, collectively known as the New Wave or New Romanian Cinema, served as an eye-opener to the horrors of communism, and that they (re)affirmed the liberal values which Romania has allegedly always cherished, but was unjustly denied during socialism.

Deploring the decoupling performed by the Iron Curtain as arbitrary, demoniacal and cruel, scholarship on contemporary Eastern European cinemas has betrayed a deep anticommunist and therefore anti-Eastern phobia; based on this phobia, scholars have called for the return of Eastern Europe to its protective and nurturing Western "cradle," from which this region had been violently and unjustly torn. In recent studies on Eastern European cinema by authors as diverse as Dominique Nasta, Dina Iordanova, Aga Skrodzka and Chris Robé, there emerges – aside from an otherwise sharp and pertinent analysis of the cinema of "The Other Europe," as Iordanova has rightly called it (Iordanova 2003) – a tendency to re-Europeanize the region.

Dominique Nasta, who has confessed to having previously titled her monograph on Romanian cinema *Eastern Europe's Unexpected Cinderella*, thus sums up her contributions to the field of scholarship:

> After difficult beginnings, uneven improvements, sparse moments of accomplishment during a short thaw, Stalinist-inspired state censorship control over all aspects of the film industry, and post-Communist difficulties in catching up with Western standards, several encouraging conditions marked a twenty-first-century revival of Romanian cinema. Over the last decade, the emergence of an authentic New Wave secured Romania more prizes in film festivals than any other country: Romania, a peripheral European country, has turned into a bright spot on the map of world cinema (Nasta 2013, 231).

While Nasta has seen the emergence of the New Wave as a reaffirmation of "true" Romanian values formerly stifled by Communist propaganda, her understandable euphoria also betrays an inferiority complex related to Romania's peripheral status in Europe and the marginality of Romanian culture at large. This is evident in her reading of Cristi Puiu's iconic film *The Death of Mr. Lăzărescu* (*Moartea domnului Lăzărescu*, 2003), for example, as vindication for the unjust oppression of socialism. While the film is indeed a marker of new realism, Nasta has evaluated the film's quality in reference to its Western reception alone. Following a lengthy summary of the film's plot and a description of its style, in order to demonstrate the film's superior value, Nasta has summarily enumerated the "top five" lists that the film made in the West, concluding that "*The Death* got no less than forty-seven international prizes, among which was the BBC World Cinema award" (Nasta 2013, 162).

Film scholar Doru Pop has rebalanced this argument somewhat, noting that, "if there is anything like a New Wave in the Romanian cinema, it is first of all a wave of prizes" (Pop 2014, 9). Film critic Sam Littman has furthermore underscored the importance of the Cannes film festival in promoting the New Wave (Littman 2014). The Western reception of New Wave films at Cannes has in fact encouraged and nourished the Romanian affectation with low-key lighting, minimalism and miserabilism, to the point that New Romanian Cinema became a side-effect of the international festival market and partially dependent on Western European approval. Theorizing a film's value in relation to its Western-conferred status, however, runs the risk of justifying an axiology based on awards and prizes alone, thus substantiating the argument that it is not so much the New Wave's aesthetic that helped win the hearts and minds of some critics and theorists, but the paradigm shift from an ignorance of Romanian national values to the current recognition of the no-longer-Othered status of Romanian cinema in the West.

Redoubling from the Romanian perspective, as it were, the positive reception of Chen Kaige's and Zhang Yimou's films in the West, Nasta has not only aligned Romania's values with Occidental ones, but she gone on to claim that Romanian filmmaking practices are so influenced by Western film schools that they are essentially descendants of cinematic styles originating in the West. She has identified these styles with the ones advanced by the practices of Italian Neorealism, the French New Wave and the British Kitchen Sink, in what is ultimately a political gesture partially following the criticism and theory of her forerunners. Adding insult to injury, film director-turned-critic Ioana Uricaru has posited that "Romanian cinema did not have a New Wave in the 1960s or 70s" (like Czechoslovakia, for example), and that the year 2000 marked the real beginning of the only genuine cinema that the country ever experienced (Uricaru 2008). In other words, while Romania missed its chance to renew its filmmaking practices in the 1960s and to rejuvenate itself, and while it did not adhere to the modernism promoted by Italian, Czechoslovak, Polish and Yugoslav cinema at the time, it received that opportunity in the early 2000s and heartily embraced it. Ironically, this negativist attitude on Romania's cinematic past mirrors that of Polish postsocialist intellectuals, who, much aware that there was an undeniable Polish School that launched Andrzej Wajda's career in the 1950s, decried the same apparent absence of a new wave for equally political reasons (Piwowarska et al. 2008). Not unlike arguments vying for a retributive return of Romanian cinema to Western filmmaking schools, the main case in favor of this statement is that films made by Andrzej Wajda, Andrzej Munk and Jerzy Kawalerowicz, among others, did not contest Communist power strongly enough and were therefore not important enough to establish a new style.

In spite of this overly vindictive assessment of Romania's cinematic past, it would be hypocritical not to find in the films of early Lucian Pintilie and Andrei Blaier, as well as in those of Savel Ştiopul and Mircea Săucan, for example, enough elements to warrant that the 1960s can only be categorized as modernist; that they were influenced by the work of Michelangelo Antonioni and the French New Wave; and that they effected a transition to a style that aesthetically differed from early 1950s socialist realism. Doru Pop is among the few Romanian scholars to admit that Ciulei and Pintilie's works did amount to an "old-New Wave" of sorts (Pop 2014, 22). Leo Şerban, the trailblazer of postsocialist film criticism, has believed that Pintilie's debut, *Sunday at Six* (*Duminică la ora 6*, 1966) "takes a cue from the French New Wave" (Şerban 2010, 7) and is for all intents and purposes a modernist film.

Responding to the exaggerated negative criticism of her postsocialist predecessors with a question, film scholar Rodica Ieta has justifiably wondered: "Why does Eastern European cinema still have to demonstrate that it is worthy of the West's attention, time, and financial investment? Why is it always that 'the second world' has to prove itself to 'the first world'?" (Ieta 2010, 32). While Ieta's question can only be answered with a postcolonial reading of Eastern European cultures, it is also essential to decouple the character of the Romanian New Wave from filmmaking schools in Western Europe. For that reason, it is important to point out that both Neorealist and Kitchen Sink dramas depict in stark tones the challenges faced by impoverished post-war Italy, on the one hand, and the rough proletarian world in the long aftermath of the war in Britain's industrial towns, on the other. While economic development in both the East and the West of Europe may point to comparisons in spite of the different timeframes in which these movements emerged, equating the Western European filmmaking schools of the late 1940s and 1960s, respectively, with the Romanian cinema of the 2000s overlooks a number of important stylistic and aesthetics differences as well as obvious artistic practices, while skipping over half a century of filmmaking history.

The most pertinent of these overlooked aspects is Neorealism's reliance on classical hard lighting and balanced compositions. Italian Neorealism rarely practiced the type of minimalism promoted by New Wave auteurs, favoring brightly lit locales (interiors as well as exteriors), and only loosely employing the stark naturalism evidenced in the *mise-en-scènes* of Puiu's or Mungiu's films. One will have to look hard to find in a classically composed Rossellini shot, for example, or in the high-key lighting of De Sica's *mise-en-scènes* in *Umberto D* (1952), for example, the grimness exhibited by *The Death of Mr. Lăzărescu*. It is true that representatives of both Romanian and Chinese New Waves claim influence from Italian Neorealism, with Cristi Puiu and Jia Zhangke being the most prominent (Mak 2008). But so do directors from various other postcolonial cultures. Drawing on Hamid Naficy, Alina Haliliuc has correctly observed that Italian neorealist influences birthed what she has called "global neorealist" movements, which are also visible in countries such as Iran (Haliliuc 2015, 155), although Turkey, China and post-Soviet Russia could easily fit the mold as well. In lieu of Europeanization, the celebrated global rejuvenation of postsocialist and postcolonial cinemas endorses the reading of Verdery and Chari, who have considered that the postcolonial and postsocialist projects should be joined to benefit the creation of a shared transcultural geographical as well as ideological space, distinct from the globalizing drive of Western capital.

If theorists have agreed that Romanian New Wave films were influenced at all by non-Western sources, these were exclusively identified with the "dissident" cinema of Lucian Pintilie, Dan Pița and Mircea Daneliuc, because *Reenactment*, *The Contest* and *Glissando*, among a handful others, staged resistance to the regime (Nasta 2013). Singling out only dissident auteurs and Western European filmmaking schools as predecessors of New Romanian Cinema, however, betrays what is essentially a political postsocialist project attempting to subsume the New Wave to the European Union with a view to commanding attention, yet again, for the once ignored and unjustly ostracized Romanian culture.

Furthermore, the arguments promoted by the Europeanizing drive have led to a theorizing that amounts to a special type of Eurocentrism seeking to distance white postsocialist filmmaking from the rest of postsocialist cinema, by effectively splitting the existing cultural and aesthetic continuum that dominated Eurasian film practices during half a century of socialism. While political reasons for this endeavor in the context of Eastern Europe's rocky accession to the European Union are understandable, this monolithic practice enacts a Manichean rupture between Romania's socialist past and its capitalist present, and it ultimately constitutes an impassioned plea for the ignorance of history, or at least its reconceptualization as exclusively part of the Western narrative. It also betrays a sense of nationalism that is ironically equivalent to the one pervading socialist-era filmmaking practices.

Even a meticulous scholar such as Dina Iordanova, who at one time almost single-handedly spearheaded the quest for a common identity of Balkan and Eastern European cinemas, has encouraged scholars in her famous work *The Cinema of the Other Europe* to adopt "a more inclusive and comprehensive understanding of European cinema, one that is necessary for a new and unified Europe which has extended towards its eastern periphery" (Iordanova 2003, 1). While de-Sovietizing the region for a generation living under the boots of Stalinism and their descendants is understandable, projecting the miserabilism of the Romanian New Wave onto the entire period of real-existing socialism by applying adjectives such as "miserable" and "monstrous" to everything from ideologies to apartment buildings and even garbage disposal bins (Nasta 2013, 145) is not only subjective, but it also betrays the politicization of culture. This unjustifiably and retroactively enforces a reading of Eastern European film through the lenses of the contemporaneous European Union project and through Western standards at large.

Continuity or Rupture?

The rupture instated by critics between socialism and postsocialism carries not only a chronological connotation. It functions, as Katherine Verdery has prefigured, as the recuperation of a not only liberal, but also bourgeois nationalist and even fascist heritage that characterized the interwar period and was readily available in the cultural underground during socialism. Anticommunist films inspired by *Somewhere in the East* used this artificially created rupture to allow otherwise dangerous ideologies such as fascism to find their way to the surface. Furthermore, while postsocialist directors such as Mărgineanu championed religion as a counterpoint to Communist indoctrination, they also rehabilitated fundamentalist rightist intellectuals and militants such as Ogoranu, who had otherwise been dormant for half a century. This stands in contrast to early socialist filmmaking which rarely if ever attacked religion.[1]

[1] Except for a decade between the late 1940s and the late 1950s, the socialist state collaborated with the clergy, rather than shutting down religious establishments, therefore allowing an impressive number of churches of diverse denominations (with the exception of the Uniate Church) to continue to function from the 1960s until the

Radu Jude is the only filmmaker aligned with the Romanian New Wave to call out the rehabilitation of fascism in postsocialism. Set in the Wallachia of the nineteenth century, *Aferim!* (2015) is centered on the figure of a police constable who is in hot pursuit of a runaway gypsy slave. Motivated by financial gain as well as by his own ingrained racism, the protagonist ultimately captures and returns the slave to his master, who bestially castrates the Roma man for his alleged guilt of having had sexual relations with his wife. Mirroring the fate of African Americans in the United States, the Roma in Wallachia were an enslaved ethnic group until 1856. Conceived as a predatory sexual symbol in the Romanian imaginary, Roma males suffered from discrimination and abuse in the modern period; they still face vicious racism in contemporary Romania. Unlike in the filmography of Emir Kusturica, a Yugoslav-Serbian director who has made Roma characters the stars of various of his films since the socialist period, the plight of the gypsies had not been depicted in a Romanian film until Radu Jude's *Aferim!* While the black-and-white cinematography, which is reminiscent of modernist filmmaking of the 1960s, on a certain level repairs the intentional absence of the topic from Romanian screens, the movie raises awareness about the persistence of ethnic discrimination in Romanian social practices from the early modern period to the fascistic interwar episode and even today.

If *Life Triumphs*, *Alarm in the Mountains* and *The Waves of the Danube* all focused on Romanian Communists fighting fascists and their sympathizers, little has been shown on the silver screen about the period before and during World War II, when the country was allied with Nazi Germany. In *The Dead Nation* (*Țara moartă*, 2017), Jude presents a handful of pages from a Jewish doctor's diary while photograms discovered in a local archive show the gradual rise of anti-Semitism in the 1930s and 1940s. What is surprising in this documentary film is not necessarily the eager embrace of right-wing ideology by the majority of interwar Romanians, but the realization that present-day Romanians still deny that the country was an active participant in the Holocaust. As made evident by Grant Harward's research in the military archives, this denial is unsustainable because "Romanian soldiers were far more motivated to fight the Soviets and commit atrocities against Jews than I had been led to believe by previous historians who claimed Romania joined the Axis under duress" (Harward 2021, 1).

Jude takes up Holocaust denial in *I Don't Care If We Go Down in History as Barbarians* (*Îmi este indifferent dacă în istorie vom intra ca barbari*, 2018) by condemning the Romanian wartime government's explicit racist policies and the barbaric slaughtering of Odessa Jews dictated by fascist leader and close

regime's demise. The clergy, in fact, became a known helping hand for the Securitate and was also known to occasionally engage in informing on the population. Ironically, the same church collaborated with the Nazi regime of Ion Antonescu before the Communist take-over. For more information on the collusion between state and church during this period, see Popa 2017.

Hitler ally Ion Antonescu.[2] In the film, a female theater director prepares the staging of a street performance that details the fate of the thousands of Jews who were burned alive by the Romanian Army during World War II. She is, however, continuously frustrated in her attempts by a city official who relativizes the importance of the event and attempts to minimize it. Moreover, and most importantly, she faces passionate contempt by the general public who, upon seeing the performance, sides with the assailants rather than with the victims.

To highlight the persistence of conformism and denial in Romanian culture, Jude in 2021 also made *Bad Luck Banging or Looney Porn* (*Babardeală cu bucluc sau porno balamuc*), in which he subtly condemns the re-emergence of bourgeois morals and the generalized fascism that threatens to return among the general public. He also comments negatively on the nouveau riche who replaced the working class in postsocialism and are in a position to dictate societal trends while engendering a surplus of tacit yet real violence.[3] While suppressed during real-existing socialism, right-wing values after 1989 returned to demonstrate yet again the past oppressiveness of Communism. Coming on the heels of what Baudrillard has ingeniously referred to as a "total orgy" of liberation everywhere in modernity (Baudrillard 1993, 3), right-wing values imperceptibly joined hands with capitalism to reassert Romania's Europeanness. The New Wave was unjustly associated with the political movement purported to bring out the truth about that past by tearing down the walls of oppression, even though in effect few New Wave films ever envisioned such a task.

While Cristian Mungiu's *4 Months, 3 Weeks, and 2 Days* does take place during the last year of real-existing socialism, the film is a character study and a portrait of human resilience in the face of patriarchal oppression and dire economic conditions, not an attack on a particular ideology. Despite this, the film has been interpreted as showing the inefficiency of socialist state power (Sarris 2008, Nasta 2013, Robé 2017, Eggert 2020), to which their commentators opposed the capitalist imaginary as offering a better alternative.

[2] According to Wiesel's *Final Report of the International Commission on the Holocaust in Romania*, Antonescu was responsible for the deaths of 280,000 to 380,000 Jewish people. These were perpetrated on Romanian soil as well as in lands occupied by the Soviet Union during Antonescu's "Holy War" in which Romania and Nazi Germany attacked the USSR. A quasi-forgotten documentary about the army's murderous actions in the Ukraine, where 30,000 Jews were shot and burned alive by Romanian and German soldiers, is Florin Iepan's *Odessa* (2012). In a memorable scene in the film, Iepan confronts Sergiu Nicolaescu with documents about the army's massacre, leaving the veteran director baffled and quasi-apologetic for making the controversial feature *The Mirror*, which glorifies the figure of the fascist dictator on grounds of patriotism. The burning episode was followed by the killing of another estimated 100,000 Ukrainian Jews by Romanian and German forces. For my reading of the rise of fascism in Romania, see Tion 2021.

[3] For a close reading of *Aferim!* see Gorzo 2022a; for Jude's critique of nationalism, see Tion 2022b.

This attitude validates as truthful only the capitalist-sponsored, postsocialist attempts to describe socialist reality. Real-existing socialism, in this view, can only be painted in broad anticommunist strokes to be believable. This enacts a forced rupture between the two eras, which the New Wave is expected to describe as different from the previous one in order to prophesize the abhorrence of the Communist past in contrast to the luminous capitalist present.

Corneliu Porumboiu's *12:08 East of Bucharest* is one of the first New Wave films to deal with this rupture in the guise of a discussion about the Romanian revolution.[4] The film is inspired by a show that the director saw on a regional TV channel and found inspiring. It is centered on three main characters who meet in a studio to discuss whether a splinter of the Romanian revolution that started in Bucharest has reached the small backwater town of Vaslui, a few hundred kilometers east of the capital, where the action is set. The film is both funny and complex as it discusses the conversational and psychological clichés recognizable in Eastern Europe as a tendency to bicker over insignificant details and to be right at all costs. It moreover employs a tendency to deviate into absurdist catchphrases and situations reminiscent of playwrights such as Eugene Ionesco, who highlighted this tendency not only in the Romanian culture from which he hailed, but in human behavior in general. Unable to establish whether their town experienced a revolution or not, therefore losing sight of its goal along the way, the film subtly brings to the discussion adjacent questions related to national identity, socialist heritage and the painful transition to capitalism – all tropes that necessitate as much debate as the memory of the revolution itself.

Discussing Porumboiu's film in the context of the Romanian national psyche, film scholar Alice Bardan has identified a series of metonymical signs that are used to avoid reliving the trauma of the event; she has informed us that "[a]t the heart of 12:08 is not only a question of language and of naming an event but also of characters being trapped by language structures and often relying on cliché-ridden vocabulary to find their way out of an impasse" (Bardan 2012, 128). The fact that, as Bardan has put it, "there is no consensus as to what really happened in December 1989 and what name should be given to the political event that opened the way for democracy in Romania" (Bardan 128) further references not only the confusing transition from one regime to another, but, in oftentimes comedic (if not tragic) treatment, the

[4] The other is Radu Muntean's *The Paper Will Be Blue* (*Hârtia va fi albastră*, 2006). Muntean's film is the only one that ultimately suggests that the shooting during the Romanian Revolution arose from confusion, and he advances the alarming possibility that, instead of the army fighting Ceaușescu's secret police, several army units were shooting at each other. A postmodern moment by definition, the revolution was interpreted up to that point as either a KGB plot, an internal coup, or as a popular movement that was "stolen" by the neocommunists who took power thereafter. The discourse on the revolution is still attempting to come clear of facts, such as that of revealing the real identity of "terrorists," alleged hired mercenaries fighting on the side of the secret police, whose presence has never been factually confirmed.

many disagreements and lack of unity between key participants in the event. This disunion, as Porumboiu has implied, characterizes not only the bickering guests on the TV show, but also the Romanian national psyche at large, as infighting after 1989 gradually came to replace (as in Pița's prescient forewarning) the socialist collective and the stability that human relations knew under the former regime.

Discussing the revolution, Baudrillard's statement that "Romanian eyewitness accounts speak of being dispossessed of the event [...], deprived of the lived experience" (Baudrillard 1994, 56) makes sense because most Romanians did not participate in the Revolution (in other words, were not physically present on the streets), except via their TV screens. Similar to Barthes' description of the way in which students were rioting in May 1968 because the radio was broadcasting news about their own rioting (Barthes 1986), the Romanian revolution was in part created by its own TV broadcast. Baudrillard's observation that "spectators then become exoterics of the screen, living their revolution as an exoticism of images, themselves exogenous, touristic spectators of a virtual history" (Baudrillard 1994, 56) alludes to the fact that the participants' experience was made possible only via the media, which played a performative part in creating the experience of the revolution for them. In line with Baudrillard, this demonstrates that it is the media performance of the event that largely creates the event.

It is in this sense that we should interpret contemporary theories related to the New Wave as well. Because truth exists only in fragments,[5] rather than recording a factual reality or stating an evident truth about the movement, theorists discussing the New Wave – to paraphrase Derrida – proceed to "saying" the rupture. This "saying," however, ends up creating a real rupture between socialism and postsocialism. Much like early socialist realist messages reinforcing Communist dignity, postsocialist rupture is performative. Yet, its performativity is a self-fulfilling prophecy that moves reality in the direction of the capitalist project.

Jia Zhangke and Cristi Puiu's Miserabilism

While not claiming that the Romanian New Wave was influenced by sixth-generation Chinese cinema or *vice versa*, enough parallels can be drawn between the two styles to warrant their reconceptualization outside the bounds of Western European movements alone. Although it belongs to the fith generation, *One and Eight*, a 1983 film about conscripts fighting in the anti-Japanese war, was rightly hailed as groundbreaking for ushering in a new style of filmmaking centered on realistic portrayals of character psychology. Zhang Junzhao's film was also considered innovative because it purportedly shed a different light on the canonical events of the past. Discussing the innovations brought about by *One and Eight* and Chen Kaige's *The Yellow*

[5] A film that makes this case even clearer is Andrei Ujică and Harun Farocki's *Videograms of a Revolution* (1992).

Earth (*Huang tu di*, 1984), film critic Ying Zhu has stated that "the illusion of shadow and sharp angles created by chiaroscuro lighting in the cell scenes in *One and Eight* and the cave scenes in *Yellow Earth* determined such scenes' dominant mood of anguish, contributing to the clarification, intensification, and interpretation of the scenes" (Zhu 2001, 463).

This parallels the minimalism of 2000s Romanian films whose use of ambient lighting and preference for location shooting, primarily in socialist-built apartments, conveys a sense of intimacy while offering audiences the interpretative key to the oftentimes browbeaten fates of their protagonists. If this filmmaking style helped Chinese sixth-generation filmmakers distinguish themselves from their predecessors, it equally made New Wave Romanian films different from their 1990s counterparts. While *One and Eight* was hailed as revolutionary for the fifth generation and while it put an end to the heroic representation of socialist realist characters, Cristi Puiu's *Stuff and Dough* (*Marfa și banii*, 2001) was unreservedly considered by a majority of critics as marking the beginning of the New Wave (Popa 2017, 9; Gorzo 2021), because it depicted an uncosmeticized everyday world which was rough around the edges and strikingly representative of postsocialist realities.

The film follows three young characters, two males and a female, on a trip between the Black Sea coast and the capital (Figure 6.1). They make the trip because the protagonist was tasked by his shady and uncouth boss, portrayed with malicious gusto by the same Răzvan Vasilescu who had played the doctor in Pintilie's *The Oak*, to deliver an unnamed merchandise to a given address in Bucharest. At first, time goes by without major incidents, until the group realizes that they are being followed by a suspicious car. Then suddenly, at a road stop, their car is bashed in by a man sporting a baseball bat. Although the heroes manage to drive away before they are physically hurt, the three spend the rest of the film in fear because they do not know the identity of

Figure 6.1 The opening of Puiu's *Stuff and Dough*.

the assailant nor the reason why they were attacked. Neither of these will be revealed by the film's finale, which seems to convey that the importance of the diegesis lies in the proverbial journey, not in the destination.

Film critic Andrei Gorzo has observed that it is strange for a road movie in which initially nothing happens to shock audiences in the way in which *Stuff and Dough* did (Gorzo 2021). The film manages to maintain its unrelenting tension because, despite being essentially confined to the interior of a car for more almost ninety minutes, the audience affectively relates to the fear of the protagonists from the moment of the attack to the very end of the film. Despite the claustrophobic *mise-en-scène*, the film moreover is interesting because it introduces realistic everyday characters who, as Gorzo has observed, are not "communists, neo-communists and former secret police officers" but small-time boutique vendors, petty entrepreneurs and even black marketeers with no elevated interests. Puiu's film succeeded, Gorzo has argued, because the director abandoned "the major obsessions of 1990s' Romanian cinema" (Gorzo 2021) and adapted a Hollywood-trafficked formula to the harsh surroundings of the postsocialist 1990s. However, as we shall see later, this happened with a twist.

It is noteworthy that, although Cristi Puiu did not make a politically engaged film – that is, he declaredly refused a political interpretation for *Stuff and Dough* (Gorzo 2022b) – the film is clearly about the violence and oppression related to the wild capitalism of the 1990s, and not at all about the memory of socialism. Because Vasilescu's character treats his young employees much like a despot would treat his serfs, the film stresses the unbridled authoritarianism of new relations of productions smacking of corruption and tyranny, which were strongly condemned in the social realist dramas of the 1980s. Although Puiu incontrovertibly has little to do with socialist politics, and although he rejects the very label of "social realism" to describe his films (Gorzo 2017), *Stuff and Dough* is indebted to both 1980s dramas and the emerging affectivity of capitalism, which would condition the entire generation of New Wave directors coming on Puiu's heels.

These conditions are similar to those describing the sixth generation in China. Although less cohesive than Romania's New Wave and "characterized by its lack of a unified aesthetic canon ever since the day they were labeled" (Nie 2021), sixth-generation directors were less interested in condemning the politics of socialism and more interested in expressing "the authenticity of their individual experiences," which, accumulated from their own past, provided them with "initial inspiration and energy" (Nie 377, 380). This ensured that their films would be authentic rather than ideological and would accentuate the continuity, rather than the rupture, between the socialist past and the postsocialist present. In fact, as in *Cellphone*, where the protagonist returns to the village which he had left behind as a child in order to reconnect with himself, sixth-generation directors betray a certain nostalgia for the past.

One reason for the absence of a date that clearly marks the start of the sixth generation could be related to China's smooth transition from the "scar films" of the 1980s to a more tolerant memorialization of the Cultural Revolution in the eyes of early 2000s directors. This is most evident in Jia Zhangke's *Platform* (*Zhantai*, 2000), which is a trailblazer in that sense. Although it has often been described as a film about a theater troupe which roams the countryside in Deng Xiaoping's China while taking in the dramatic transformations marked by "the historical divide between the planned economy and the market economy" (Nie 391), *Platform* is also a film about childhood and growing up. In that sense, it is an authentic and lively coming-of-age film indebted to the director's personal experiences, and it is replete with the romanticism characteristic of this genre.

The protagonist Cui Mingliang is a brooding young intellectual who, aside from directing a group of like-minded youths to sing and dance in theater propaganda works, is also interested in developing a meaningful relationship with his girlfriend. Although the girlfriend leaves him halfway through the film for reasons that remain confusing, she does an about-face in the film's finale when she invites Mingliang to her house and back into her life. In the temporal arc described by these events, Jia's emphasis lies mostly on describing the group as a tightly woven collective which resembles those in Lou's and Mungiu's films. As a group, characters are seen watching animated sex-education videos and Raj Kapoor comedies in dilapidated theaters, as well as listening to popular music which becomes increasingly Western as the movie progresses. In tune with the cultural transformations and the country's opening to the West, in the second half of the film the troupe is seen dancing to Western pop, such as Modern Talking, and to rock tunes (Mello 2019, 99), recalling Tian Zhuangzhuang's *Rock Kids* (*Yaogun Qingnian*, 1988), a surprisingly honest film about punk culture which describes the exuberance of the late Deng era, in an environment that is almost depoliticized. While Jia's film does make political references, the film's politics is not overbearing or overly determinant. Although the troupe's members at various times are seen participating in the "one-child policy" as well as the "save electricity" campaigns, they do so in a performative way. Jia does not attach a negative political meaning to these scenes, treating them as natural occurrences in his characters' lives; therefore, he does not make it a priority to contest the propaganda undoubtedly present in his milieu as he was growing up.

A scene in the film further shows that characters never take propagandist messages seriously. In a work meeting with his actors, Mingliang half-heartedly criticizes one employee for singing the parody of a revolutionary song when returning from a live performance on the back of a truck. Reflecting on what appears to be a comic situation for him, the latter does not appear to be very affected by Mingliang's criticism (Figure 6.2). As in Yurchak, politics for Jia's characters becomes constative. Unlike in the films of the 1980s, we are a long way here from a toxic depiction of the Cultural Revolution, which negatively impacted the lives of those characters who took part in it.

The elements that are impacted by politics, however, are those that ironically have to do with political liberalization. While fifth-generation directors imbued their female characters with extreme sensuality, Eros is never glamorized in *Platform*. On the contrary, it is treated with irony: because villagers

Figure 6.2 Mingliang talks to the dancers in an empty courtyard in *Platform*.

demand increasingly "sexier" performances from the troupe, Mingliang is compelled to commercialize their sing-and-dance acts. For this reason, the female group members in the second part of the film are repeatedly seen putting on something of a sexualized performance. But Jia does not make comments on his material, and it is in such instances that he tacitly lampoons the decaying quality of theater art. Ironically, although no one expected the revolutionary agitprop of the 1980s to further decrease the quality of the troupe's acts, Jia makes it clear that it is the emergence of capitalism that gradually transforms the troupe into a producer of cheap (and sexualized) entertainment.

Romanian as well as Chinese critics noted that both Puiu and Jia provoke audiences at levels that transcend the political. While Gorzo drew attention to Puiu's obliterating of borders between fiction and documentary films (Gorzo 2021), Ray Chow referred to Jia's cinema as expressing a "fondness for making films that look like documentaries" (Chow 2014, 26). If politics is commented on, this is done via the film's form rather than in programmatic dialogue or narrative structure. Long shots in which the surroundings almost dwarf the characters in *Platform* bespeak the littleness of people in relation to something that could be interpreted as the overpowering political system. These allusions, as in Tian's *Horse Thief*, are however mostly metaphorical, as they can be read in a purely realist key.

Another stylistic element that makes Jia's film similar to Puiu's, which would come out only a year later, is the preferred use of ruins as backgrounds. Literally or metaphorically, numerous scenes (both interior and exterior ones) use dilapidated rooms and buildings or run-down spaces as an interpretative key. The drab grays of a warehouse courtyard used as a scrapheap for semi-abandoned farm machinery in one scene in *Platform* contrast with the red costumes of the female dancers. In another scene, the same dancers are shown performing in the back of a truck parked on a highway, while a crumbling workers' wagon flanks the composition on the right-hand side of the frame. Such *mise-en-scènes* are comparable to Puiu's use of the makeshift boutique owned by the protagonist's mother in *Stuff and Dough*, which appears in the first shot of the film, or the gloomy, blue-tiled kitchen that dominates the composition at the end.

These shots are important because they reference Fernando Solanas and Octavio Getino's "aesthetic of garbage"; the two theorists have advocated for the establishment of a Third Cinema which should valorize the ugliness of postcolonial surroundings in order to draw attention to the plight of formerly colonized peoples. They have argued that the exposure of postcolonial "garbage" would ultimately help turn ugliness into beauty. In their 1969 manifesto, the South American anticolonial theorists considered this type of filmmaking revolutionary because it challenged European art cinema, particularly the French New Wave, as well as bourgeois Hollywood, which, via their cosmeticized settings, detracted from the tragedies that colonialism had brought about in the Third World (Solanas and Getino 1969).

Both *Platform* and *Stuff and Dough* engage with this "aesthetic of garbage" to recall the crumbling Communist project. This aesthetic is also employed in Puiu's *Sieranevada* (2016), in which characters are seen crowding the minuscule space of a dark socialist-era apartment that becomes the setting for a conflict between the old and the new. Standing in the crowded kitchen, the thirty-something female protagonist passionately blames her neighbor for the criminality of Ceaușescu's policies. The neighbor, a former Communist, disagrees that the policies were criminal, exemplifying that the apartment in which the niece lives – old and ugly as it may be – would never have been built had it not been for them, the Communists. She further accuses the niece, a monarchist, of being blinded by the figure of the former king and by her idealism calling for a return to religious practices that would exploit poor, innocent people. The scene is both realistic and incredibly dramatic because the conversation makes the niece erupt into a hysterical crying bout, even though the funeral wake that she is there to attend does not extract a single tear from her. Influenced by *Chernukha Cinema*, Puiu's *mise-en-scène* points to a post-kitchen sink or socialist sink style rather than the British one, as I have argued elsewhere (Țion 2020). This happens when he positions his characters in front of walls or backgrounds that recall the atmosphere of the socialist past. In doing so, he imbues the spaces with an affectivity that reflects the memory of the socialist-era collective, thus altering the predominantly negative connotation of socialism. Similarly, the backgrounds of many conversations in *Platform* become characters themselves, nostalgic markers of a recent history that help render the ugliness of the past haptic. By integrating the ruins into the diegesis, Jia directly connects the affectivity of his characters to the landscape in which they live, in a way that makes the ruins a personification of a tangible past.

Ugliness – as inherited from the crumbling project of utopian socialism – aspires, via Jia and Puiu, to become the new beautiful. Beauty in both postsocialist new waves is not the classical ideal made famous by the bourgeoisie and valorized as the standard of Western art since the fifteenth century, but the ruins of a political project beginning to take on new life as the background for a new East. Because postsocialist misery is beauty, miserabilism is not just a building bloc towards yet another bourgeois era, but an actualization of Solanas and Getino's revamped "aesthetic of garbage."

Unlike writers advocating for Romania's return to Europe or the incorporation of mainland China into a transnationalist cinema – which are as utopian as socialist realism was in its heyday – the beautified ugly of Jia's and Puiu's films forges the necessary aesthetic connections not between Eastern and Western Europe, but between the East and the Far East. It recreates the intra-national links of the former Eastern bloc, therefore reconstituting a postsocialist space that inherits the political heritage, history and forms of expression of a generation raised on the dialectical relationship between utopia and reality.

Authority Figures and Patriarchy

Ruins are also central to Wen Jiang's *In the Heat of the Sun* (*Yang guang can lan de ri zi*, 1994), yet another Chinese example of a coming-of-age film that treats the past in a benevolent manner. Although set during the tumultuous Cultural Revolution, the film concerns a group of teenagers whose shenanigans, much like those of Jia's characters in *Platform*, bespeak an interest in interpersonal relationships more than in politics. Ma Xiaojun (who is nicknamed "Monkey" and played by Yu Xia, the protagonist of *Electric Shadows*) is a rambunctious teenager deprived of a father's love; he focuses on breaking door locks and peeping into other people's homes until he makes the acquaintance of an older mysterious girl who captures his fancy. What is important in Jiang's film, besides Monkey's pursuit of Mi Lan, is the close friendship which he establishes with his roguish peers and their engagement in continued acts of lawlessness, such as sneaking into movie theaters and crashing dinner receptions staged in honor of political guests.[6] An act of barely acknowledged resistance, which recalls the orphans running away from the children's home in Mihileș's film, this identifies the teenage collective as powerful enough to defy the politics and the turmoil of the Cultural Revolution.

Both Chinese and Romanian film directors found the coming-of-age genre suitable to show their own versions of the Cultural Revolution and the socialist past, a version predicated not on the official anticommunist discourse but on the authors' personal experience. Romanian directors used the genre to negotiate a version of the socialist past that was in counter-distinction to what Doru Pop has called the *cinema du papa* of the old regime (Pop 2010, 12), but, even more so, one that was entirely different from the anticommunist films of the 1990s. Marginally recalling both the equidistant recounting of the past

[6] Incidentally, one of the receptions they plan to crash is given on occasion of Romania's national day.

in *The Blue Kite*, in which socialist history is portrayed through the eyes of a child, as well as *In the Heat of the Sun*'s adolescent focus, Cătălin Mitulescu's *How I Celebrated the End of the World* (*Cum mi-am petrecut sfârțitul lumii*, 2006) is a Romanian film that, although set in the last year of totalitarianism, does not condemn the politics of the socialist era. Unlike 1990s films which usually portrayed Ceaușescu as exaggeratedly malicious, Mitulescu reframes the dictator's image to make it appear less infused with vindictive judgment. His figure in the film, in fact, serves merely to introduce us to the protagonists, middle-school student Lali and his older sister Eva, whose endearing coming-of-age story mirrors the country's rocky transition to capitalism. The plot follows the pursuits of the two siblings during the months before the 1989 revolution and shortly thereafter. Forefronting the precarity of a middle-class neighborhood in Bucharest, the film offers an understanding of socialist life as filtered through Lali's eyes. For this reason, the narratological structure allows for surreal dream sequences to blend with reality, therefore offering a subjective and rather innocent view of a totalitarian society, which renders reality less terrifying and thoroughly livable.

As Aga Skrodzka has theorized in reference to Eastern European cinema, "magic realism helps the provincial subject to make sense of the center-enforced currents of history by introducing a pause in history, by exposing history as always a mixture of magic and logic" (Skrodzka 2012, 2). We see this type of magic in Mitulescu's film when Lali, in response to his family's victimization at the hands of history, compensates for their powerlessness by dreaming of building a submarine which would take his family across the border. This dream proves prophetic, as Eva's boyfriend does make his dramatic escape across the Danube in the film's finale. Furthermore, featuring a pseudo-uncanny power vaguely reminiscent of Emir Kusturica's hero from *Time of the Gypsies* (*Dom za vesanje*, 1988), Lali secretly brews a plan to kill the country's leader when he is selected to sing in a children's choir at a Ceaușescu rally. The surreal exploit concocted in Lali's imagination, indeed his "mixture of magic and logic," is depicted as having a direct bearing on Ceaușescu's downfall. But like all fairytales, Lali's victory is accompanied by loss – in his particular case, the prefigured loss of childhood and of the affective connections with the other members of his family. To confirm this, in partial fulfillment of Lali's escapist dreams, Eva leaves home and emigrates to the West. This is less a personal victory for her than imagined, however, as the scenes showing Eva as a stewardess on a cruise ship convey her shock and alienation rather than the expression of liberation, prefiguring the difficult times laying ahead for her and her country for an indefinite time in the future. The parallelism between reality and fiction mirrors the one between Lali's father and the figure of Ceaușescu. Because the father sometimes does impersonations of the leader to amuse his children, we realize that Lali's imagination confounds the father figure with that of the so-called "father of the nation," a phrase which Ceaușescu used to refer to himself. This symbolically equates the last decade of socialism with the protagonist's childhood and Ceaușescu's demise with the loss of an influential father figure.

Enveloped in the film's predominantly bluish tint and dream-like atmosphere, this loss evidences the ambivalent nature of Ceaușescu's downfall. In an overlooked scene at the end of the film, Lali and his friends watch, disturbed, as revolutionaries set a car ablaze only to wonder afterwards why they did so. This scene is followed by another in which, unsure of their political future, the same revolutionaries cheer Lali's imaginary return to the neighborhood riding in a luxurious automobile, in an eerie reminder of Ceaușescu's authoritarian style. The scenes do not celebrate the annihilation of an inclement political system as much as they reflect the loss of a community predicated on socialist affect.

Careful to revoke any possibility of nostalgia for socialism or *Ostalgie*, literary theorist Angelo Mitchievici has intimated that Mitulescu does not pine for a specific political regime, but for the attractiveness of a utopian past which just happened to coincide with the socialist period (Mitchievici 2011, 182). As in Jia's *Platform*, however, the transition between the two eras evinces rather nostalgically not only the disappearance of a community-oriented lifestyle, in which neighbors were as important as family members, but also the emergence of a society dominated by material concerns and individualism. This means that the end of the world mentioned in the film's title references not only the demise of a system that was overpowering and oppressive, but also the anxiety felt *vis-à-vis* the rise of a new bourgeoisie, which brutally awakens the characters from their oblivious slumber. It also awakens the audiences from theirs, of course, when the latter witness this anxiety already in Puiu's *Stuff and Dough*.

Another trait that the Romanian New Wave and China's sixth generation have in common is the focus on parental and authority figures. In contrast to the Romanian anticommunism of the 1990s, where militia men, secret police officers and apparatchiks were memorialized in a manner disproportionate to reality, as in Mărgineanu's films, the police in Chinese films of the 2000s, despite their connection to a (still) authoritarian party-state, are credibly portrayed. For example, regardless of their intimidating posture, the two police officers in *Platform* who interrogate an unmarried couple as to why they requested to sleep in the same hotel room, do not have the same authority as their Mao-era predecessors. Moreover, there is enough hesitation in the way in which the actors deliver their lines to intuit a slight depreciation of power. Likewise, the honest portrayal of a friendship between a policeman and a street urchin in Ying Liang's *Taking Father Home* (*Bei yazi de nanhai*, 2005) also reflects the crumbling of central authority on the heels of Maoism's demise, which is truthfully represented in the work of both directors.

If Romanian anticommunist films created caricatures of authority figures well into the second decade of the 2000s, as in Mărgineanu's *White Gate* (*Poarta albă*, 2014) – a stilted portrait of conscripts working on the Danube-Black Sea Canal in the 1950s – New Wave directors would change that. The first to look with a questioning eye at contemporary authority is Corneliu Porumboiu in *Police Adjective* (*Polițist, adjectiv*), a 2009 film about the hesitations of a cop tasked with arresting a teenager for the possession of a small amount of marijuana. Featuring long takes and static shots, Porumboiu paints an intimate portrait of the law at a time when former authoritative discourses were beginning to lose their relevance in a postsocialist age riddled with precarity, corruption and instability. Bringing to the table a realistic description of the loss of confidence which authority figures experienced in early postsocialism, Porumboiu paves the way not only for Călin Peter Netzer's portrayal of the corruptible police force of *Child's Pose* (*Poziția copilului*, 2013), but also for Eugen Jebeleanu's *Poppy Field* (*Câmp de maci*, 2020), a strikingly intimate portrait of a police officer ridden with guilt while in the middle of a professional crisis.

In *Poppy Field*, although Cristi is gay and has an ongoing relationship with Hadi, a French foreign national of Arabic descent who visits him in Bucharest, he cannot come out to his co-workers. His crisis is brought about by a standoff to which the police are called to mediate, between an ultranationalist religious group who interrupts the screening of a gay-themed movie in a theater and the progressive audience. Siding with the conservatives, like most of his colleagues do, would go against Cristi's conscience, while taking the side of the homosexual-rights group would inadvertently out him. He chooses to do the former by punching a gay acquaintance who tries to establish contact with him based on a previous sexual encounter that the two had shared in the past. This has the effect of isolating Cristi from the rest of his peers while also endangering his colleagues by tainting the image of the police in general.

The first part of the film, which takes place in Cristi's home, is shot in a bluish tint conferring a certain coldness on the lovers' intimate encounter, yet the rest is dominated by the red interiors of the movie theater (Figure 6.3). Contrary to what should have been a close relationship with his lover and a colder one with his colleagues, respectively, Jebeleanu chooses to invert the color palette in order to show Cristi's special if unattainable attachment to his

Figure 6.3 Cristi in the empty movie theater in Jebeleanu's *Poppy Field*.

coworkers. This attachment is confirmed in the film's finale by his superior: he confesses to having known all along that Cristi is gay and offers his tacit support. Although this support contravenes the unwritten machismo of the police institution, it humanizes the workspace while returning something of an affective closeness to a collective which vaguely resembles the lost if utopian one of the socialist era.

Although Jebeleanu's effort represents a first for postsocialist Romanian cinema, gay-themed films involving authority figures were surprisingly common in both China and Romania beginning in the late 1990s, despite the countries being traditionalist post-authoritarian cultures. Considered the first gay film to come out of China, *East Palace, West Palace* (*Dong gong xi gong*, Zhang Yuan, 1996) is a film about the unlikely encounter and increasingly intimate contact between a young gay man and a police officer who takes the former in for questioning. Vaguely reminiscent of *Poppy Field* in its theme, Zhang's film is shot in a dark and mysterious chiaroscuro lighting that makes the characters appear distant and ethereal while also uncannily real.

Fish and Elephant (*Jin nian xia tian*, Yu Li), a film by a female director and about a lesbian relationship between a TV host and a saleswoman, was first screened at an international festival in 2001, while Tudor Giurgiu's *Love Sick* (*Legături bolnăvicioase*) was released in Romania in 2006. Both are rather formulaic films that pale in comparison with Cristian Mungiu's more sophisticated *Beyond the Hills* (*Dincolo de dealuri*, 2012), which follows the intimate yet barely averred emotional relationship between two young nuns in an ultra-traditionalist convent dominated by an authoritarian clergy. In 2019, Marius Olteanu would make *Monsters* (*Monștri*), about a gay man who is married to a woman despite having an actively gay lifestyle. *Monsters* is a staple of late New-Wave cinematography, featuring brooding interiors and nocturnal cityscapes in which a deliberately slow-paced narrative and self-critical, ruminating characters give a captivating impression of apathy and inertia.

This inertia and a society unchanged by the advance of democratic reforms are the main topics of Mungiu's *Graduation* (*Bacalaureat*, 2016). By forefronting the fact that they live in a corrupt culture, Mungiu's law enforcers find excuses to behave immorally themselves. This is in fact the reason why the police are in collusion with other authority figures, such as the father in the film, who is a doctor, and it is also why the father believes that tampering with the results of his daughter's graduation exam is well within his rights. This shows the specific entitlement that comes with allegedly being exceptional – that is, being exempt from following the rule of law on the grounds that society is unlawful in the first place. *Graduation* is therefore about the belief that one can go against the system because the system is vitiated. And since the corruption of the system comes from a long series of crimes of which Communism was the most recent culprit, this provides the sanctioned anti-communist excuse one needs in order to also become corrupt. The equation of the totalitarian regime with crime, as in the government's decree of 2007 – an equation ironically consecrated by democracy – ultimately works not only against the system, but also against the people that live in it, perpetuating the self-destruction of the system and, moreover, the self-destructive attitude of the components of the system, the "little" people.

Because the father in *Graduation* insists that his daughter accept his meddling in the system on her behalf, Mungiu shows how corruption is corroborated by paternalism and patriarchy. The same paternalism comes across in Netzer's *Child's Pose*, a film reminiscent of the overbearing father from Callas-Dinescu's *Too Hot for the Month of May*, in which a mother's over-protective attitude towards her adult child becomes increasingly toxic after she insists on evading the law in order to absolve him of a manslaughter conviction with which the latter was charged following a traffic accident. The counterpart to the mother in Netzer's film is the character played by Vlad Ivanov, the ambiguous abortion doctor from Mungiu's *4, 3, 2*. Emerging in the aftermath of the car accident as the only witness, he blackmails the perpetrator for financial reward, yet seems unsure whether he wants to put himself in the position of a blackmailer. These characters' attitude confirms, as in Georgescu's articulation, that postsocialism is more libertine than liberal, and that the only law that consistently applies in postsocialism is the dialectics of the hazard. Their attitude also validates the argument put forward by film scholar László Strausz who has claimed that authority and parental figures in postsocialism experienced a crisis of masculinity and vulnerability, which forced them to reconsider their roles in family and social life (Strausz 2017). Indeed, it made them more authoritarian than the authoritarianism that they consistently decried.

As in the case of fifth-generation Chinese directors reviving the themes of Maoist cinema, this however is a hackneyed theme that postsocialist filmmaking in Romania inherited from the socialist era. It appears in *Too Hot for the Month of May*, where ethics takes center-stage in a similar yet lower-stakes manslaughter case, and yet again in Lucian Pintilie's *Reenactment*. In comparison to its successor, socialism ironically comes across as the more humane of the two antonymic systems because, unlike the corrupt postsocialist legal system, the prosecutor in *Too Hot* insists on the execution of justice despite the father's intervention on behalf of the culprit. Similarly, the Militia in Pintilie's film insists not on punishing the two youths, but on making them understand (via re-education) that their behavior is anti-social.

What Western individualism accuses the socialist state of is its very ability to interfere in private life. But, when George Mihăiță, the actor playing one of the two rebellious youths in *Reenactment*, declared in a postsocialist interview that the film was taken to a festival in the United Kingdom, and that British audiences were shocked by the state's negotiating, if paternalistic, attitude when confronted with what was essentially a public misdemeanor, the question that emerged was the following: what constitutes interference in the capitalist versus the socialist systems?[7] Although Pintilie pejoratively

[7] One of the few Romanian jokes of postsocialism asks: "What was totalitarianism?" Playing on the word "tot/total" = "everything," the answer is: "Totalitarianism is that type of regime in which everything is permitted."

portrays the Militia as incompetent, what transpires in *Reenactment* is the image of a state engaged in promoting the observance of the law, not by exerting force, but by using persuasion. This is entirely absent in postsocialist films where concern for ethics is sacrificed for the rule of democracy, which shows no regard for the rule of law. Ironically, postsocialist films demonstrate that capitalism lost the previous system's concern for ethical behavior while preserving its patriarchy.

The Abortion Film in Romania and China

Referring to the solidarity of the protagonists in *4, 3, 2*, film scholar Constantin Parvulescu has claimed that Mungiu's film is less about totalitarianism; rather, it is in fact "the story of two friends and a friendship" (Parvulescu 2022). He has further stated that, while the film does offer a snapshot of Romanian society as a web of close-knit relationships built, among other reasons, in response to the much-quoted oppressiveness of the police state, it is not primarily about such a state. The Communist "structures of feeling," which Chris Robé has correctly identified (but misinterpreted) in Mungiu's film, not so much contest authoritarianism as describe a particular (and after all trivial) *modus vivendi* in socialism, one that was predicated on poverty, precarity and economic want. But this lifestyle also reveals the almost symbiotic bond between Găbița and Otilia, for whom the student dorm epitomizes their solidarity, and for whom friendship not only means running errands for each other, but also being prepared to literally sacrifice one's wellbeing for one another. In this way, their relationship personifies the robustness of a socialist collective which does not point to the memorialization of oppression, but to the safety of an interpersonal female space which appears tinted with nostalgia, especially when framed in contrast to the callous individualism of capitalism.

This individualism is represented in *4, 3, 2* by the screen persona of the "douche" abortion doctor played by Vlad Ivanov, that unprincipled and heartily dislikable Mr. Bebe who, in order to perform the abortion, convinces both women to sexually submit to him. The sociologist Dušan Bjelić has seen Ivanov's character "not as […] a commentary on the Romanian Communist past, but rather as a critical allegory of the Romanian neoliberal future" (Bjelić 2018). This point of view is sustainable because Bebe is not interested in using the oppression of state power to achieve his goals. Unlike the above-mentioned Militia which educated rather than punished, Mr. Bebe is only interested in financial transactions. Therefore, he punishes Găbița not for being careless, as the Militia would have done, but for defaulting on her financial commitment. He is, moreover, solely interested in attaining self-gratification and profit, thereby acting as a true capitalist.

As Verdery has observed in her analysis, Romania was Marxist in name only (Verdery 1991), which allowed for its social fabric to be perforated by the intrusion of capitalism. This intrusion agrees with Nasta's belief that Romania purportedly never cherished Communist values and instead was all along capitalist "at heart" all along. This would make Bebe a poster child for the "return to Europe" theory, and a promoter of both the capitalist values from the interwar past as well as those coveted by socialist Romania underneath the veneer of its Communist agenda. If Bebe is a promoter of capitalist values, however, he is also a deeply unethical character who uses patriarchal rather than political power to ultimately subdue the girls and profit from their suffering.

While I agree with Bjelić's reading of Mr. Bebe as an allegory of neoliberalism, Mungiu's protagonist is also a reification of the patriarchal leftovers of an over-traditionalist society which Communism could not fully eradicate. This is evident not only in the way in which he uses verbal violence, emotional abuse and intimidation to overpower the women, but also in the way in which he treats other characters. A scene in the middle of the film shows Bebe in the background of a long shot, chastising his mother for resting on a bench in front of her socialist-era apartment building. The scene is not essential to the diegesis, and Mungiu could have easily left it out. Staged in deep space with Otilia's figure in the foreground waiting for him in the car, the scene was, however, necessary to convey Bebe's compulsive need to control other people. The lines that he speaks to his mother – "You're driving me crazy; I don't want you to leave the house" – betray not only a pathological need for control but bespeak the abusive treatment of the weak by those in a position of power. Ironically, this power is not a derivative of socialist oppression but, via his status as caregiver and provider for his elder mother, of patriarchy.

Although empowered by his patriarchal position and financial security, Mr. Bebe is also an outcast. Because his occupation does not allow him to fit in, he lives on the fringes of both underground capitalism and real-existing socialism, inhabiting a confusing inbetweenness which makes him the quintessential Other. Although he abuses his patriarchal powers, his character is not entirely negative. He is also a courageous man who fights state oppression by breaking what is ultimately an unjust law – that of professing control over someone else's body. After all, he risks his life to perform an illegal abortion for which the capital punishment would not be excluded. Because he operates (pun intended) in the interstices between what is lawful and what is illegal, he cuts a dubious figure who aspires to be elsewhere, maybe in the "civilized West," because only the arbitrariness and political turmoil of the "East" rendered him despicable. A mixture of Guattari's and Deleuze's "fascist inside" us (Guattari and Deleuze 1987), on the one hand, and the personification of transgression, on the other, Mr. Bebe is the reification of ambiguity developed in the throes of Communist dialectics. In that way, he is a pure product of socialism hailing from the polysemous human environment of that era.

In fact, much like the fifth generation in China, Mungiu reprocessed and imported his character from the past. The film that featured an earlier (female) replica of Mr. Bebe is the 1975 production of *Postcards with Wildflowers* (*Ilustrate cu flori de cîmp*), by the veteran 1950s director Andrei Blaier. Not unlike Pintilie's doctor who was adapted from *Red Apples* and refigured in *The Oak*, whether consciously or not, Mungiu had the opportunity to look back to this film to find his model. *Postcards* was made in the long aftermath of the Party's notorious 770 decree instated in 1966, which banned the performance of abortions. Laura, a naïve romantic, is forced to abort because of an illicit affair which she has had with a Bucharest architect who refuses responsibility for his act. When she arrives in a small city to perform the abortion illegally, she becomes the victim of an incompetent middle-aged female shopkeeper doubling as abortion doctor and her local accomplice, who cannot help but involve the former's sensitive young daughter in the affair. While undergoing the dangerous procedure, Laura befriends the doctor's daughter; before long, their relationship acquires something of a bond resembling that between Otilia and Găbița. But in Blaier's version, Laura dies of complications, and the tragedy leads to the young daughter's suicide. Faced with the consequences and overcome by panic, the accomplices ponder running away but eventually give in to the psychological pressure which wears down both of them. Because Blaier unfolds the simple plot with the hand of a self-restrained tragedian and imbues the film with a half-melancholy key, he chooses to leave the ending open.

Mungiu sets his narrative in the socialist period immediately predating the 1989 revolution and similarly chooses a provincial town as location. This time, however, what stands out are the graying socialist blocks, which loom depressingly triumphant over the dead-end lives of a pregnant college student and her roommate. The focus is on the patient/doctor relationship (a favorite motif of Romanian filmmakers since Tatos) and on the minutia of the abortion itself, laboriously described throughout all its grim and unsanitary stages. Nobody dies, and life goes on after the successful abortion. Yet, with Communism itself showing no signs of abating its oppression, the future continues to look grim for both protagonists.

While *Postcards*' clear propagandist design forced Blaier to keep the condemnation of the anti-abortion decree to a minimum, Mungiu did not have his hands tied by the regime, so to speak. In spite of this, he fortuitously adopted Blaier's formula rather than an anticommunist one. This helped preserve the film's sense of neutrality towards state power while refocusing its thrust on the development of characters. While in Pintilie's *The Oak*, for example, character realism is sacrificed on the altar of anticommunism, Mungiu's film focuses on human behavior rather than politics. This helps not only shed an ambivalent light on the alleged rupture experienced in the time elapsed between the two regimes but demonstrates that the restraint adopted in the socialist era by social realist directors bode well for their descendants, and that creative restrictions – in this case, paradoxically – engendered objectivity rather than conventionality. What endures in both Mungiu and Blaier is the affective community that is created – pessimistic as it may be – in response to power: in both films, characters bond (whether in tragedy or hope) in their collective rapport with political leadership. Therefore, the affective community thus created not so much opposes socialism as it plays a counterpart role to the imagined individualism of capitalism.

It is surprising that yet another abortion drama made in 1988, this time in China, resembles Mungiu's film in several aspects.[8] This is Tian Zhuangzhuang's *Unforgettable Life* (*Te bie shou shu shi*), about which its director once said: "My films are made for people of the next century" (Tian, quoted in Yaping 2022, 106). Since the film was not released until 2005 (only two years before *4, 3, 2* came out), history has proven him right. Aside from sharing similar themes and release dates, both Tian's and Mungiu's movies were chronologically set at the crossroads of two political eras, both were partially funded by the state, and both have strong female leads. The similarities do not stop here. Tian's film forefronts the same type of female companionship that is featured in *4, 3, 2*, this time between Lu Yun and Yuanyaun, two women in their thirties who develop a strong connection with each other.

In the beginning of the film, Lu Yun, a TV news anchor *cum* producer, walks into a hospital to abort an unwanted pregnancy from her philandering young boyfriend and immediately takes a liking to Yuanyuan, her female abortionist. Thanks to Yuanyuan facilitating contact with other women like Lu Yun, who resort to abortion in order to end their unwanted pregnancies, the reporter decides to produce a TV program meant to advance knowledge on the topic and help influence social policy. However, her initiative comes at a price: Lu Yun will only recieve permission from the station manager to go ahead with her program if she agrees to sleep with him.

Following Lu Yun's development of a strong friendship with Yuanyuan, the narrative describes the highs and lows of their oftentimes intimate relationship and is interspersed with Lu Yun's interviews of various women who visit the hospital. The documentary feel of these sequences imbues the film with a surprising naturalness which is further assisted by the jazzy 1980s soundtrack and Tian's haptic camera that lingers long enough on the protagonists' faces in close-up to reveal their innermost doubts and hesitations. During recurring scenes set in their comfortably modern apartments, where they talk while listening to Julio Iglesias and sipping canned sodas, the two women open their hearts to each other and reveal their most intimate thoughts on marriage and sex. When Yuanyuan confesses that her husband suffers from impotence, which she tacitly ascribes to her unattractiveness, Lu Yun complains of her boyfriend's insatiable sexual appetite and infidelity, while fearing that she is inhibited, which leads to her being generally dissatisfied and unfulfilled by any sexual activity. The honesty of their revelations helps bring the two women so close to each other that their relationship starts to resemble a homoerotic friendship.

The film's finale is highly surprising in its similarity to Blaier's *Postcards with Wildflowers*. Yuanyuan and Lu Yun track down a pregnant patient who refuses their services and instead calls on a private clinic run by an incompetent

[8] It is unlikely that one film influenced the other, although the copyright infringements of which Mungiu was accused in Romania prove that the topic was "in the air" in various cultures processing the memory of authoritarian leadership. This includes capitalist countries, as later shown in the case of *The Janes*.

female abortionist. Lu Yun feels particularly guilty because it was her innocent mistake that forced the patient to run away from the hospital. For that reason, although she tries to intervene in time to save the patient's life, she and Yuanyuan arrive too late on the scene to prevent a tragedy. Despite the final melodrama, the film is entirely realistic. The blackmailing that Lu Yun experiences moreover sheds much-needed light on the patriarchal system that characterized Deng's China, which extended up the professional ladder, from the lowest to the highest echelons of power. This blackmailing, as well as Lu Yun's boyfriend's philandering attitude, also reveal the everyday challenges that women had to face when fighting unwanted attention from men and recalls the dominant role that patriarchy plays in their lives. Unlike Mungiu's film, which was widely read as a critique on Communism, Tian's focus on patriarchy intimates that Communism's failure lies not in having fostered authoritarianism, but rather in failing to completely eradicate it. In a surprising side-by-side reading of the Romanian and Chinese films, it appears that neither of the two traditionalist societies suffered from too much Communism but, surprisingly, from too little of it.

Although this does not diminish the oppressiveness of one regime relative to another, China faced an issue different from Romania's. While Romania's nativist policies concentrated on expanding the population and therefore made abortion illegal, the one-child policy encouraged it. Although the three films mentioned so far do not attack state policies head on, this does not make them any less courageous in their realistic portrayal of a social issue that found little room for expression in other parts of the world until that time. The three films' blunt portrayals of abortion illustrate the progressive side of socialist cinema, even when that cinema was employed in the service of the state. This can be considered audacious for a time when Hollywood itself had difficulty tackling subjects such as sexual impotence and female inhibition, let alone abortion.

A recent American documentary film makes that difficulty clear. *The Janes* (Tia Lessin and Emma Pildes, 2022)[9] portrays the sexist, male-centric medical world of the 1970s, when abortion was illegal in most of the United States. Chicago is particularly shown to be a conservative environment in which white doctors sexually abuse pregnant women while the establishment turns a blind eye on female pleas for legalization. The documentary highlights the courage of the *Jane Collective*, a leftist group of militant feminists who between 1969 and 1973 risked their freedom to perform an estimated 11,000 illegal abortions. When contrasted with Mungiu's film, *The Janes* serves as a call to decouple generalized perceptions of Communism from the postsocialist criticism with which it is often associated. A comparative reading furthermore makes clear that the culprit behind the loss of freedom is not always ideological and that cultures should not only be measured, in monolithic fashion, against their degree of alleged indoctrination and authoritarianism, because,

---

[9] Phyllis Nagy dramatized the same story in the fiction film *Call Jane*, released in the same year.

as Žižek has warned, such ideological readings work to expiate capitalism of its own propaganda (Žižek 2001).

Rather than a cliché narrative pitting the oppressive state versus the defenseless individual, Mungiu's film garners more interest if read in connection with a particular affective regime emerging in the negotiation between the "nanny state" and the individual, and moreover between individuals themselves. The fact that both Mungiu and Tian focus on female friendships in their films shows that the collectives thus created empower individuals in socialism as much as their capitalist counterparts. Furthermore, the same collectives strike a note more harmonious than the dissonant ones portrayed in postsocialism (recall the bickering guests on the TV show in *12:08*). What both directors intimate is that oppression comes not from an authoritative state but from patriarchy, and the protagonists of both films become sufficiently enlightened to develop the necessary skills to fight against it. That is what determines both Găbița to leave her boyfriend at the end of *4, 3, 2* and Lu Yun to launch a TV program advancing sexual education in a society dominated by traditional and paternalistic power structures.

Although Mungiu does not ascribe to the world of cinema a meta-textual commentary on the oppressiveness of the Communist system, he accurately describes the realistic inner workings of a community ruled by traditionalism and dogma. He also prefigures, however, that this community is bound to be changed from within by its unruliest and most progressive subjects: the women born and raised on the principles promoting an equalitarian socialist society.

The Western View of the East

The first international "splash" of New Romanian Cinema in the West, Cristi Puiu's *The Death of Mr. Lăzărescu* appears to shine a caustic light on the apocalyptic public health system of postsocialist Romania, seen as a leftover of the disastrous socialist state dissolved through revolution in 1989. But, as Puiu himself agrees, it is not so much the negative socialist heritage that becomes a target of the director's criticism as are the human relations, and even the human condition in general (Gorzo 2017).

The story of the film is painfully simple. Lăzărescu, a man in his sixties who is suffering from stomach ulcers, suddenly and without forewarning experiences great pain and thinks it necessary to find hospital care immediately. When trying to contact his children and relatives, no one seems available to accompany him to the hospital, this obligation falling into the hands of his neighbors. The neighbors, despite showing some initial concern for his wellbeing, end up abandoning him to the whims of the medical services. This is only the beginning of a long ambulance trip, which Lăzărescu shares with a nurse who takes the place of his relatives and who genuinely wants to help him, even though she faces the brutal apathy of a medical system in disarray. After several hospitals in the capital refuse to register him as a patient, he ends up on the operating table of a feisty doctor who at first shows as much reluctance to treat Lăzărescu as the previous ones before him. The director abruptly ends the narrative at the culminating point, and, apart from the innuendo in the film's title, audiences never find out what ultimately happens to the protagonist who is last seen lying on a stretcher, prepared to be wheeled into the operating room.

The film's style sealed the fate of New Romanian Cinema and became emblematic for other directors who employed realism to describe the social conditions of postsocialism. Film scholar Monica Filimon has jokingly written that "Romanian critics, such as the late Alex Leo Şerban and Andrei Gorzo, have underlined the major leap made by Romanian cinema after Puiu's 2005 Cannes prize," because *The Death of Mr. Lăzărescu*, as Şerban has written (Şerban 2011), went so far as to separate the history of cinema "into two major 'eras' – BC and AC (before and after Cristi)" (Filimon 2014, 58).[10] This rupture, however, as we have previously seen, generated as much confusion as enthusiasm.

Chris Robé has quoted filmmaker Lucian Pintilie to explain that Cristi Puiu's film *The Death of Mr. Lăzărescu* reflects the unfavorable consequences of socialism in the present. According to the director of *Reenactment*, "Communism disappeared as a regime, not as a mentality" (Robé 2017, 1). This statement is further supported by film scholar Alina Haliliuc who has identified in the neurotic way in which characters in the film communicate with each other "terrifying language mannerisms inherited from communist times" (Haliliuc 2015, 158). Although these critics have believed that the social system depicted in Cristi Puiu's film is a remnant of Soviet authoritarianism, they have equally claimed that the film's style is solely connected to Western filmmaking practices.

In this section, I question the assumption put forth by these theorists, by claiming that, firstly, although Puiu's film does indeed depict the bad influences of socialism, it is not judgmental about the ideology of Communism but about the people who ended up (not) putting it into practice; in this way it is similar to Chinese films of the sixth generation and very dissimilar from 1990s anticommunist films. Secondly, I claim that the system described in the film is a product of postcolonialism rather than an inheritance of socialism, and Puiu's style belongs to the Eurasian postsocialist cultural sphere rather than a principally Western European filmmaking school. Finally, because the film is also evocative of universal concerns (such as the state of the medical system in developed parts of the world), I argue that, by accentuating the Communist influence, the above theorists Orientalize the film, much like the fifth-generation directors Orientalized China for Western audiences.

Yurchak has correctly identified in his critique that what blurs Western understanding of socialism (and implicitly, socialist filmmaking) is the West's

[10] Although Filimon's reference is correct, the notations are somewhat confusing because, in a separate article, Şerban has also used them differently ("BCP" and "AM," respectively) to refer to the phrases "Before Cristi Puiu" and "After Mungiu" (Şerban 2010, 3).

reliance on what he has identified as the authoritarianism/freedom binary (Yurchak 2005). According to this ultimately political principle, equally promoted by Havel, films made under socialism are seen as unable to express the full reality of the state's oppressive power, even if they were not directly concerned with it. Theorists of New Romanian Cinema have carried this binary over into the postsocialist age when they have categorized films according to their alleged political agendas, which betrays the use of cultural politics first and film studies second, and it is an eminently colonialist attitude in evaluating the worth of a cinematic product.

In *The Protestant Ethnic and the Spirit of Capitalism*, cultural theorist Rey Chow has subtly captured the entitlement of the West to speak for the rest of the world. Based on the mistaken belief that the "politically correct white subject, who imagines that he has already successfully disaffiliated from his culture's previous, more brutal forms of racism" (Chow 2002, 14), can understand cultural behavior that is foreign to his cultural space, Chow has warned us to beware of the self-legitimizing forms of Western criticism. Even if she does not mention socialism *per se*, one can extrapolate her comments about the perpetuation of racism in Western cultural approaches to China to include the rest of the socialist Bloc and make one think twice about the locus and political position from where the discourse is being enunciated.

While it would amount to discrimination to deny Chris Robé the right to identify "a communist structure of feeling that predominated during its official heyday" in socialism and to identify that structure with Communist power, it is too stereotypical and too simplistic to equate this structure of feeling with "oppressiveness." Such an act, not unlike the anticommunism of 1990s films, amounts to caricaturizing real-existing socialism, something that film critic Andrew Grossman called in relation to the Chinese New Wave the selling of (Eastern) suffering to a Western audience (Grossman 2009). Furthermore, while it is true that Puiu's hand-held camera, the pale color palette underlining the depressing blues and greens of the hospital interiors, as well as the dimly lit interiors of the protagonist's home shot mostly at night point to an overbearing anxiety and melancholic yet haptic distance, this is neither Kitchen Sink nor Italian Neorealism, as Robé, Haliciuc and Nasta have claimed. Although the long opening scene, which follows the protagonist in his kitchen (Figure 6.4), reverberates with echoes of the British New Wave, where this part of the house was used to hotly debate the domestic and economic challenges faced by the films' middle-class characters, as in Lindsay Anderson's *This Sporting Life* (1963), Puiu's *mise-en-scène* calls to mind the interiors of *Chernukha* kitchens such as that in Pitchul's *Little Vera* or even that of Bela Tarr's *The Prefab People* (*Panelkapcsolat*, 1982) which, foreshadowing the *Chernukha* style in Hungary, is set in a crammed and dark 1980s apartment in Budapest. Despite claiming the influences of Cassavetes and Wiseman, *Lăzărescu* is therefore more comparable to homegrown Eastern European films made famous shortly before the collapse of the socialist system.

Figure 6.4 Lăzărescu in his kitchen in *The Death of Mr. Lăzărescu.*

Furthermore, Puiu's film is less interested in showing Lăzărescu aimlessly carried by ambulance from one hospital to another because of a broken medical system inherited from the socialist era and more interested in pointing out that the staff's incompetence is primarily caused by an unwillingness to help. As Andreescu has written, "what was thought to be a reliable system is just a product of humans with prejudices, who give priority to personal interests over their work interests" (Andreescu 2013, 76). Quite literally, this means that medical personnel do not care in the least about Lăzărescu's wellbeing – they indeed make a "boisterous parody of caringness" (Bradshaw 2006) – with the single exception being, of course, the nurse that "takes charge" of him based on an unexplained personal whim and who sticks with him until the end of his journey. The conclusion is that neither his friends and family (who have largely defected from his life) nor his neighbors (for whom Lăzărescu is but an embarrassing nuisance) come out of their selfish shell to lend a hand to another human being in distress.

This scenario – while not necessarily radical in an individualist society – becomes something of a shock in the new democratic era, particularly when contrasted with the memory of socialism, a system in which, for better or worse, the individual was never alone. Whether in the company of friends and family (as in *Too Hot for the Month of May*) or that of enemies (as in *Too Young for Wrinkles*), protagonists in socialist cinema were always surrounded by a collective to which they willy-nilly belonged. In a parallel to Yuri Nazarov, the actor playing the father in *Little Vera*, who was well-known from socialist realist films for playing Soviet heroes, it would be more appropriate to see Lăzărescu as the dead image of a socialist-era ideal. As Andreescu has correctly observed, Lăzărescu is "strikingly different from the young and idealistic characters built during communism," as the film instead "focuses on a retired, sick, lonely, and cynical character that lives with his three cats in a shabby, dirty apartment in Bucharest" (Andreescu 2013, 75). Furthermore, when contrasted to *Red Apples* and the optimism of that film's protagonist, Lăzărescu seems to be grieving the loss of something amounting to the idealism of a past age.

Because Puiu himself has commented that his film is about "disappearance" (Nasta 2013, 162), I take this to refer not only to the disappearance of the protagonist, but of that of a social system. Because he can no longer relate to his capitalist milieu in postsocialism, he pines for the affective environment of neighbors and relatives who, even though equally incompetent, at least *performed* that they cared. While this performativity would not have cured his perforated ulcer, it would have given him the fallacious but necessary hope that he would survive. What is therefore deplored in the film is the very performative nature of socialism. The "rupture" in the movie thus comes not from a defamatory assessment of socialism but from missing, and even longing for (much alike in Mitulescu's film) the familiarity of a bygone world. As outrageous as this may sound, Lăzărescu misses Communism; therefore, far from being an *ad literam* condemnation of socialism (or its chaotic aftermath), *The Death of Mr. Lăzărescu* appears as a violent critique of capitalism.

The first (exuberant) response to *Lăzărescu* in the West was that, quite straightforwardly, there is no East and West. This reinforces the Bordwellian view held by some Romanian scholars that the New Wave originates in Western filmmaking schools and that the language of film is universal. Moreover, when Western audiences saw Puiu's film, they underscored the universality of human suffering, irrespective of political context. In support of this statement, I shall quote the non-professional remarks belonging to an anonymous author of the French newspaper *Diocese du Lyon* who, upon seeing a connection between the main character's name and the biblical text as signaling the universality of Christian motifs, resignedly declared:

> We understood from the very first images that this particular Lazarus here had little hope for resurrection. The few hours spent with Lăzărescu […] end up convincing us of the absurdity of our hyper-medicalized societies, hyper-technicized yet almost dehumanized. Suffice to spend a Saturday night in the emergency room to understand, on one's own skin, the meaning of the word "compassion."

Peter Bradshaw of *The Guardian* has equally seen the film as revelatory for the behavior of medics and medical staff the world over (Bradshaw 2006), and Ruthe Stein of *SFGATE* has mentioned: "[I]f Puiu only intended to condemn socialised medicine, 'Mr. Lăzărescu' wouldn't have made it much further than theaters in Bulgaria" (Stein 2006). Finally, returning to the film's style, Robert Sklar in *Cineaste* has contended that Puiu's *mise-en-scène* is reminiscent of Robert Altman's in *The Long Goodbye* (1973), while his pace reminds one of a Frederick Wiseman documentary or a Samuel Beckett play (Sklar 2006, Bradshaw 2006). Factoring in the 2016 release of Ken Loach's *I, Daniel Blake*, a poignant critique of Britain's insurance and medical systems, with which Puiu's film shares some criticism, nothing would strike the Western viewer as particularly "Romanian" or "postsocialist" about the topic; as screenwriter

Rădulescu himself has stated, there is no intent to "nationalize" Lăzărescu in Puiu's film.[11]

Despite these readings, the insistence of Haliciuc and Robé that the protagonists in both *4, 3, 2* and *Lăzărescu* are victims of a Communist-inspired system makes one wonder whether this amounts to self-victimization. Predicated also on Filimon's credo that "disillusionment followed the euphoria of 'revolution'"[12] and "concern for the other, never fully cultivated in communism, diminished even further" (Filimon 2017, 3), this reading enforces a political understanding of art which is influenced by the negative memorialization of Communism; in that sense, it is less film criticism than cultural politics. Furthermore, it recalls Buck-Morss' warning that the West's embracing of Malevich represents the West's antagonistic stance against Communism. This is a tricky road to follow because such critical interpretations of Puiu's film (but also of Mungiu's *4, 3, 2*) induce the necessary fantasizing of the imagined Other personified by the capitalist West. In other words, critiques blaming the frustrations of Puiu's characters and the shortcomings of the medical establishment on the negative inheritance of socialism facilitate the proliferation of Occidentalism as an antidote for the ills of postsocialism.

Similar to the anticommunist discourses that put an end to the Communist project in Romania after the 1989 revolution, the writings of Chinese-American literary theorist Xiaomei Chen have discussed the role of Occidentalist utopias in relation to the Chinese national psyche. Chen has considered *River Elegy (He shang)*,[13] a national six-part television series aired in 1988, as relevant for this topic because the film asserted that Chinese civilization desperately lagged behind the accomplishments of the West and that, despite Communist slogans purporting to have developed the country since 1949, China was stuck in the throes of backwardness. Claiming that Chinese civilization was hurting and in decline because of the "passive defeat over the past century that has conditioned us psychologically," the film concluded that "since 1840 people tended to cover up our weakness and backwardness with the greatness and splendor of our past."[14] In *Occidentalism: A Theory of Counter-Discourse in Post-Mao China*, Chen has contended that the film "can be best understood neither as an example of Chinese naïveté nor of Western imperialism, but as a potent anti-official discourse employed by the Chinese intelligentsia to express what was otherwise politically impossible

[11] This was imparted by the film's screenwriter at the *Secvențe* workshop held in Bucharest in 2011.

[12] The word is placed between quotation marks in the original text, signifying the purportedly fallacious nature of the popular movement and its orchestration by Communist forces.

[13] The Chinese characters making up the title, 殇, are literally translatable as "river of premature death."

[14] The "shame" purportedly refers to the so-called "century of humiliation" and 1840 to the forced opening up of China by Britain's Opium Wars, which pushed the country down the path of semi-colonization.

and ideologically inconceivable" (Chen 1995, 24). In a statement reminiscent of Marchetti, Chen has considered that the concept of "Occident" is used in the film in order "to liberate" what has formerly been repressed by the promoters of the "Open door policy."

Given that she wrote this in 1995, Chen may be exonerated of being unable to foresee the developments of the "Open door policy," which ultimately led to a veritable Westernization of all things cultural (and of course economic) in post-Deng Xiaoping China. To her defense, history seems to ultimately validate Chen, as it very much appears that what she has called the "liberating" Occidentalist discourse has "won out" despite the repression of Tiananmen, which Chen has feared would represent "the end of Deng's 'pro-Western' era and the beginning of a closed-door policy once again" (43). This argument presumes – and this is comparable to the Romanian postsocialist discourse – that because nationalism only brought poverty and isolation, China needed to de-nationalize and look to the West. Yet, such a view replaces one evil with another: the nationalist one with the Western one. It substitutes national identity with a Western-sanctioned view of China, which produces an essentialized culturalism and represents the country's ultimate defeat. Furthermore, this eminently Occidentalist view itself has been borrowed from the West, which has been using it since the beginning of the Cold War to fight against the frightening Communist project. Its adoption is clearly shown in *Lăzărescu*, and it demonstrates the negative effects of Westernization while capturing the painful transition to capitalism.

If one is to see the release of *The Death of Mr. Lăzărescu* in the same context as the fifth generation's charming of the West in the 1990s, one might understand the position of both Chinese and Romanian anticommunist critics. Craving Western attention, they saw in Puiu's and Zhang Yimou's films an alleged return to a Western filmmaking style that they felt socialism had unreasonably denied Romanian and Chinese cinemas until that time. This is more than self-orientalism, however; it is self-victimization. By inferring that socialism is the culprit for all capitalist-era evils, critics of the New Waves looking solely westward amount to nothing short of pitying their own fate. As such, they seek outside (Western) validation for what they conceive as the national wretchedness of their countries' postsocialist condition, without noticing that postsocialist wretchedness spans the entire expanse of postsocialist Eurasia. The only salvation from their self-labeled deplorable condition is another cry for help, along the lines of Milan Kundera. This approach, however, denies Central Europe its local character because it aligns it – via the glamorization of authors such as Kafka, whom Kundera instrumentalizes to demonstrate the region's Western heritage (Kundera 1984) – with the unitary cultural sphere of the West. Clamoring, like Nasta and her followers, for a reunion with the West would furthermore delegate the sphere of Kundera's "totalitarian Russia" to backwardness, therefore enacting more separation and distance in a gesture that is eerily reminiscent of the present political context.

If there is a cinematic alternative to the Europeanizing and transnationalizing drives of Nasta and Marchetti, as well as a way to effect unification by not excluding and creating other "Others," then it is not a turn westwards, but a turn to the condemned intra-Eurasian brother, and Jia Zhangke is the one to show us how this process can be put into practice.

The World and the Eurasian Postsocialist Condition

If the Chinese fifth generation reformulated the theses of socialist realism in the language of cognitivism, as I have argued, the same power of cinema to fight against injustice inherited from socialist film is also the topic of the celebrated sixth-generation films of Jia Zhangke. Seen by a few critics (Marchetti 2018, Lu 2007b, Rosenbaum 2019) as a straight-forward condemnation of the nefarious effects of transition from communism to capitalism in China, *The World* (*Shijie*, 2004) acts as an appropriate Chinese counterpart to Romania's *Lăzărescu*.

Forced by dire conditions to migrate to Beijing and work in a theme park that offers Chinese tourists a miniature replica of Western attractions, Tao, a woman in her early thirties, discovers the urban blues and dissatisfaction that come with her less-than-glamorous job. While working in the park, she realizes that her relationship with Taisheng, her visiting village boyfriend, needs to end because of the latter's infidelities. It is also here that she meets a Russian coworker, Anna, who was pushed to emigrate from her home country by precarious circumstances similar to the ones that forced Tao to find a job in the city. Anna, however, is forced by the park's exploitative management into a semi-bondage condition bordering on prostitution. Using animation and dreamlike sequences, Jia gives the park a particularly oneiric character, which is in tune with Tao's imagining of capitalist modernity. However, this modernity equally features a dystopian character that forces Tao to develop her friendship with Anna. Because Anna stands for a more classical view of the world, to which Tao can better relate, the latter finds her relationship with Anna soothing and compensatory for the cold-heartedness of her capitalist surroundings.

Not only does the theme park, as Marchetti has correctly pointed out, personify China's disenchantment with globalization and capitalism (Marchetti 2018), but it also symbolically references the Outside and represents the Occidentalized attraction of the Western Other. This is made even clearer because the park mimetically copies the West, whose superficiality and artificiality echo Baudrillard's simulacrum. If the West in the socialist imaginary during Maoism appeared as a trope permitting the socialist subject to cope with the difficult realities of socialism, the West in postsocialism, as in the French philosopher's understanding, has not merely become a copy of the real, but the new real itself. In other words, the theme park *cum* simulacrum is the reification of Occidentalism, an upside-down mirror image of Orientalism, imagining the West as a land of plenty that contrasts with Second- and Third-World precarity. That is why the response of American film critic Jonathan Rosenbaum to the film is valid. He has stated that "[o]ne reason *The World* is such a potent companion piece to *Platform* [Jia's earlier film], which views the Cultural Revolution over many years from the vantage point of a traveling theater troupe, is that it can be said to describe another failed cultural revolution – capitalism, seen from the vantage point of Chinese communism" (Rosenbaum 2019).

The World is therefore not so much about migrants and globalization as it is about the destruction of the socialist-era utopia personified by the Western Other. Tao's attitude towards Anna is molded by her socialist experience, during which the Other personified the hope of escape, the promise of an alternative reality that would counterbalance the grim economic reality of socialism. However, in the postsocialist landscape, escape is no longer predicated on the illusory presence of the Western Other, but on that of the re-fraternized Other of the intra-socialist world. In the friendship between the Chinese and the Russian characters, the film conjures up nostalgia for a community of "fraternal nations" and, implicitly, for the proletarian slogan calling for unification across borders, seen here as devoid of its socialist-era bravura – to paraphrase Dostoyevsky – as a unity of the humiliated and insulted, of those left behind by the dismantling of a world that never came into being, yet a world whose utopian character deeply contrasts with that of the indeed dystopian character of capitalism. *Lăzărescu* and *The World* in fact fantasize the imagined Other – both the Other of the disappearing collectivism of socialism and that of the individualism of the West. They are, therefore, not only staples of postsocialist "miserabilism" (both thematically and aesthetically), but also socio-political markers descended from the dogmatic era of socialism.

In that sense, Jia's film is an apt response to Chen's Occidentalist predictions, because it shows how China's adoption of Occidentalism failed to guarantee the much-coveted progress of humanism. Contrary to Chen's argument, Jia's film reinforces the theses of socialist-era films which saw liberation as attainable via internal struggle. Such is the message put forth by Nicolaescu's *Hot Days* or by the protagonist in *Breaking with Old Ideas*: adapting national values to the international context makes more sense than adopting international values to fit local history. Interestingly, the same Occidentalism promoted by Chen in China was used by anticommunist Eastern Europeans to effect a disproportionate destruction of the country's socialist heritage. In a pessimistic coda to *Hot Days*, Romanian journalist Ovidiu Amălinei has shown how, as result of an inefficient privatization process, the industrial infrastructure formerly used to manufacture ship propellers under socialism was dismembered and sold for spare parts and scrap metal. Lamenting the demise of the "largest non-ferrous foundry in South-Eastern Europe" (Amălinei 2022), his article has bemoaned an act of destruction which brought profit to postsocialist robber barons and destitution to its former employees.

What we know from the bifurcated paths of Romania and China as instantiations of Occidentalist discourse – the Other knows better; the Other does better; the Other is superior – is highly characteristic of subaltern cultures all over Eurasia. Postsocialism reproduces an image of the Balkans which Todorova has described as self-orientalist via discourses claiming that Eurasia is lagging behind the West. These developmentalist discourses, however, represent appropriations of the Western gaze by postsocialist and postcolonial Eurasian thinkers, which promote a view of postsocialist Eurasia as defective. Throwing away the nationalizing drive of Communist ideology plays into the hands of a postsocialist capitalism that is only predicated on the Western imaginary. Adopting this discourse, both Chinese and Romanian postsocialisms perform an act of self-denial, which negates the political identity of both countries. Since self-denial is predicated on the scapegoating of the socialist period – seen as the sum of all evils – promoters of this discourse have adopted the hypostasis of total defeat, a hypostasis bespeaking the domination of Western capital and centuries-old imperialism, which the Communist episode prevented only on a temporary basis. This indicates, one more time, that Eurasian socialist economies suffered not from too much Communism, but from not enough of it.

7 Postsocialism and Occidentalism

When they came out in the 1990s, anticommunist films promoted a bipolar view of the world, replacing the ambivalence and symbolism of 1980s productions with a Manichean treatment of the past. Their discourse regarded socialism as an evil that capitalism would root out. New Wave films made in the capitalist period, however, did not turn out to be an open window onto the horrors of Communist regimes. On the contrary, they revived the polysemy and ambivalence, which anticommunist film through its promotion of binaries and revalorization of the once-buried ideals of fascism had succeeded to root out.

The New Waves in both Romania and China inherited the polysemy of earlier generations, not because they finally gave voice to the oppressed bourgeois humanism repressed by Communism (as it happens in Mărgineanu's films, for example), but because they preserved the contradictory nature of the Communist project with its ambiguous (if uncertain) track-record of attempting to instate change. As *4, 3, 2* demonstrates, they revisit the past from a contestatory position which is critical of the anticommunist one. An aspect ignored by the Western reception of both the Romanian and the Chinese New Waves is that these films, by rejecting the "before and after" binary, attempt to perfect the already emancipatory platform of Communism.

If this is not performed in a systematic, observable fashion, it is because, as László Strausz has rightly argued, the distinct realism of Romanian New Wave characters comes from their hesitation, from their being unable to "make sense of the complex, often impenetrable social realities they are faced with" (Strausz 2017, 2). Following Gorzo and identifying a Bazinian "ambiguity of the real" in modes of narration associated with Puiu's cinema and the Romanian New Wave in general, Strausz has assigned this hesitation and ambiguity to a historical mode of being in the world which "can be traced back to the Ceaușescu years, during which the authoritarian state used to write and rewrite versions of the national past to conform to political motivations" (2). While this is both true and untrue, as writing and rewriting versions of the national past is attributable to both the Ceaușescu years and the fascist ones, which rearticulated the romantic nationalism of the nineteenth century, postsocialist hesitation harks back to what I have termed performance under socialism.

Oscillating between performing dignity and engaging with the West in a dialogue that films were supposed to mediate, the affect thereby created what amounted to a national identity of sorts, which withstood the artificiality caused by ruptures. Rather than hailing from an immaterial, distant past in which capitalism and Christianity purportedly locate the origins of humanism, postsocialist New Wave cinemas, in Romania as well as China, did not instrumentalize the past in order to legitimate fascist ideology, but highlighted their continuity with the past while questioning the values of both past and present. In that, both New Waves are as dialectical as their socialist-era counterparts.

While Radu Jude shows this better than other directors in his generation, his *Don't Expect Too Much from the End of the World* (*Nu aștepta prea mult de la sfârșitul lumii*, 2023) highlights the continuity between the past and the present more prominently than his earlier work. By contrasting the completely exhausted, overworked female delivery driver in his film to the female taxi driver in Lucian Bratu's 1981 *Angela merge mai departe*,[1] Jude draws a clear parallel between the two political systems. The dialectical synthesis emerging from this parallelism via intercutting between scenes of the present and the past (Jude manipulates Bratu's footage to draw explicit parallels) foregrounds the resemblance between the female condition under socialism and capitalism, emphasizing that both female protagonists are exploited by the systems in different ways. By *questioning* rather than *combatting* Communist heritage, as well as capitalism, Jude's film articulates the voices of the otherwise mute(d) postsocialist subjects.

In highlighting continuity rather than rupture, another merit of the Romanian New Wave and of the sixth generation in China is that of having questioned the erstwhile Occidentalism of their immediate predecessors: the anticommunist generation in Romania and the fifth generation in China. A good example is Mungiu's debut film *Occident* (2002), in which the director contests the saccharine version of the West created in the national imaginary. Even if his satirizing of crude Westernization does not follow the politically correct norms of late capitalism, Mungiu shows that adopting the capitalist imaginary as panacea for the very real pains of postsocialist Romania is unrealistic.

As an alternative to the transnationalizing drive that subsumes the socialist past to the capitalist present and the former Second World to the First, Jia's *The World* similarly upholds the realistic version of an un-Occidentalized Eastern Bloc. While the early 1950s' "Friendship of Nations" or *Druzhba Narodov* slogan, which became the cultural *porte-parole* for international cooperation throughout the socialist bloc, may have been limited and naïve, the program contributed to the creation not of an entirely "New Man," as the early Communists had hoped, but that of a Different Man. Different, that is, from Western capitalism. This difference was based on the dissemination of socialist affect as a means of achieving rapprochement between the vastly different

[1] While some websites translate this film title literally as *Angela Goes On*, which does the Romanian original a disservice, IMDB prefers to keep the Romanian title untranslated.

cultures of the Soviet Union and, later, of the entire Communist Bloc. The result for postsocialism, as shown in Jia's film, is that, instead of feeding on the utopian values of Communism, this Different Man and Different Woman appropriated the ambiguity and polysemy of the failed socialist project and incorporated it into the real-existing lives of postsocialist subjects.

Despite its failure as a system, therefore, aside from a depressed postsocialist world, Communism created a rather homogenous Second World from Bucharest to Beijing, one in which fraternity and idealization interpenetrated each other to mold an *avant-la-lettre* transnational postsocialist subject. Not unlike Benedict Anderson's print capitalism (Anderson 1983), Communism birthed a certain Screen Socialism, which ended up uniting not exactly the proletarians dreamed of by Lenin, but the middle-class intellectuals of the Eastern Bloc. Because audiences saw roughly the same films in China and Romania, the by-product of the original goal of socialist internationalism – the forging of ties between peoples subjugated by capitalism – turns out to have been more successful than originally thought. This may also be the reason why audiences in China and Romania today have more in common with each other than with the First World.

Another upshot of the "Friendship of Nations" was the creation of respect for the Other, whereas the privilege of the Enlightenment had only managed to create condescendence. Although visible in Jia's films, this respect however was never fully unearthed from under the rubble of the Eastern Bloc collapse. This is because, as Verdery has put it, Communism continues to be under-researched due to Western scholars' lack of access to socialist countries during the Cold War, an era that required non-interference in national affairs, but came to mean the non-understanding thereof (Verdery 1996). In response to postsocialist pessimism with the erstwhile goals of the internationalist movement, Russian literary critic Nadejda Averyanova has suggested using the term "enmity of nations" to highlight the slippage that had taken place from *druzhba* to *vrazhba narodov* (Karasyov 2010).[2] Despite this slippage, films produced by China's sixth generation and Romanian New Wave directors continue to show that the old Eastern Bloc cooperation project holds promise for the twenty-first-century scholar, mainly because it offers enormous potential for reassembling a conceptual and historical puzzle that has never been seriously studied in the political sciences, anthropology, or (even less) film studies.

This cooperation literally comes alive in Porumboiu's *12:08 East of Bucharest*, where one of the commentators who phones in to join the discussion about the revolution happens to be a Chinese ethnic and small boutique owner who lives in the same town as the protagonists. Chen respects honesty and reciprocity, unlike other callers who regularly disparage the guests on the show. He also maintains that an honest search for truth, like the one which the TV producer is performing, cannot take place in the absence of respect for one another and for oneself, which he believes Romanians as a people are

[2] While "druzhba" in Russian means "friendship," "vrazhba" means "enmity."

generally lacking. Offended by his remarks, the talk-show host mocks Chen in response, referring to him as "the Chinese," and reproves him for meddling in a revolution that is "none of his business." However, Chen's concerns regarding the treatment of the guests on the show are entirely legitimate. Referencing the generally abject treatment of the Other in Romanian culture over time, as shown in Jude's films, Chen represents the missing link between Romanian and Asian rapprochement, and on a certain level he repairs the slippage that occurred in Romanian-Chinese relations after the much contested "Asianization" of the country.

It is rare that the figure of the Other is featured in Romanian films, but effective – especially when treated critically, as in Cristian Mungiu's *RMN* (2022), another film that portrays the figure of the foreigner in Romanian culture. In a story inspired by real events, a group of Sri Lankan workers hired by a rural bakery are violently assaulted by a bigoted village crowd. The only one to stand up for their rights is their female boss, who finds the food that the Sri Lankans cook for her, their courtesy and their determination to move to a foreign country to help their families endearing. The position of the Sri Lankan guest workers in Romania mirrors the status of Romanian immigrants in Germany. Although mistreated there at the hands of his Western employers, the protagonist of the film shows his opprobrium of the Sri Lankans and joins the anti-foreigner crowd himself, promoting ethnic hatred upon his return to Romania. The film not only gives evidence of the astounding hypocrisy of one subaltern nation towards another but also bemoans the prejudice intervening after the traumatic decoupling of capitalist Romania from socialist-era internationalist goals, which used to treat socialist and postcolonial subjects as brethren in a common anti-imperialist crusade. The film also shows that, following the downfall of Communism, the intra-socialist brotherhood has been replaced with intra-Eurasian phobia and discrimination.

Porumboiu's oblique commentary on Romanian disrespect via "the Chinese" in *12:08* and Mungiu's commentary on hypocrisy via the treatment of the Sri Lankans in *RMN* point to an ambivalent national self-image that is divided between aspiration to the Western capitalist imaginary, on the one hand, and the haunting of the socialist past, on the other. In the anticommunist narrative, the socialist past acts as an obstacle for full membership to the Western club, which creates hatred for the past, and therefore hatred for oneself as a nation. This is the very contradiction that "the Chinese" in Porumboiu's film identifies as paramount for the shaping of a faulty national image. Chen further intimates that self-hatred comes from a lack of self-acceptance, which China, even though equally Occidentalist, partially avoided due to a more accepting view of the past.

Performing Difference

A common question at film festival Q&As following the screenings of East European films is: "How come your film represents us, too?" This sounds as if national neighbors did not quite expect the difficulties of a postsocialist country such as Romania to be similar to those of Bulgaria, for example. Echoing *Lăzărescu*'s reception in Western Europe and the US, the producers answer that audiences all over the world, postsocialist *and* Western, from France over Russia to the United States, make similar comments about their films.

In counter-distinction to the producers' remark, I ask whether films made in the politically subaltern cultures of the depressed Second World, which the Romanian and Chinese New Waves represent, do not perchance articulate the voices of a mental collective that is different from that of the First World. While creating a new division between the East and West is farthest from my mind and while truly believing that binaries separate rather than guard us against precarity, destabilization and war, I nevertheless ask whether the bifurcated postsocialist paths of Eurasia and the West do not require a conceptualization of their economies, national histories and cultures that is different from the one employed at present. Before we attempt to make postsocialist filmmaking into a copy of capitalist filmmaking, we need to question the validity of Bordwell's cognitivism. While cognitivism argues that Eurasian postsocialist films can be integrated to a universal way of filmmaking which is the product of the leveling effects of Enlightenment values, I argue that, while for Western audiences postsocialist films are about the human condition, for the postsocialists themselves they are about subalternity. This makes the spectating act of Eurasian audiences different from that of Western capitalist ones, in spite of apparent similarities in reception.

This differential is caused by the thematic concern of the films themselves. Via their display of precarity and poverty, which is reminiscent of Third Cinema theories, Eurasian cinemas perform an expiative ritual to which subalternity confines them. Moreover, Eurasian cinema performs the cultural and civilizational fears of the West, literalizing the West's innermost fears of its hidden traumas and, metaphorically speaking, acting as a bandage of sorts for the West's hemorrhage. This is why, although Puiu's *Lăzărescu* identifies the absence of care as a universal concern, the film's iteration of this absence in a Eurasian context performs the West's fear of regression to a primitive social state and thus accomplishes a cathartic intervention which absolves the West of its own absence of care. This further means that the East takes upon itself – in almost Christ-like manner – the "sins" of the West and, by way of Dostoyevskian suffering, redeems them. By positioning themselves as metaphorical sacrificial lambs for the First World, as it were, subaltern films not only imbue the Romanian and Chinese cultural conditions with a melodramatic responsibility that shapes their national characters, but they also mold a specific affect, indeed create an affective subalternity, that is both recognized and recognizable onscreen as reification of the dialectical postsocialist/postcolonial "soul" of the Eastern Other. In other words, they effectively spell the East's alterity as identity.

Therefore, when Doru Pop has asked in reference to the Romanian New Wave whether "this group of filmmakers, and a few others who followed in their footsteps, adhere to a coherent cinema aesthetics" and whether "there [is] a 'code,' or a language, or a syntax, or maybe just a common ground on which their international success can be explained in terms of film theory and movie criticism" (Pop 2014, 12), the answer is clear: not only do they share something in common, but they also share a postsocialist common language understandable from Beijing to Bucharest, as well as an aesthetic that is strikingly similar, from Cristi Puiu to Jia Zhangke. Therefore, even though Pop has argued that "[t]his new cinema happening in Romania during the last decade is fundamentally a part of the European cinema" (13), which achieves "[t]he process of integration of the so-called 'new Europe' into the 'old European' world" (14), Romanian cinema's newly found affinity with China in postsocialism begs for a reorientation of cultural politics, in a direction that is primarily rooted in a collective (post)socialist affect. Indeed, this communal transnational "structure of feeling" further brands Eurasianism as a distinct type of subalternity born out of poverty and oppression, on the one hand, and out of shared Occidentalism and a sense of self-hatred, on the other. These help to redefine the national mental collective along an axis that is different from that of the West's history of colonialism, dominance and imperialism.

As we have seen in Jia Zhangke's *The World* and Cristi Puiu's *The Death of Mr. Lăzărescu*, these films are mini-comments on the theory of Occidentalism as liberation. Standing in opposition to the anticommunist discourse, however, their miserabilism and Third Cinema-derived aesthetics shows that nothing about and through themselves is liberatory. They agree to act as what Jacques Derrida in reference to Plato has called "pharmakon" – that is, as both medicine and poison (Derrida 1981). That is, they are medicine in as much as their effect cures the West, and they are poisonous in that they represent the East's ultimate sacrifice. This sacrifice, however, is deceptive because what lies beneath it is an offering, an opening for dialogue, an invitation to reciprocation which the West has not been able to "get" since the time of socialist realism and since the Chinese-made Korean War films of the 1960s. Despite their misrecognition in the West, these films are still more empowering for the subaltern than importing Occidentalism into Eurasia, because they force the West to openly confront its Eurasian counterpart in sincere dialogue.

This dialogue has been previously attempted, yet its participants have failed to communicate with one another. When Italian filmmaker Michelangelo Antonioni and his crew visited the impregnable fortress that China was in the 1970s to make *Chung Kuo*, an impressive documentary that was to explain China to the world, the Italian and the Chinese sides ended up in conflict. Although invited by Mao's premier, Zhou Enlai, to make a film about the New China, the Italians were fascinated by the very aspects of everyday life that the Chinese found shameful. While Antonioni often filmed poor-looking subjects and structures in ruins because he found them – as in the Third Cinema manifesto – real and beautiful, Zhou Enlai had hoped that the Italians would focus on their newly built factories and found the Italians' behavior insulting.

Reading the film, Rey Chow has branded Antonioni's fascination with a civilization up to that point unknown to the Italian director as coeval with Othering (Chow 2014). Since the film was rejected by the Chinese government and only partially distributed in China, this apparently reinforces the veracity of Chow's position. However, what was lost in translation between the two cultures and perceived incorrectly by Zhou Enlai himself – as attested by Jia Zhangke in his revealing documentary *I Wish I Knew* (*Hai shang chuan qi*, 2010) – is the unavoidability of Othering in intercultural dialogue. What Antonioni is mainly surprised about in *Chung Kuo* is not the cliché of rural China as an uninterrupted civilization, but his own ignorance. This misunderstanding is what creates the rupture between the two cultures, and not some deeper commentary on physiological differences bordering on exoticization and even racism, as has been subtly implied by Chow. Allowing to exoticize each other might signify a first step towards understanding, as opposed to feigning understanding of each other.

Of course, the sense of awe and wonder of the Western gaze, which cannot help but *gaze* in the most literal sense of the word, is Eurocentric, but it is neither intruding, nor defining of its object of perception: "We don't pretend to explain China. We'd like only to begin to observe this large repertoire of faces, of gestures, of customs," says the narrator in the film. Antonioni's is a gesture of befriending, an invitation that says: I see you, and I realize that I know nothing. This, however, escapes the consciousness of the object of perception, who can only see Westerners as Westerners, a picture which reinforces the divide. Chow is in perfect agreement here with both Zhou Enlai and the Gang of Four, who hated the film. In her take on *Chung Kuo*, she is disappointed because, despite his alleged love for Chinese civilization, an enlightened person such as Antonioni in fact does not know China or its people.

Is Chow right in allowing that Antonioni "Others"? Undoubtedly. Because of the centuries-old burden of colonialism, however, the only alternative approach to the Other is to fake sameness. This, incidentally, personifies the current transnationalist drive of academic discourse, which theorist Dan Vukovich has criticized as the forced "becoming sameness" of China (Vukovich 2012, 1), because this discourse forces China to become the same as Western civilization. Going a step further, Žižek has ridiculed transnationalism for its belief that under the skin of every Chinese person hides an American wanting to break free from the shackles of dictatorial politics (Žižek 1998).

When Chow reads Western fascination as an essentialist gesture, she implies that this approach needs to be stamped out in order to avoid Othering (Chow 2014). What is missing in Chow's response, however, is the fact that Othering also carries a performative element that inscribes the interrelationship between the two worlds with a quality of reverence, of respect, of awe. No dialogue between the postsocialist world and the West in the wake of colonialism can avoid the ghosts of Othering, nationalism and fascism. To claim otherwise is to ignore and repress history in the name of faking sameness. And while Othering, nationalism and fascism should not be validated or encouraged, if any dialogue is to take place between postsocialist Eurasia and the West, it does mean that they have to be *performed*.

As seen in the example of the Korean War films, what Eurasia wants, and this may reflect the melodrama that Dissanayake has called the East's primordial condition (Dissanayake 1993), is most literally to play – that is, to perform; to carnivalize *à la* Bakhtin the East-West divide, therefore to *performatize* the political and thus to finally dispense with the burden of binary formations. The East wants to bring back Bhabha's contestatory angle via play. In this type of dialogue, the ambassadorial function of film – its inherently performative mediating power – can be reused, as it was in the age of high socialism when film, no matter how differently spectated across cultures, acted as a gift, which induced an obligatory feeling of reciprocation and, ultimately, of compromise. Incidentally, this would save Eurasia's sought-after dignity and make Iepan's question why the Second World has to "prove itself" to the First unnecessary.

What follows from a crude parallel of *modi vivendi* between Eurasia and the West – at least as far as cinema is concerned – is that the very concept of "identity" is but a privilege of the rich, and the "true" nature of the Second and the Third Worlds lies in *performing* their identity. In an alternative to a classical reading of identity, Slovenian philosopher Alenka Zupančič has proposed the model of the mask as the truth. Claiming in her study on comedy that "[e]verything is deceptive, only the mask never lies" (Zupančič 2001, 103). Zupančič has argued that theatricality is the fastest and most effective strategy to short-circuit the Lacanian symbolic order. Arguing that the Other in effect structures the symbolic coordinates of our world (100), Zupančič has concluded that our true identity comes to the surface via the façade, or the mask that we choose to present to the others. In our example, referencing the Eastern sacrifice mentioned earlier, the Other in effect stands for the genuine (but concealed) identity of the West.

If Eurasia stands for the Other in this renewed Western/postsocialist divide, the postsocialists would only be able to admit to their inferiority in dramatized form, only knowing that the mask that they present to others is their shared Occidentalist dream meant to offer the subaltern access to the world of the former colonizer. While this may hark back to Havel's dishonesty of thinking one thing while performing another, the subaltern's new engagement with the West via theatricality is different from the authoritarian context in the former socialist bloc, which Havel had in mind. In this new scenario, the subaltern does not perform their adherence to performative truths, as in Yurchak, but chooses to adhere to Western values willfully, hoping that in response they will be appreciated for doing so.

While the subaltern appears voiceless and oppressed in relation to the more powerful West – recall the Chinese soldiers burying themselves in snow in *Battle of Lake Changjin*; the rejection that Lăzărescu faces in several of the hospitals he visits; or even, more evidently, the friendship between Tao and Anna in the face of authoritarian capitalism in *The World* – the subaltern is only apparently defeated. This is because, while performing her subalternity (her hypostasis of defeat in the face of the West) so as to ingratiate herself with the dominant powers, the subaltern also knows that she is more powerful than the Westerner. While for the Westerner subalternity is only subalternity, for the Easterner subalternity amounts to what the African-American sociologist W. E. B. Du Bois over a century ago has called "double consciousness" or the ability of "looking at one's self through the eyes of others" (8).[3] This is because the subaltern knows more about the Westerner than *vice versa* and because the subaltern is conscious that she is being seen (but not understood) by the locus of power. This not only allows the subaltern access to additional knowledge about authority, but it also gives the Eurasian freedom to use this knowledge in order to negotiate with any dominant and overpowering force, such as neocolonialism.

As Netzer shows in *Child's Pose*, where the mother saves her adult child from prison by corrupting the police force, the precarity of the postsocialist-postcolonial world allows the subaltern not only to play second fiddle to the West, but also to get away with anything – in this case, quite literally, murder. This freedom not only endows the postsocialist Eurasian with the necessary agency to engage in dialogue with the West, but it also puts Eurasian culture in the privileged position of being both dangerous and unpredictable. This gives the subaltern the same advantage as the oppressed collectives in Mungiu's *4, 3, 2* or in Lou's *Summer Palace*.

When contesting the authoritarianism of the Soviet Union in the late 1980s, Milan Kundera called for the integration of Central Eastern European culture into the Western sphere of influence, therefore admitting the defeat of the subaltern in the face of Soviet authoritarianism. Before Kundera, however, a group of anonymous Chinese journalists writing in the national daily *Renmin Ribao* (*People's Daily*) in 1977 had based their contestation of Soviet authoritarianism on Mao's erstwhile theory of contradictions as well as international cooperation: "If unity is sought through struggle, it will live; if unity is sought through yielding, it will perish" (Renmin Ribao 1977). Unlike Kundera, the Chinese journalists called for unity across the Second and Third Worlds for defense against what Khrushchev's opponents at the time of the Sino-Soviet split called "revisionism." This position was still congruent with the socialist project of fraternity among the oppressed, and therefore determinedly against both Soviet and American imperialism. It is this position of renewed fraternity that *The World* as well as films of the Romanian New Wave could perform, if only allowed to cooperate with each other, as it were, from positions of empowered subalternity.

[3] At the turn of the century, Du Bois sought to apply his concept to black folk in a racist America, but it has since been expanded to cover subaltern groups in other parts of the world, among them also Eastern Europe.

Defeat as Victory

Paul Pickowicz, a scholar of Chinese cinema, has described the post-war nationalization of the film industry by the Communists in 1949 as a defeat masked by the sign of Communist victory. Portraying the way in which the Communists confiscated and nationalized the studios formerly controlled by the Japanese, Pickowicz has derided the Chinese government for "declaring its intention of going into the postwar motion picture business," which "was a first for China" (Pickowicz 2013, 123). In his thinking about the transfer of power from capitalism to Communism, Pickowicz has obviously employed a mindset predicated on what the British commander leading the Yugoslav brigades in the 1940s had termed incomprehensible to a person who has learned to think only in the "code of capitalism." Moreover, Pickowicz has ignored that the Communist film directors prior to 1949 were working under what in his monograph *Dianying* Jay Leyda has called "the threat of the two most repressive political systems in modern history, the Kuomingtang and the Japanese occupation" (Leyda, 1972 71). Other historians have equally discussed the danger to which leftist filmmakers and actors prior to the Communist revolution were exposed under Chiang Kai-shek's regime, which slaughtered Communists at every opportunity. The literary scholar Yingjin Zhang has written that "[t]he impact of leftist film criticism was immediate, and its penetration to the heart of the KMT-controlled newspapers disturbed the Nanjing government, which had tried every means possible to curb the spread of pro-Communist or pro-socialist ideas. As in film production, the crackdown on the leftists was relentless" (Zhang 2004, 66).

I have brought into discussion Pickowicz's argument in order to underline a common postsocialist strategy used to describe both the Chinese Civil War and the War of Japanese Resistance as "defeats," despite their being antinationalist and anticolonial movements lasting a remarkable two decades and resulting in millions of victims. Not unlike the (Western) collective forgetting of bombardments of the US-led alliance in the Korean War which, according to new research, caused four million casualties among the civil population alone and destroyed 95 percent of Pyongyang,[4] this projection of a Western ideological framework onto the history of subaltern nations tells us something about the power of cultural hegemony in a world in which socialism, like Romania in the anticommunist imaginary, was rerouted from victory to defeat, and the memory of victory became trapped in the capitalist underground.

---

[4] The famous director of *Shoah*, Claude Lanzmann in his second-to-last documentary, *Napalm*, which was distributed in 2017, one year prior to his death, recounts the director's visit to Pyongyan as a young man in the 1960s, when he was sent there as a volunteer on the Communist side. Using the touching yet unconsumated brief affair with a Korean nurse, Lanzmann describes the horrific effects that mass-scale American napalm bombing had on the North Korean capital. One of the victims of this campaign was the nurse herself, who had lost one of her breasts in the bombing.

Accepting that progress in postcolonial modernity was achieved – particularly in the Chinese context – through struggle, the primordial Marxian concept appealed to by Mao, the theory of contradictions remains, as far as I am concerned, a valid category to explain the evolution of the socialist and postcolonial worlds. Maoism here synthesizes the difference between socialism and postsocialism: while the postsocialists attempt to recuperate Kundera's self-Orientalizing subjection of the Second World to the First, socialists (particularly the Chinese ones) advocated for subaltern agency through (mostly) cultural cooperation among the Second and Third Worlds, as evident on the cultural front in the rich exchange of films between China and Eastern European countries such as Romania, Albania, or Yugoslavia. While this cooperation may not have materialized as the front of the struggle against imperialism that it literally advocated, it did create, so I argue, a very diverse international community. This community became, with the help of transnational socialist cinema and socialist affect, effectively (and affectively) homogenous, regardless of whether their spectators went with or against the socialist project. Turning on its head Pickowicz's statement on Communist victory in Mao's China, according to which the Chinese went from victory over the Japanese to being defeated by the Communists in 1949, socialism instituted a mode of idealizing defeat which comes close to the representation of powerlessness in Third Cinema. Despite being a failed economic experiment, Communism created cultural interrelational patterns, as well as societal and individual behaviors that offered a semblance of self-dignity to the entire space affected by its ideology. The cultural changes brought about by socialist programs during half a century of Communism were as real as the economic failures. To ignore these changes is to deny historical truth.

Slavoj Žižek is right when he claims that the only real consequence of the indiscriminate portrayal of socialist history in a negative light is the possible whitewashing of capitalism. While *Lăzărescu*'s critics claim that Communism, as a beastly system, is still alive underneath the veneer of a developing yet corruptible democracy, Puiu's film shows that the erstwhile goals of collectivism have already solidified into a particular Eurasian character – that of real-existing postsocialism – which, instead of questioning Communism, is critical of democracy. This is because the Eurasian sees (and inevitably judges) the ideals of democracy merely as ornamental as the propagandist ones of erstwhile socialism. The generation of film directors brought up under totalitarianism (to which both New Wave Romanian and sixth-generation Chinese directors belong) sees through the fakeness and hypocrisy of democracy, of the values trumpeted by the West during the Cold War, because it can equally see through the fakeness of totalitarianism. This double sight – or Du Bois' double consciousness – gives their generation an advantage: that of seeing the effects of totalitarian democracy in action.

Unlike critics claiming that socialist-era film is indoctrinating, the examples from the socialist period used here show that film should be read at the polysemous level at which it was intended – that is, as a dialectical work documenting the twofold relationship between the socialist state and its audiences. Socialist film, as Zupančič's mask, does not lie, because it reifies an instance of performative truth. Indeed, the more totalitarian the regime and the more propagandistic the image, the easier it is to unearth the political objective from under its surface. The obverse, however, is equally true, and in light of Žižek's warning, equally relevant: the more democratic the image, the more suspicious the reader/decoder should become. By promoting the capitalist ideology as normal, as non-ideological, First World filmmaking is less polysemous than the socialist one and, therefore, less rich in nuance and substance. The New Wave in Romania and the sixth generation in China fortunately return to Eurasian filmmaking some of its socialist-era polysemy, without fully adhering to Western aesthetics, film form, or film style to tell their stories.

Moreover, what the combined voices of Romanian and Chinese postsocialist directors are saying is that the current postsocialist/postcolonial dystopia is not as pessimistic as it looks at first glance. The answer to the postsocialism conundrum, as in Jia's playful animations of *The World*, is not Occidentalist escapism, but utopic collectivism predicated (if only aesthetically) on the same goals of the Third International that gave agency to the workers, with the only difference that it is not proletarians, but a cultural collective of the oppressed that should become the agents of change. Such a utopia would bring to the fore the neighbor[5] as the intra-Other of the former socialist bloc, as opposed to the Western Other, who is currently held as universal panacea for the ills of the East in a typical process of Occidentalization. Rather than following Xiaomei Chen's perspective of liberation through the idealization of the West, it is the idealization of the neighbor, the ignored intra-Other of the bloc that should become the target of the postsocialist or neo-socialist collective.

Given the similarity of Romanian and Chinese cultures and their perceived disadvantage in the face of Western dominance, this collective of the oppressed is attainable in the same way in which Mungiu's and Jia's films used contestation to build collectives based on socialist affect. Because cultural Romanianness as well as Chineseness are two categories predicated on the common recognition of "aesthetic of garbage" markers (such as dilapidated apartments, ruins and precarity), these markers become interchangeable in the postsocialist space at large, acting as levelers of cultural borders. The Eurasian's disadvantage in this way becomes an advantage, not only because misery loves company, but because subalternity creates collectivity.

Furthermore, these markers are negotiated in similar ways at the level of both the Chinese and the Romanian national psyche. This is made clear when Rey Chow disagrees with Antonioni's Western understanding of

---

[5] There is a lot of theorizing of the neighbor in current continental philosophy from Thomas Elssaesser to Zupančič, which was spurred, among other reasons, by the immigrant crisis in Europe. This philosophy, itself with roots in Levinas, can equally be de-Europeanized and reapplied eastward to the Eurasian landmass where it would not fall on deaf ears.

Chineseness. According to Chow, there is a Chineseness that is unique to Chinese people and not what the West or even Western philo-Chinese think it to be. Nevertheless, as Chow has beautifully stated when talking about her mother's response to Bernardo Bertolucci's *The Last Emperor* (1987), the Chinese only recognize Chineseness when it is the Other who defines what it is (Chow 1991, 24). What Chow has implied here is that the Other does not know Chineseness at all, but in the Other's representation of Chineseness the Chinese "family" performs a negotiatory response to the Other's portrayal that comes closer to defining it. In other words, the Chinese "family" is defined via contestation of the Western definition of the Chinese "family." It is in *performing* the Chinese reaction to the Westerner that the definition of the "family" is created.

This scenario is at play in some of the Romanian films discussed in this book. It is the response of the talk-show host to the Chinese character in *12:08* that strengthens the identity of Romanianness. Until the Chinese character phones in, the guests are caught in a relentless game of bickering; they are victims of their own "language structures," as Bardan has put it. Once the conversation with the Chinese takes place, the Romanians – insulted, like Chow's mother, that a Chinese knows them so well – become more aware of who they are. The presence of the Other (a Eurasian fraternal Other, in this case) confers the diffuse character of Romanianness a more stable (if not necessarily convenient) identity.

This identity is also evident in narrative structures. Not espousing the Western styles with which New Wave Romanian filmmaking is usually associated, *Stuff and Dough*, for example, does not apply cognitivism's classic scenario of normalcy interrupted by disturbance, followed by a return to normalcy. This is so even though Puiu's film is apparently structured in that way. The universe we witness alongside our three protagonists who are confined to the interior of the car is a universe of continuing contingency, in which the inciting incident (the attack from the unseen assailant) is a deceptive plot point. Because nothing concrete happens after the attack (we do not know more about the merchandise which the protagonists carry, nor about what is happening to them), the attack itself does nothing more than create anxiety. Although it suddenly places the protagonists in the middle of an extreme life-and-death paradigm, we do not understand what that paradigm is. We can only feel its affective result.

For that reason, Puiu's *Stuff and Dough* is representative of the generalized anxiety that consumes, for reasons having to do with postcolonialism and subalternity, the Eurasian subject. Unlike Bordwellian narratology, the Eurasian plot is one delayed *ad infinitum*, both before and after the inciting incident happens, which is also observable in Jia's *Platform*. The film drags on in wait for an inciting incident that never really comes about until the end – in which Mingliang's girlfriend/wife is seen nursing a baby – which is too late in the narrative to represent a plot point. The Eurasian plot, in that way, encapsulates the anxiety of an ending without an end in sight, and it also reinforces the unpredictability of the subaltern's universe. As seen in both *Stuff and*

Dough and *The World*, this universe presents the affective potentiality to evoke the contestation of the dominant power of capitalism, without making use of the transnationalist trope.

While the new inability to theorize the Other forced academia to capitulate to the (barely theorized) hegemon of plurality, yet another binary was unwillingly created – that of accepting or rejecting plurality and fragmentation, with the First World creating the binary of an "enlightened" versus "traditional" or reactionary worldview. This discourse, however, robs the subaltern of speech, even though it is comparable to the transnationalist philosophy seeking to incorporate the Other into a particular schema of thought propagated by the West. And since this binary eschews the problem of difference, what follows for the Other, yet again, is either self-Orientalization or (cultural) nationalism and fascism – two outcomes only too familiar at the close of a convoluted postcolonial twentieth century.

In this book, I have tried to demonstrate that, while Chinese and Romanian filmmakers are aware of the paradigm in which they find themselves, they are not aware of each other. Although having similar symptoms, Chinese and Romanian cultures do not share a unified view of postsocialism, which would allow the Eurasian underclass to form a family of sorts. This family cannot be obtained, as transnationalist theorists have argued, by condemning the wrongfulness of the past in hope of "liberation." Reviling socialism, as we have seen in Romanian anticommunist films of the 1990s, condemns the postsocialist masses to self-flagellation.

The alternative is to reconstruct a sense of Eurasian identity, which Romanian and Chinese cinemas have been tacitly attempting to build in isolation of each other. This reconstruction would lead to a different memorialization of socialist history in Romania and China, one that stands apart from the current narrative of economic malaise. It would also provide an alternative to conceptualizing Communism as an abusive and criminal regime meant to serve humanity a lesson. Accentuating Communism's help in staving off fascism and (for a while) nationalism, while promoting women's liberation and rebuilding the industrial base of the Romanian and Chinese economies destroyed after the war, would lead to a reconceptualization showing that the masses working to promote these goals were not unnecessarily duped by the Communist experiment and made unnecessary victims of a cruel and harmful ideology.

Comparative literature scholar Sheldon Lu has put it well when he warns of the risks of taking an excessively critical view of the past, arguing that "to denounce the political excesses of the socialist era is one thing. But generations of people grew up, grew old, and lived their lives in those years. They devoted all their youth and adulthood to what was believed to be a meaningful cause. To completely deny their past would be like not having lived at all" (Lu 2007, 144). This equally applies to cinema histories. Denying that films under socialism expressed the genuine thoughts and emotions of their filmmakers, even though they were made under duress, amounts to these films not having been made at all, which further amounts to consciously erasing half a century of history because that history does not fit our current capitalist outlook. Chinese sixth-generation and Romanian New Wave filmmakers agree with transforming this view and choosing an alternative, which would rescue the past from what Walter Benjamin, in reference to Friedrich Nietzsche's condemnation of reinterpreting history as theology (Nietzsche 1997),[6] has termed the dogmatic way of making use of history in the present (Benjamin 1968).[7]

What lies ahead for Eurasian postsocialism is the realization that a progressive understanding of the future involves the validation and acceptance of the past. In as much as commonalities between Romanian and Chinese postsocialist filmmaking practices are concerned, this may constitute the key to the creation of a transnationalism different from the one predicated solely on a Western understanding of cinematic semiology. The alternative would promote a return to polysemy and enrich our understanding of both the socialist past and its cinematic history. This approach would equally constitute the initial gesture towards the creation of a postsocialist Eurasian community that would engage in an honest dialogue with the West. Only such an alternative would enable us to move past the East/West binary and eventually help us recontextualize World Cinema from another angle, an angle which will allow more agency to the currently disempowered postsocialist and postcolonial subject.

[6] Nietzsche's thoughts on history can be found in his essay "On the Use and Abuse of History for Life," included in *Untimely Meditations*. In the 1997 edition, edited by David Breazeale, this essay has been translated as "On the Uses and Disadvantages of History for Life."

[7] Walter Benjamin has expounded his views on history in his short essay "On the Concept of History," published in the edited collection of his writings, *Illuminations*.

Bibliography and Works Cited

Agerpress. 1960. Spectacol de gal⊠ cu filmul chinez 'Fiicele partidului' (Gala Night with Chinese Film 'Daughters of the Party')." *Scînteia*, 30 September, vol. 4952 (30), p. 3.

Ahmed, Sara. 2004. *The Cultural Politics of Emotion*. New York: Routledge.

Amălinei, Ovidiu. 2012. "ELNAV, distrusă din nepricepere şi jaf la drumul mare (ELNAV, Destroyed by Incompetence and Theft)." *Viaţa liberă*, 7 September, https://www.viata-libera.ro/economie/34031-viata-libera-galati. Accessed 5 May 2022.

Anderson, Benedict. 1983. *Imagined Communities: Reflections on the Origin and Spread of Nationalism*. London: Verso.

Andreescu, Florentina C. 2013. *From Communism to Capitalism: Nation and State in Romanian Cultural Production*. New York: Palgrave Macmillan.

Anonymous. [n. d.]. "La mort de Dante Lăzărescu." *Jeunes Cathos: Le portail des jeunes de l'Eglise catholique*, www.jeunes-cathos.fr/actus/culture/la-mort-de-dante-Lăzărescu. Accessed 8 August 2019.

Arendt, Hanna. 1951. *The Origins of Totalitarianism*. New York: Harcourt, Brace and Co.

Arnold, Gary. 1976. "'Ideas': Maoist Doctrine on Film." *Washington Post*, 4 December, p. E5.

Arrigo, Anthony Francis. 2010. "Imagining the Dam: The Visual Rhetoric of Hoover (Boulder) Dam in Popular and Public Print Media, 1920–1975." PhD diss., University of Minnesota.

Bakhtin, M. M. 1981. *The Dialogic Imagination*. Austin: University of Texas Press.

Ban, Cornel. 2014. *Dependenţă şi dezvoltare: Economia politică a capitalismului românesc (Dependency and Development: The Political Economy of Romanian Capitalism)*. Cluj: Tact.

Bardan, Alice. 2012. "Aftereffects of 1989: Corneliu Porumboiu's 12:08 East of Bucharest (2006) and Romanian Cinema." In *A Companion to Eastern European Cinemas*, edited by Anikó Imre. Chichester: Wiley-Blackwell, pp. 125–147.

Barthes, Roland. 1972. *Mythologies*. New York: The Noonday Press.

Barthes, Roland. 1986. *The Rustle of Language*. New York: Hill and Wang.

Bassin, Mark. 2015. "Narrative Kulikovo: Lev Gumilev, Russian Nationalists, and the Troubled Emergence of Neo-Eurasianism." In *Between Europe and Asia: The Origins, Theories, and Legacies of Russian Eurasianism*, edited by Mark Bassin, Sergey Glebov and Marlene Laruelle. Pittsburgh: The University of Pittsburgh Press, pp. 165–187.

Baudrillard, Jean. 1993. *The Transparency of Evil: Essays on Extreme Phenomena*. London: Verso.

Baudrillard, Jean. 1994. *The Illusion of the End.* Cambridge: Polity Press.

Bazac, Ana. 2017. "Jaful adus la zi: Responsabilitatea specialiștilor (An Update on Theft: The Specialists' Responsibility)." In *Marele jaf postcommunist: Spectacolul mărfii și revanșa capitalismului* (*Grand Postcommunist Theft: The Spectacle of Merchandise and Capitalism's Revenge*), edited by Emanual Copilaș. Iași: Adenium, pp. 28–43.

Benjamin, Walter. 1968. *Illuminations.* New York: Schocken Books.

Benjamin, Walter. 2008. *The Work of Art in the Age of Its Technological Reproducibility, and Other Writings on Media.* Cambridge: The Belknap Press.

Berry, Chris. 1995, "Seeking Truth from Fiction: Feature Films as Historiography in Deng's China." *Film History*, vol.7 (1), pp. 87–99.

Berry, Chris, and Mary Farquhar. 2006. *China on Screen: Cinema and Nation.* New York: Columbia University Press.

Betea, Lavinia, Florin-Răzvan Mihai and Ilarion Țiu. 2018. *21 August 1968: Apoteoza lui Ceaușescu* (*21 August 1968: Ceaușescu's Apotheosis*). București: Corint.

Bhabha, Homi. 2004. *The Location of Culture.* London and New York: Routledge.

Bjelić, Dušan. 2018. "4 Months, 3 Weeks and 2 Days at the Moment of Neoliberal Catastrophe." *Ejumpcut*, No. 58, Spring, https://www.ejumpcut.org/archive/jc58.2018/index.html. Accessed 30 July 2020.

Blaga, Iulia. 2010. "Când vrei să discuți despre un film, e bine să-l vezi – Portretul luptătorului la tinerețe (It's Advisable to Watch a Film Before You Want to Discuss it – Portrait of the Fighter as a Young Man)." *Liternet.ro*, February, https://agenda.liternet.ro/articol/10699/Iulia-Blaga/Cand-vrei-sa-discuti-despre-un-film-e-bine-sa-l-vezi-Portretul-luptatorului-la-tinerete.html. Accessed 8 March 2024.

Boia, Lucian. 1997. *Istorie și mit în conștiința românească* (*History and Myth in Romanian Consciousness*). București: Humanitas.

Bordwell, David. 1985. *Narration in the Fiction Film.* London: Routledge.

Bordwell, David. 1996. "Contemporary Film Studies and the Vicissitudes of Grand Theory." In *Post-Theory: Reconstructing Film Studies*, edited by David Bordwell and Noel Caroll. Madison: The University of Wisconsin Press, pp. 3–37.

Bordwell, David. 2000. *Planet Hong Kong.* Cambridge, MA: Harvard University Press.

Bradshaw, Peter. 2006. "The Death of Mr. Lazarescu." *The Guardian*, 14 July, https://www.theguardian.com/film/2006/jul/14/worldcinema.comedy. Accessed 1 July, 2024.

Brinkema, Eugenie. 2014. *The Forms of the Affects.* Durham: Duke University Press.

Buck-Morss, Susan. 2000. *Dreamworld and Catastrophe: The Passing of Mass Utopia in East and West.* Boston: MIT Press.

Butler, Judith. 1993. *Bodies that Matter: On the Discursive Limits of "Sex".* London: Routledge.

Buzura, Augustin. 1974. *Fețele tăcerii* (*Faces of Silence*). Bucharest: Cartea românească.

BZI. 2016. "Cea mai spectaculoasa cale ferata din Romania, 39 de tuneluri, 35 de poduri si viaducte pe o lungime de 31 de kilometric." *BZI*, 7 March, https://arhiva.bzi.ro/cea-mai-spectaculoasa-cale-ferata-din-romania-39-de-tuneluri-35-de-poduri-si-viaducte-pe-o-lungime-de-31-de-kilometri-foto-1188879. Accessed 15 March 2024.

Căliman, Călin. 2011. *Istoria filmului românesc* (*The History of Romanian Cinema*). București: Contemporanul.

Călinescu, Paul. 1982. *Proiecții în timp: Amintirile unui cineast* (*Projections in Time: Memories of a Cineaste*). București: Editura sport-turism.

Camhi, Leslie. 1999. "Surviving an Era of Maoist Tumult with Calm Intact." *New York Times*, 25 April.

Caranfil, Tudor. 2008. *Dicționar universal de filme* (*World Film Dictionary*). București: Ed. Litera Internațional.

Chakrabarty, Dipesh. 2008. *Provincializing Europe: Postcolonial Thought and Historical Difference*. Princeton: Princeton University Press.

Chan, Jessica Ka Yee. 2019. *Chinese Revolutionary Cinema: Propaganda, Aesthetics and Internationalism, 1949–1966*. London: I. B. Tauris.

Chen, Jian. 2001. *Mao's China and the Cold War*. Chapel Hill: University of North Carolina Press.

Chen, Xiaomei. 1995. *Occidentalism: A Theory of Counter-Discourse in Post-Mao China*. Oxford: Oxford University Press.

Chenaktshang, Dorje Tsering. 2003. "Reflections on Tibetan Film." *Proceedings of the Tenth Seminar of the IATS, Tibetan Modernities*, vol. 11. Leiden: Brill, pp. 267–281.

Chow, Rey. 1991. *Woman and Chinese Modernity: The Politics of Reading between West and East*. Minneapolis: University of Minnesota Press.

Chow, Rey. 2002. *The Protestant Ethnic and the Spirit of Capitalism*. New York: Columbia University Press.

Chow, Rey. 2014. "China as Documentary: Some Basic Questions (Inspired by Michelangelo Antonioni and Jia Zhangke)." *European Journal of Cultural Studies*, vol. 17 (1), pp. 16–30.

Cioroianu, Adrian. 2005. *Pe umerii lui Marx: O introducere în istoria comunismului românesc* (*On Marx's Shoulders: An Introduction to Romanian Communist History*). București: Editura Curtea Veche.

Cistelecan, Alex. 2019. *De la stânga la stânga: Lecturi critice în câmpul progresist* (*From Left to Left: Critical Readings in Progressive Thought*). Cluj: Tact.

Clark, Katerina. 1981. *The Soviet Novel: History as Ritual*. Chicago: University of Chicago Press.

Clark, Paul. 2011. "Closely Watched Viewers: A Taxonomy of Chinese Film Audiences from 1949 to the Cultural Revolution Seen from Hunan." *Journal of Chinese Cinemas*, vol. 5 (1), pp. 73–89.

Coates, Paul. 2005. *The Red and the White: The Cinema of People's Poland*. London: Wallflower Press.

Comisia națională pentru statistică. 1990. *Anuarul statistic al României 1990*. București: Combinatul poligrafic.

Comisia prezidențială pentru analiza dictaturii comuniste din România. Raport final (*Presidential Committee for the Study of the Romanian Communist Dictatureship*). București, 2006, https://www.wilsoncenter.org/sites/default/files/media/documents/article/RAPORT%20FINAL_%20CADCR.pdf. Accessed 13 March 2024.

Cosașu, Radu (Belphegor). 1971. "Răsună Valea." *Cinema* (6), June, http://aarc.ro/articol/rasuna-valea. Accessed 20 March 2024.

Deletant, Dennis. 1999. *Romania under Communist Rule*. Iași, Portland: Center for Romanian Studies in cooperation with the Civic Academy Foundation.

Derrida, Jacques. 1981. *Dissemination*. Chicago: University of Chicago Press.

Dirlik, Arif. 2017. "Neoliberal Socialism/Global Capitalism: Boom and Gloom in China Watching." *Development and Change*, 48 (2), pp. 387–96.

Dirlik, Arif. 2005. *Marxism in the Chinese Revolution*. Lanham: Rowman & Littlefield.

Dissanayake, Wimal. 1993. "Introduction." In *Melodrama and Asian Cinema*, edited by Wimal Dissanayake. Cambridge: Cambridge University Press, pp. 1–8.

Dissanayake, Wimal. 1996. *Narratives of Agency: Self-Making in China, India, and Japan*. Minneapolis: University of Minnesota Press.

Du Bois, W. E. B. 2007. *The Souls of Black Folk*. New York: Oxford University Press.

Du, Weijia. 2015. "Beyond the Ideology Principle: The Two Faces of Dubbed Foreign Films in PRC, 1949–1966." *Journal of Chinese Cinemas*, vol. 9 (2), pp. 141–58.

Duara, Prasenjit. 1995. *Rescuing History from the Nation: Questioning Narratives of Modern China*. Chicago: University of Chicago Press.

Dunford, Michael. 2022. "The Chinese Path to Common Prosperity." *International Critical Thought*, vol. 12 (1), pp. 35–54.

Eggert, Brian. 2020. "4 Months, 3 Weeks and 2 Days." *Deep Focus Review*, 30 May, https://www.deepfocusreview.com/definitives/4-months-3-weeks-and-2-days/. Accessed 20 March 2024.

Eyal, Gil, Ivan Szelenyi and Evelyn Townsley. 1998. *Making Capitalism without Capitalists: Class Formation and Elite Struggles in Post-Communist Central Europe*. London: Verso.

Feng, Dongneng. 2007. "Aesthetics after Propaganda: The Second Coming of the Cultural Revolution Performing Arts." In *Theatres of Thought: Theatre, Performance and Philosophy*, edited by Daniel Watt and Daniel Meyer-Dinkgrë. Newcastle: Cambridge Scholars Publishing, pp. 65–79.

Fifield, Anna. 2017. "Why Does North Korea Hate the United States? Let's Go Back to the Korean War." *Washington Post*, 17 May, www.washingtonpost.com/news/worldviews/wp/2017/05/17/why-does-north-korea-hate-the-united-states-lets-go-back-to-the-korean-war/?utm_term=.cbd968e52ff5. Accessed 8 August 2019.

Filimon, Monica. 2014. "Beyond New Romanian Cinema: Old Traps and New Beginnings." *Cineaste*, vol. 39 (2), pp. 30–34.

Filippi, Gabriela. 2017. "Comori ascunse: Receptarea după 1989 a filmelor interzise în perioada comunistă (Reception after 1989 of Films Banned during Communism)." In *Filmul tranziției: Contribuții la interpretarea cinemaului românesc „nouăzecist"* (*Transition Cinema: Interpretative Contributions to the Films of the 1990s*). Cluj: Tact.

Foucault, Michel. 2003. *Society Must Be Defended: Lectures at the Collège de France, 1975–1976*. London: Picador.

Foucault, Michel. 1978. *The History of Sexuality: An Introduction*. New York: Pantheon Books.

Fulger, Mihai. 2020. "Mitul 'Reconstituirea,' după 50 de ani (The 'Reenactment' Myth 50 Years Later)." *Adevărul.ro*, 7 July, https://adevarul.ro/blogurile-adevarul/mitul-reconstituirea-dupa-50-de-ani-2033968.html. Accessed 15 March 2024.

Georgescu, Florin. 2018. *Capitalul în România postcomunistă, Vol. I* (*Capital in Postcommunist Romania, Vol. I*). București: Editura Academiei Române.

Gillespie, David. 2014. *Russian Cinema*. London and New York: Routledge.

Goldiș, Alex. 2018. "Moromeții I: O lectură în cheia naratologiei ideologice (The Moromete Family I: A Reading Based on Ideological Narratology)." *Vatra*, vol. 6–7, pp. 59–62.

Gorzo, Andrei. 2017. "In the Name of 'The Ambiguity of the Real': Romanian Cinematic Realism after the 2000s." *Film Criticism*, vol. 41 (2), pp. 1.

Gorzo, Andrei. 2018. *Un film cu o fată fermecătoare* (*Charming Girl*). București: Next-Liternet.

Gorzo, Andrei. 2021. "20 de ani de la 'Marfa și banii.'" *Lucruri care nu pot fi spuse altfel*, 11 January, https://andreigorzoblog.wordpress.com/2021/01/11/20-de-ani-de-la-marfa-si-banii/. Accessed 22 March 2024.

Gorzo, Andrei. 2022a. "… and Gypsies Get Many a Beating …: On the Significance of Radu Jude's Aferim!" *Revista Transilvania*, vol. 6–7, pp. 1–11.

Gorzo, Andrei. 2022b. "În dialog cu Aurelian Giugăl despre filmul românesc contemporan." *Lucruri care nu pot fi spuse altfel*, 12 November, https://andreigorzoblog.wordpress.com/2022/11/12/in-dialog-cu-aurelian-giugal-despre-filmul-romanesc-contemporan/. Accessed 22 March 2024.

Grossman, Andrew. 2009. "Beyond the Western Gaze: Orientalism, Feminism, and the Suffering Woman in Nontransnational Chinese Cinema." In *Chinese Connections: Critical Perspectives on Film, Identity and Diaspora*, edited by Gina Marchetti, See Kam Tan and Peter X. Feng. Philadelphia: Temple University Press, pp. 138–52.

Groys, Boris. 1992. *The Total Art of Stalinism: Avant-Garde, Aesthetic Dictatorship, and Beyond*. Princeton: Princeton University Press.

Guattari, Félix, and Gilles Deleuze. 1987. *A Thousand Plateaus: Capitalism and Schizophrenia*. Minneapolis: University of Minnesota Press.

Guneratne, Anthony R. 2003. "Introduction: Rethinking Third Cinema." In *Rethinking Third Cinema*, edited by Anthony R. Guneratne and Wimal Dissanayake. London and New York: Routledge, pp. 1–29.

Haliliuc, Alina. 2015. "What Is So Funny about The Death of Mr. Lazarescu?" *The Journal of Popular Culture*, vol. 48 (1), pp. 154–67.

Hall, Stuart. 2019. "Encoding and Decoding in the Television Discourse." In *Essential Essays: Stuart Hall*, edited by David Morley. Durham: Duke University Press, pp. 257–277.

Hann, Chris, Caroline Humphrey and Katherine Verdery. 2002. "Introduction: Postsocialism as a Topic of Anthropological Investigation." In *Postsocialism: Ideals, Ideologies and Practices in Eurasia*, edited by C. M. Hann. London and New York: Routledge, pp. 1–28.

Harward, Grant. 2021. *Romania's Holy War: Soldiers, Motivation, and the Holocaust*. Ithaca: Cornell University Press.

Havel, Václav. 2018. *The Power of the Powerless*, London: Vintage Classics.

He, Laura. 2021. "China's Korean War Propaganda Movie Smashes Box Office Record." *CNN Business*, 4 October, https://edition.cnn.com/2021/10/04/business/battle-lake-changjin-china-box-office-intl-hnk/index.html. Accessed 12 January 2024.

Hegel, G. F. 1988. *Introduction to the Philosophy of History*, translated by Leo Rauch. Indianapolis and Cambridge: Hackett Publishing Company.

Huntingon, Samuel. 1996. *The Clash of Civilizations and the Remaking of World Order*. New York: Simon & Schuster.

Ieta, Rodica. 2010. "The New Romanian Cinema: A Realism of Impressions." *Film Criticism*, vol. 34 (2/3), pp. 22–36.

Imre, Aniko. 2016. *TV Socialism*. Durham: Duke University Press.

Iordanova, Dina. 2003. *Cinema of the Other Europe: The Industry and Artistry of East Central European Film*. London: Wallflower Press.

Iovănel, Mihai. 2021. *Istoria literaturii române contemporane: 1990–2020* (*History of Romanian Contemporary Literature: 1990–2020*). Iași: Polirom.

Jameson, Fredric. 1986. "Third-World Literature in the Era of Multinational Capitalism." *Social Text*, vol. 15, pp. 65–88.

Jinhua, Dai. 1995. "Invisible Women: Contemporary Chinese Cinema and Women's Film." *Positions: East Asia Cultures Critique*, vol. 3 (1), pp. 255–80.

Jitea, Bogdan. 2021. *Cinema în RSR: Conformism și disidență în industria ceaușistă de film* (*Cinema in the Socialist Republic of Romania: Conformism and Dissidence in Ceaușescu's Film Industry*). Iași: Polirom.

Johnson, William. 1978. "Breaking with Old Ideas." *Film Quarterly*, vol. 31 (3), pp. 42–48.

Kang, Liu. 1997. "Popular Culture and the Culture of the Masses in Contemporary China." *Boundary 2*, vol. 24 (3), pp. 99–122.

Kaplan, E. Ann. 1993. "Melodrama / Subjectivity / Ideology: Western Melodrama Theories and Their Relevance to Recent Chinese Cinema." In *Melodrama and Asian Cinema*, edited by Wimal Dissanayake. Cambridge: Cambridge University Press, pp. 9–28.

Karamanić, Slobodan, and Ivana Momčilović. 2017. "Cinema Antikomunisto, or How Ideology Doesn't Move Anything." *Studies in Eastern European Cinema*, vol. 8 (3), pp. 211–31.

Karasyov, Alexander. 2010. "ПОЛИТИКА – ДЛЯ БАРЫШНИ ГИБЛОЕ ДЕЛО (Politics – Bad Job for a Young Lady [interview with Nadia Averyanova])." *Литературная Россия*, vol. 47, 19 November, http://web.archive.org/web/20130813163457/http://www.litrossia.ru/2010/47/05757.html. Accessed 9 August 2019.

Karl, E. Rebecca. 2010. *Mao Zedong and China in the Twentieth-century World*. Durham and London: Duke University Press.

Kiossev, Alexander. 2004. "Grand Narratives and Imagined Communication: Literature and the Symbolic Patterns of Emancipation." *Neohelicon*, vol. 2, pp. 9–17.

Kiss, Endre. 2004. "Does Mass Psychology Renaturalize Political Theory? On the Methodological Originality of 'Crowds and Power.'" *The European Legacy*, vol. 9 (6), pp. 725–38.

Kovačević, Nataša. 2008. *Narrating Post/Communism: Colonial Discourse and Europe's Borderline Civilization*. London: Routledge.

Kracauer, Siegfried. 1975. "The Mass Ornament." *New German Critique*, vol. 5, pp. 67–76.

Kundera, Milan. 1984. "The Tragedy of Central Europe." *New York Review of Books*, vol. 7 (31), pp. 33–38.

Leyda, Jay. 1972. *Dianying/Electric Shadows: An Account of Films and Film Audience in China*. Cambridge, MA: The MIT Press.

Li, Jing. 2010. "Xin shiqi tizhi yanbian zhong de dianying jinkou yanjiu (The Study of Film Imports during the Evolution of the System in the New Era)." PhD diss., Shandong University.

Li, Lily. 2021. "Fatal Betrayal and Persistent Memory in Lou Ye's Summer Palace." *Canadian Review of Comparative Literature*, vol. 48 (2), pp. 276–95.

Liehm, Antonin, and Mira Liehm. 1977. *The Most Important Art: East European Film after 1945*. Oakland: University of California Press.

Littman, Sam. 2014. "The Long Take as a Reaction to the Past in Contemporary Romanian Cinema." *Senses of Cinema*, issue 71, June.

Liu Yong. 2006. *Sino-Romanian Relations: 1950's–1960's*. București: Institutul Național pentru studiul totalitarismului.

Losurdo, Domenico. 2011. *Liberalism: A Counter History*. London: Verso.

Lu, Sheldon. 2007. *Chinese Modernity and Global Biopolitics: Studies in Literature and Visual Culture*. Honolulu: University of Hawai'i Press.

MacFarquhar, Roderick, and Michael Schoenhals. 2008. *Mao's Last Revolution*. Cambridge: Belknap Press.

Maddison, Angus. 2006. *The World Economy* (Vols 1 and 2). Paris: OECD.

Mak, Edwin. 2008. "Postsocialist Grit: Contending Realisms in Jia Zhangke's Platform and Unknown Pleasures." *Offscreen*, vol. 12 (7).

Mao, Tse-Tung. 1952. *On Contradiction*. Beijing: Foreign Language Press.

Marchetti, Gina. 1998. "Transnational Cinema, Hybrid Identities and the Films of Evans Chan." *Postmodern Culture*, vol. 8 (2).

Marchetti, Gina. 2006. *From Tian'anmen to Times Square: Transnational China and the Chinese Diaspora on Global Screens, 1989–1997*. Philadelphia: Temple University Press.

Marchetti, Gina. 2018. *Citing China: Politics, Postmodernism, and World Cinema*. Honolulu: University of Hawai'i Press.

Mauss, Marcel. 1954. *The Gift: The Form and Reason for Exchange in Archaic Societies*. New York: W. W. Norton & Company.

McGrath, Jason. 2010. "Cultural Revolution Model Opera Films and the Realist Tradition in Chinese Cinema." *The Opera Quarterly*, vol. 26 (2–3), pp. 343–76.

Mello, Cecília. 2019. *The Cinema of Jia Zhangke: Realism and Memory in Chinese Film*. London: Bloomsbury Academic.

Mendelson, Scott. 2021. "Box Office: China's 'Battle at Lake Changjin' Tops $400M." *Forbes*, 5 October, https://www.forbes.com/sites/scottmendelson/2021/10/05/box-office-china-battle-at-lake-changjin-starring-wu-jing-jackson-yee-tops-400m-passes-tops-tenet-black-widow-and-shang-chi/?sh=984357462b19. Accessed 10 January 2024.

Mignolo, Walter. 2006. "Theorizing from the Borders: Shifting to Geo- and Body-Politics of Knowledge." *European Journal of Social Theory*, vol. 9 (2), pp. 205–21.

Miller, Jamie. 2010. *Soviet Cinema: Politics and Persuasion under Stalin*. London: I. B. Tauris.

Mitchievici, Angelo. 2011. "Nostalgia, marile speranțe și spectrul eșecului (Nostalgia, Great Expectations, and the Specter of Failure)." In *Noul cinema românesc: De la tovarășul Ceaușescu la domnul Lăzărescu (New Romanian Cinema: From Comrade Ceaușescu to Mr. Lăzărescu)*. Iași: Polirom.

Mittler, Barbara. 2016. "Just Beat It! Popular Legacies of Cultural Revolution Music." In *Listening to the Cultural Revolution: Music, Politics, and Cultural Continuities*, edited by Paul Clark et al. Camden: Palgrave Mcmillan, pp. 239–268.

Naficy, Hamid. 2001. *An Accented Cinema: Exilic and Diasporic Filmmaking*. Princeton: Princeton University Press.

Nasta, Dominique. 2013. *Contemporary Romanian Cinema: The History of an Unexpected Miracle*. London: Wallflower Press.

Necșulescu, Iulia. 2022. "Masculinitate și ideologie în Răsună Valea (Masculinity and Ideology in *Reverberates the Valley*)." *Film Menu*, 21 August, https://filmmenu.wordpress.com/2022/08/21/eseu-masculinitate-si-ideologie-in-rasuna-valea/. Accessed 15 March 2024.

Ngai, Sianne. 2005. *Ugly Feelings*. Cambridge, MA: Harvard University Press.

Nie, Wei. 2021. "The Generation, Transformation, and Dissipation of the 'Sixth Generation' Cinema in China: The Entropy Change of a Concept." *Journal of Chinese Film Studies*, vol. 1 (2), pp. 377–397.

Nietzsche, Friedrich. 1997. *Untimely Meditations*. Cambridge: Cambridge University Press.

Orwell, George. 2019. *Nineteen Eighty-Four: A Novel*. London: Penguin Books.

Paddington, Arch. 2000. *Broadcasting Freedom: The Cold War Triumph of Radio Free Europe and Radio Liberty*. Lexington: The University Press of Kentucky.

Parvulescu, Constantin. 2009. "The Cold World behind the Window: 4 Months, 3 Weeks and 2 Days and Romanian Cinema's Return to Real-Existing Communism." *Jump Cut*, No. 51, Spring, https://www.ejumpcut.org/archive/jc51.2009/4months. Accessed 27 July 2022.

Parvulescu, Constantin. 2015. *Orphans of the East, Postwar Eastern European Cinema and the Revolutionary Subject*. Bloomington: Indiana University Press.

Pickowicz, Paul. 2013. *China on Film: A Century of Exploration, Confrontation, and Controversy*. Lanham: Rowman & Littlefield Publishers.

Piwowarska, Barbara, Łukasz Ronduda and Marcin Wawrzyńczak. 2008. *Polska Nowa Fala: Historia zjawiska, którego nie było / Polish New Wave: The History of a Phenomenon That Never Existed*. Warsaw: Centre for Contemporary Art Ujazdowski Castle.

Poenaru, Florin. 2017. *Locuri comune. Clasă, anticomunism, stânga* (*Common Places: Class, Anticommunism, the Left*). Cluj: Tact.

Pop, Doru. 2010. "Cinematic Symptoms: Psychoanalytical Keys to Understanding the Romanian 'New Wave.'" *Studia Universitatis Babes-Bolyai-Dramatica*, vol. 2 (19), pp. 3–19.

Pop, Doru. 2014. *Romanian New Wave Cinema: An Introduction*. Jefferson: McFarland.

Popa, Bogdan. 2017. *Sexul și capitalul: O teorie a filmului românesc* (*Sex and Capital: A Theory of Romanian Cinema*). București: Tracus Arte.

Popa, Bogdan. 2018. "What's Wrong with the Romanian New Wave? Auteur Cinema, the Communist and the Production of the Violent Working Class." *Studies in Eastern European Cinema*, vol. 9 (1), pp. 89–102.

Popa, Ion. 2017. *The Romanian Orthodox Church and the Holocaust*. Bloomington: Indiana University Press.

Popescu, Cristian Tudor. 2011. *Filmul surd in România mută* (*Deaf Film in Mute Romania*). Iași: Polirom.

Popovici, Iulia. 2017. "'De mult vreau să te fut': Sexul femeilor și puterea bărbaților în filmul de tranziție (It's Been Long Since I Wanted to Fuck You: Women's Sex and Men's Power in Transition-Era Cinema)." In *Filmul tranziției: Contribuții la interpretarea cinemaului românesc „nouăzecist"* (*Transition Cinema: Interpretative Contributions to the Films of the 1990s*), edited by Andrei Gorzo and Gabriela Filippi. Cluj: Tact, pp. 133–150.

Povestea unei căi ferate unicat: Bumbești – Livezeni (@Exclusiv în România), https://www.youtube.com/watch?v=hndm0fd3a7s, 8 November 2014. Accessed 25 January 2023.

Radu, Carmen. 2021. "Oficial: Companiile din China vor fi excluse de la licitațiile pentru infrastructură: Ordonanța, publicată în Monitorul Oficial (Official: Chinese Companies Will Be Excluded from Infrastructure Tenders: The Decree Was Published in the Official Journal of the Government)." *Economedia.ro*, 5 April, https://economedia.ro/oficial-companiile-din-china-vor-fi-excluse-de-la-licitatiile-pentru-infrastructura-ordonanta-publicata-in-monitorul-oficial.html. Accessed 1 August 2023.

Renmin Ribao. 1977. "Chairman Mao's Theory of the Differentiation of the Three Worlds is a Major Contribution to Marxism-Leninism." *Renmin Ribao*, 1 November, www.marxists.org/history/erol/ncm-5/theory-3-worlds/. Accessed 10 August 2019.

Rîpeanu, Bujor T. 2005. *Filmat în România (Repertoriul filmelor de ficțiune – Cinema și Televiziune), vol. II, 1970–79* (*Filmed in Romania: The Repertoire of Fiction Films – Cinema and Television, vol. II, 1970–79*), București: Editura Fundației PRO.

Robé, Chris. 2017. "The Specter of Communism: A Communist Structure of Feeling within Romanian New Wave Cinema." *Film Criticism*, vol. 41 (2), p. 1.

Rosenbaum, Jonathan. 2005. "The World in a Beijing Theme Park." *Chicago Reader*, 29 July, www.jonathanrosenbaum.net/2005/07/the-world-in-a-beijing-theme-park/. Accessed 8 August 2019.

Said, Edward W. 2014. *Orientalism*. New York: Knopf / Doubleday.

Salys, Rigmalia. 2003. "The Strange Afterlife of Stalinist Musical Films." The National Council for Eurasian and East European Research, Title VIII Program, University of Colorado.

Săraru, Dinu. 1964. "Complimentul nu rezistă (The Compliment Doesn't Hold Up)." *Cinema*, vol. 6, June, http://aarc.ro/articol/complimentul-nu-rezista. Accessed 15 March 2024.

Sarris, Andrew. 2008. "A Nasty Peek Behind the Iron Curtain." *Observer*, 22 January, https://observer.com/2008/01/a-nasty-peek-behind-the-iron-curtain/. Accessed 23 March 2024.

Şerban, Alex. Leo. 2010. "Romanian Cinema: From Modernity to Neo-Realism." *Film Criticism*, vol. 34 (2/3), pp. 2–21.

Şerban, Alex. Leo. 2011. "Bridging the Gap: Where Does the Romanian New Wave Go from Here?" *Film Comment*, vol. 47 (1), pp. 12–13.

Shen, Qinna. 2021. "Female Desire, Pop Rock, and the Tiananmen Generation: The Synergy of Sexual and Political Revolutions in the Banned Chinese-German Film Summer Palace (2006)." *JCMS: Journal of Cinema and Media Studies*, vol. 60 (5), pp. 48–74.

Sklar, Robert. 2006. "The Death of Mr. Lăzărescu." *Cinéaste*, vol. 31 (3), pp. 62–63.

Skrodzka, Aga. 2012. *Magic Realist Cinema in East Central Europe*. Edinburgh: Edinburgh University Press.

Slaby, Jan. 2019. "Relational Affect: Perspectives from Philosophy and Cultural Studies." In *How to Do Things with Affects: Affective Triggers in Aesthetic Forms and Cultural Practices*, edited by Ernst van Alphen and Tomáš Jirsa. Leiden: Brill Rodopi, pp. 59–81.

Solanas, Fernando, and Octavio Getino. 1969. "Toward a Third Cinema." *Tricontinental*, no. 14, pp. 107–32.

Solonari, Vladimir. 2009. *Purifying the Nation: Population Exchange and Ethnic Cleansing in Nazi-Allied Romania*. Washington DC: Woodrow Wilson Center Press with Johns Hopkins University Press.

Spinoza, Baruch. 1992. *The Ethics: Treatise on the Emendation of the Intellect and Selected Letters*. Indianapolis: Hackett.

Stein, Ruthe. 2006. "A Sad, Affecting Journey through Romanian Hospital Hell." *SFGATE*, 30 June, https://www.sfgate.com/movies/article/A-sad-affecting-journey-through-Romanian-2532383.php. Accessed 23 March 2024.

Strausz, László. 2017. *Hesitant Histories on the Romanian Screen*. Camden: Palgrave Macmillan.

Szalontai, Balázs. 2014. "Political and Economic Relations between Communist States." In *The Oxford Handbook of the History of Communism*, edited by Stephen A. Smith. Oxford: Oxford University Press, pp. 305–321.

Suter, Emil. 1950. "Un început de drum în filmul artistic romînesc: 'Răsună Valea' (A Starting Point in Romanian Artistic Cinema: 'Reverberates the Valley')." *Contemporanul*, no. 170, 6 January, p. 9.

Tan, Hui, and Yuan He. 2018. "Romanian Films in China (1953–1963)." *Studii și cercetări de istoria artei: Teatru, muzică, cinematografie*, vol. 12 (56), pp. 105–13.

Teodorescu, Vlad. 2013. "Regretele unui brigadier: Nu ne-au amintit când au dărâmat Stadionul 23 August" (Regrets of a Brigadier: They Didn't Mention Us When They Tore Down the "23 August" Stadium)." *Evenimentul Zilei*, 3 April, pp 10.

Ţichindeleanu, Ovidiu. 2017. *Contracultură: Rudimente de filosofie critică (Counterculture: The Basics of Critical Philosophy)*. Iași: Polirom.

Tion, Lucian. 2022a. "The Socialist Leader in Film: Sergiu Nicolaescu's *Hot Days* in Romania and Post-Maoist China." *Comparative Literature Studies (Urbana)*, vol. 53 (3), pp. 468–86.

Tion, Lucian. 2022b. "The Relationship of History to the Present: Romanian Nationalism in the Films of Radu Jude." *Cineaste*, vol. 47 (4), pp. 30–34.

Țion, Lucian. 2020 "Socialist Sink: The Eastern Roots of the Romanian New Wave." *Quarterly Review of Film and Video*, vol. 39 (1), pp. 51–73.

Țion, Lucian. 2021. "The Use of Language in the Making of Romanian Nationalism from Dimitrie Cantemir and Mihai Eminescu to the Iron Guard and National Communism." *Acta Universitatis Sapientiae: European and Regional Studies*, vol. 20 (20), pp. 63–92.

Tismăneanu, Vladimir. 2003. *Stalinism for All Seasons: A Political History of Romanian Communism*. Berkeley: University of California Press.

Toderici, Radu. 2017. "Deceniul autorilor: Ce s-a întâmplat cu filmul românesc în anii '90? (The Auteurist Decade: What Happened to Romanian Cinema in the 1990s?)" In *Filmul tranziției: Contribuții la interpretarea cinemaului românesc "nouăzecist" (Transition Cinema: Interpretative Contributions to the Films of the 1990s)*. Cluj: Tact.

Taylor, Richard. 1999. "Singing on the Steppes for Stalin: Ivan Pyr'ev and the Kolkhoz Musical in Soviet Cinema." *Slavic Review*, vol. 58 (1), pp. 143–59.

Todorova, Maria. 2009. *Imagining the Balkans*. New York: Oxford University Press.

Totok, William. 2016. *Între mit și bagatelizare: Despre reconsiderarea trecutului, Ion Gavrilă Ogăreanu și rezistența armată anticomunistă din România (Between Myth and Trivialization: On Reconsidering the Past, Ion Gavrilă Ogăreanu and Anticommunist Armed Resistance in Romania)*. Iași: Polirom.

Turcuș, Claudiu. 2017. *Împotriva memoriei: De la estetismul socialist la noul cinema românesc (Against Memory: From Socialism Aestheticism to New Romanian Cinema)*. București: Eikon.

Turnock, David. 1970. "The Pattern of Industralization in Romania." *Annals of the Association of American Geographers*, vol. 60 (3), pp. 540–59.

Țuțui, Marian. 2011. "Imaginea trecutului prin ochii prezentului (The Image of the Past Through the Eyes of the Present)." In *Noul cinema românesc: de la tovarășul Ceaușescu la domnul Lăzărescu (New Romanian Cinema: From Comrade Ceaușescu to Mr. Lăzărescu)*. Iași: Polirom, pp. 231–49.

Ulieriu, Nicolae. 1984. "*Prea cald pentru luna mai (Too Hot for the Month of May)*." *Săptămâna*, 23 March, http://aarc.ro/articol/prea-cald-pentru-luna-mai. Accessed 20 March 2024.

Uricaru, Ioana. 2008. "*4 Months, 3 Weeks and 2 Days*: The Corruption of Intimacy." *Film Quarterly*, vol. 61 (4), pp. 12–17.

van Alphen, Ernst. 2019. "Reading for Affects: Francis Bacon and the Work of Sensation." In *How to Do Things with Affects: Affective Triggers in Aesthetic Forms and Cultural Practices*, edited by Ernst van Alphen and Tomáš Jirsa. Leiden: Brill Rodopi, pp. 163–176.

Verdery, Katherine. 1991. *National Ideology Under Socialism: Identity and Cultural Politics in Ceaușescu's Romania*. Oakland: University of California Press.

Verdery, Katherine. 1996. *What Was Socialism and What Comes Next?* Princeton: Princeton University Press.

Verdery, Katherine, and Chari, Sharad. 2009. "Thinking Between Posts: Post-colonialism, Postsocialism, and Ethnography after the Cold War." *Comparative Studies in Society and History*, vol. 51 (1), pp. 6–34.

Vukovich, Daniel F. 2012. *China and Orientalism: Western Knowledge Production and the P. R. C.* London and New York: Routledge.

Wang, Ban. 2016. "Third World Internationalism: Films and Operas in the Chinese Cultural Revolution." In *Listening to the Cultural Revolution: Music, Politics, and Cultural Continuities*, edited by Paul Clark, Laikwan Pang and Tsan-Huang Tsai. Basingstoke: Palgrave Macmillan, pp. 85–106.

Wang, Haizhou. 2022. *Imagined China: Research on Chinese Films in the 1980s*. New York: Routledge.
Wang, Hui. 2014. *China from Empire to Nation-State*. Cambridge, MA: Harvard University Press.
Wang, Zhuoyi. 2014. *Revolutionary Cycles in Chinese Cinema, 1951–1979*. Camden: Palgrave Macmillan.
White, Daniel. 2017. "Affect: An Introduction." *Cultural Anthropology*, vol. 32 (2), pp. 175–80.
Wiesel, Elie. 2004. *Final Report of the International Commission on the Holocaust in Romania*. Iași: Polirom.
Wilczynski, Adam. 1968. "Film z czarującą dziewczyną (Film with a Charming Girl)." *Film*, no. 21 (581), p. 6.
Williams, Raymond. 1977. *Marxism and Literature*. Oxford: Oxford University Press.
Wolff, Larry. 1994. *Inventing Eastern Europe: The Map of Civilization on the Mind of the Enlightenment*. Redwood City: Stanford University Press.
Xu Jian. 2006. "Sino-Romanian Relations: 1950's-1960's (Foreword). In *Sino-Romanian Relations: 1950's-1960's* by Liu Yong." București: Institutul Național pentru studiul totalitarismului.
Yaping, Ding, 2022. *General History of Chinese Film III: 1976–2016*. New York: Routledge.
Yurchak, Alexei. 2005. *Everything Was Forever, Until It Was No More: The Last Soviet Generation*. Princeton: Princeton University Press.
Zhai, Qiang. 2013. "Mao's China and Romania: In the Shadow of Sino-Soviet Relations." *Journal of Sino-Western Communications*, vol. 5 (2), pp. 33–61.
Zhang, Ling. 2021. "From 'Mystification' to 'Massification': Canton Counterespionage Films and Cold War Geopolitics." *The Journal of Popular Culture*, vol. 54 (6), pp. 1309–30.
Zhang, Ling. 2018. "Navigating Gender, Ethnicity and Space: Five Golden Flowers as a Socialist Road Movie." In *The Global Road Movie: Alternative Journeys around the World*, edited by José Duarte and Timothy Corrigan. Bristol: Intellect Books, pp. 150–171.
Zhang, Yingjin. 2004. *Chinese National Cinema*. London: Routledge.
Zhu, Ying. 2001. "Cinematic Modernization and Chinese Cinema's First Art Wave." *Quarterly Review of Film and Video*, vol. 18 (4), pp. 451–71.
Žižek, Slavoj. 1998. "A Leftist Plea for Eurocentrism." *Critical Inquiry*, vol. 24 (4), pp. 988–1009.
Žižek, Slavoj. 2001. *Did Somebody Say Totalitarianism? Five Interventions in the (Mis)use of a Notion*. London: Verso.
Zupančič, Alenka. 2001. *The Odd One Out: On Comedy*. Cambridge, MA: MIT Press.

Selected Filmography

4 Months, 3 Weeks, and 2 Days (4 luni, 3 saptamâni si 2 zile). Dir. Cristian Mungiu, Mobra Films, 2007.
Alarm in the Mountains (Alarmă in munți). Dir. Dinu Negreanu, 1956.
Breaking with Old Ideas (Jue lie). Dir. Li Wenhua, Beijing Film Studio, 1975.
Child's Pose (Poziția copilului). Dir. Călin Peter Netzer, Parada Film, Hai Hui Entertainement, HBO Romania, 2013.
Daughters of the Party (Dong de nuer). Dir. Nong Lin, Changchun Film Studios, 1960.
Early Spring in February (Zaochun Er Yue). Dir. Xie Tieli, Beijing Film Studio, 1964.
Eastside Story. Dir. Dana Ranga, Anda Film, 1997.
Horse Thief (Dao ma zei). Dir. Tian Zhuangzhuang, Xi'an Film Studio, 1986.
Hot Days (Zile fierbinți). Dir. by Sergiu Nicolaescu, Casa de filme Trei, 1975.
Ju Dou. Dir. Zhang Yimou, China Film Co-Production Corporation, 1990.
Life Triumphs (Viața învinge). Dir. Dinu Negreanu, 1951.
On the 38th Parallel (San Ba Xian Shang). Dir. by Wenchi Shi, 1960.
Postcards with Wildflowers (Ilustrate cu flori de câmp). Dir. Andrei Blaier, Casa de filme Trei, 1975.
Raid (Qi Xi). Dir. Xu Youxin, August 1st Film Studio, 1960.
Raise the Red Lantern (Da hong deng long gao gao gua). Dir. Zhang Yimou, Era International, 1991.
Reenactment (Reconstituirea). Dir. Lucian Pintilie, Filmstudio București, 1968.
Reverberates the Valley (Răsună valea). Dir. Paul Călinescu, Romfilm, 1949.
River Elegy (He shang). Dir. Su Xiaogang and Wang Luxiang, China Central Television, 1988.
River Without Buoys (Mei you hang biao de he liu). *Dir. Wu Tianming, Xi'an Film Studio. Serfs (Nong nu)*. Dir. Jun Li, 1963.
Somewhere in the East (Undeva in est) Dir. Nicolae Mărgineanu, Solaris Films, 1991.
Stuff and Dough (Marfa și banii). Dir. Cristi Puiu, Mandragora, RoFilms. 2001.
Summer Palace (Yi He Yuan). Dir. Lou Ye, Dream Factory, Flying Moon Filmproduktion, 2006.
The Bridge (Qiao). Dir. Bin Wang, Northeast Film Studio, 1947.
The Death of Mr. Lăzărescu (Moartea domnului Lăzărescu). Dir. Cristi Puiu, Mandragora Film, 2005.
The Red Detachment of Women (Hong se niang zi jun). Dir. Xie Jin, Tianma Film Studio, 1961.
The Waves of the Danube (Valurile Dunării). Dir. Liviu Ciulei, Studioul Cinematografic București, 1960.

The White Haired Girl (Bai mao nu). Dir. Bin Wang, Changchun Film Studio, 1950.
The World (Shijie). Dir. Jia Zhangke, Office Kitano, 2004.
Unforgettable Life (Te bie shou shu shi). Dir. Tian Zhuangzhuang, Xiaoxiang Productions, 1988.

Index

EU Authorised Representative:
Easy Access System Europe Mustamäe tee 50, 10621 Tallinn, Estonia
gpsr.requests@easproject.com

Printed and bound by CPI Group (UK) Ltd, Croydon, CR0 4YY
29/09/2026
02224981-0005